CONVERGING THEOLOGIES

*Comparing and converging terms within the
Byzantine and Pratyabhijñâ (Kashmir Shaivite)
traditions within a space for convergence*

CONVERGING THEOLOGIES

*Comparing and converging terms within the
Byzantine and Pratyabhijñâ (Kashmir Shaivite)
traditions within a space for convergence*

Desmond Nicholas Gurupada Bamford

2011

Converging Theologies: *Comparing and converging terms within the Byzantine and Pratyabhijñâ (Kashmir Shaivite) traditions within a space for convergence—* published by the Rev. Dr. Ashish Amos of the Indian Society for Promoting Christian Knowledge (ISPCK), Post Box 1585, 1654, Madarsa Road, Kashmere Gate, Delhi-110006.

ISBN: 978-81-8465-159-1

Laser typeset by

ISPCK, Post Box 1585, 1654, Madarsa Road, Kashmere Gate, Delhi-110006 • *Tel:* 23866323

e-mail: ashish@ispck.org.in • ella@ispck.org.in
website: www.ispck.org.in

Contents

Introduction

I have other sheep that are not from this fold; I must bring them back also and they will heed my voice. So that there will be one flock, one shepherd. Jn.10:16

This work is divided into two parts. The first examines the place for converging ideas within two traditions, looking at models of dialogue and comparison and converging ideas of the Byzantine and Pratyabhijñâ (philosophy proper of Kashmir Shaivism) traditions to aid the development of theological parameters through interreligious dialogue. The second part will provide a short examination of the notion of person in Pratyabhijñâ within a context of interreligious dialogue, reciprocity and openness to understand a concept of person from a Hindu philosophical-theological perspective in relation to Byzantine Christian theology. This work should be taken in the context of interreligious dialogue where I seek to converge ideas to develop a holistic notion of revelation and salvation, as Irenaeus stated that: "He (God) recapitulates in Himself all the nations dispersed since Adam".[1] He brings all those who have faith in Him to Him for as Abraham was saved by faith (Rom.4:1-5:1) the "promise comes by faith" (Rom.4:16), so that all who have faith will be "justified through faith" (Rom.5:1) and saved despite the varying practises. Although we can accept the principles of faith scattered abroad as varying manifestations of the religious *other,* we can state that those who accept Christ will receive

---

[1] Irenaeus, *Against the Heresies*, 120.

a greater portion of truth and fullness. In this sense this work seeks engagement with the religious *other* through a Byzantine-Christian perspective, but utilising Kashmir *Œaivite* terms to help further mutual understanding and to converge ideas.

Instead of looking to models of dialogical theology that seek existential ways to approach dialogue by comparing certain religions through the hermeneutic of comparison, I will incorporate an ontological dimension. This work becomes an ontological task to uncover the meaning of *being*. I shall not reduce the study to mere analysis or a process of academia, but engage with the religious *other* by recognising them as co-workers in faith through an open study by seeking that which we all have in common, our humanity, as long as the notion of humanity is not taken out of a theistic context. We should move away from understanding comparison and convergence in terms safe contexts of inclusivism or pluralism, which has a whiff of Hegelianism about it, so that the whole exercise is not reduced to an observation of sociological patterns. We should look to a depth in the meaning of dialogue through a task of finding the meaning to person, which then allows us to more fully engage in dialogue. Without this meaning dialogue becomes an outward, empty and casual conversation rather than a *koinonia* in truth. To this end I shall include hagiographical elements for the whole of Pratyabhijñâ (the philosophy proper of the Kashmir Úaivite tradition) and Byzantine tradition are centred on the notion of human becoming and it is in this context of becoming for all human persons, that this work shall be framed. In this context Religions should not be considered as outward existential representations of differing cultures, but placed within the true context of revelation, or multiple revelatory acts and the Divine purpose for us all. In this sense we are looking for the depth of the religion, what it conveys, what it means to be as a human person. We should not only look for existential convergence but an ontological one, to understand religions not only in terms of differing modes of existing, but rather seek unity and unlock a process of unity through a shared communion in God where becoming united citizens of Heaven we overcome the notion of differences. This then is a deeply spiritual task and cannot be taken out of the context of a shared faith in the Supreme Lord, who we Christians call the 'One' incarnate *Logos*, Christ, together with the Father and Holy Spirit as the Godhead the Moslems call Allah; the Jews call YHWH; the Hindus and Buddhists understand through Paramâtman and Nirvana respectively, so that we all come to understand the meaning of God's purpose and will through the many God-centred and varied revelations.

We should not qualify religions only in terms of diverging types of existing but in relation to categories of *being*, to how God creates the human condition and then conveys His will to a specific culture so that through His operational will humanity, and by faith in the One God, is called to be recapitulated to Him. All religions convey an aspect of return to the divine where the present human condition is viewed as either fallen or delusional and must return to a higher God-related state. This does not negate the reality of life but all true religions accept what is concrete and real so that we come to Him and know Him in a real way. In this return we find the true meaning of person, where return is contextualised to revelation and the divine purpose. Thus the many divine revelations are interconnected, relational, and thus a study that encourages interreligious dialogue has an important place in fostering human understanding for the purpose here is a deeply anthropological one, deeply related to the meaning of human existence.

Thus, the aim of this work is to be dialogical, inclusive and compelling: it compels us to engage with the religious other. It is not enough to stand by and watch from the side lines we must seek encounter with the religious *other*. I will utilise Indian philosophical terms within a Christian theological context of person, and in relation to Greek Patristic theology, to synthesise and converge models of person. Through such convergence I will consider the new model of person, the *Âtman-hypostasis* within a *space* for convergence or a *theology of convergence* to aid interreligious dialogue[2] and within an atmosphere of honesty[3] and openness to dialogue with other religions. Within a premise of openness, it is hoped, that this work will be able to explore terms and ideas from different religious traditions through comparison and convergence without clinging to rigid ways of doing comparative theology within an atmosphere of respect for the other's faith and without denuding faith principles of the 'other'. Such an approach will affirm the place for multiple divine revelations, which can be considered as the driving force behind inter-religious dialogue. This addresses the problem of over confessionalism within a specific tradition through a focus on what is shared; a confession of the One God who manifests divine *economia* through a multitude of divine operations, through many *events* of the divine *act,* which allows revelation to be upheld within specific faith traditions while at the same time acknowledging the place for a revelatory process that involves the whole of humanity. At the heart of understanding the misunderstandings within the dialogue of world religions is a resolution of the problem of revelation within the context of the accepting of many religions. How can religions exist-in-situ with each other? This question goes to the very heart of a concept of accepting the place for 'many religions' model of theology and indeed as to what should be categorised as a religion. But it also concerns the very purpose of many divine revelations and the reasoning for the reception of many revelatory *events*: how and why particular religions are revealed? The affirmation of many revelatory events allows a model

---

[2] As exemplified in the debate on personhood within an inter-religious dialogue highlighted by Descry, 'Unknowing and Personalism' in Bäumer (ed.), *Mysticism in Shaivism and Christianity* (Delhi: 1997); and K. P. Aleaz, *A Convergence of Advaita Vedânta and Eastern Christian Thought* (Delhi: 2000).

[3] Jacques Dupuis calls for an honest and open approach to inter-religious dialogue, see 'Christianity and Religions: Complementarity and Convergence', in Catherine Cornille, *Many Mansions: Multiple Religious Belonging and Christian Identity* (Maryknoll: 2002), pp.61-75.

of a multi-revelatory God, who manifests Himself in many ways in many religions, which seriously impacts of the way the divine operations are understood and how divine operations are correlated to a meaningful transfer and reception of grace in all religions. Of course as a Christian I argue that God reveals Himself in many ways to allow all to have faith in Him, the One Absolute God, so that through His economia He can be known partially but who is fully revealed in Christ. This work will not answer problems relating to many divine revelations directly, it will affirm the place for different forms of economic manifested grace within different traditions through convergence, to a lesser and greater extent, while affirming the place for the transformation and restoration of God-centred human persons but which are ultimately related to the salvific work of the Christ and to the divine operations (*energeia*).

PART 1

Converging Traditions

CHAPTER 1

An Eschatological Hope

Introduction

The development of comparison[1] and convergence[2] in this work shall be placed in the context of an "eschatological hope",[3] as Wolfhart Pannenberg puts it, and fulfilment,[4] that is to say in relation to fulfilment of the end (the *eschata*); the *telos* of all things so that all

---

[1] Types of theological comparison have been highlighted by William E. Paden, 'Comparative Religion', in John R. Hinnells, *The Routledge Companion to the Study of Religion* (London: 2005), pp.208-225. See also: John Hick and Paul Knitter (eds.), *The Myth of Christian Uniqueness* (Maryknoll: 1992); Gavin D'Costa, *The Meeting of Religions and the Trinity* (Maryknoll: 2000); P. L. Quinn and K. Meeker (eds.), *The Philosophical Challenge of Religious Diversity* (NY: 2000); Catherine Cornille (ed.), *Many Mansions: Multiple Religious Belonging and Christian Identity* (Maryknoll: 2002); Jacques Dupuis, *Christianity and the Religions: From Confrontation to Dialogue* (Maryknoll: 2003); Veli-Matti Kärkkäinen, *Trinity and Religious Pluralism* (UK: 2004); Paul F. Knitter (ed.), *The Myth of Religious Superiority* (Maryknoll: 2005).

[2] I will develop convergence similar to the type of K. P. Aleaz, who argues for the place of theological convergence of *Vedânta* and Eastern Christianity, see *A Convergence of Advaita Vedânta and Eastern Christian Thought* (Delhi: 2000).

[3] Wolfhart Pannenberg, 'The Task of Christian Eschatology', in Carl E. Braaten and Robert W. Jenson (eds.), *The Last Things: Biblical and Theological Perspectives on Eschatology* (Grand Rapids, Michigan: 2002).

[4] 'Revelation', in the *New Testament*, 22: 12.

things may be revealed and unified through the incarnate *Logos*. This idea of hope will be placed within the discourse of inter-religious dialogue and seeking dialogue with the 'other'[5] within the hope of fulfilment, which underlines the reasons for bringing the two traditions together in a comparison. But hope will not only be understood in terms of an outward fulfilment, but also in terms of the inner life, where in the inner experience, the *telos* of person is attained in an inner *event*. The inner *event* represents the end or completion of the person[6] within an inner mystical experience, and which represents the hope for all persons in the experience of *deification/re-cognition*. This does negate the context of what is real but allows the real life experience to be affirmed but raised so that we come to meet God in a real but transfigured way.

What will be accepted is that an eschatological vision allows for fulfilment and yet recognises the place for difference, where the divine wish to bring humankind to God reflects the recognition for the place for revelatory participations. Theological and religious paradigms must go beyond previous, exclusivist, inclusivist or pluralistic claims of religion,[7] to a cosmic[8] vision, while at the same time considering models that encourage a mindset that look to new theologies.

---

[5] John D. Zizioulas, *Communion and Otherness* (London: 2006), pp.43-55. The notion of the other will also be understood from the context of Zizioulas' Trinitarian theology, where the other becomes related to the divine *hypostasis* and thus in this work will also relate to the nature of *hypostasis* through *Âtman*.

[6] Mathew 24:13-14, where Jesus refers to a single end (ôÝëò) event, but which can also be understood in terms of an inward completion.

[7] See Perry Schmidt-Leukel, 'Exclusivism, Inclusivism, Pluralism: The Tripolar Typology–Clarified and Reaffirmed', in Knitter (ed.), *The Myth of Religious Superiority*, p.13; and see also Hick, *Dialogues in the Philosophy of Religion*, pp.186-187.

[8] Hick, *Dialogues in the Philosophy of Religion*, p.187.

Encounters of the Personal

In affirmation of this convergence approach, a comparison should be sought between Indian philosophy (*Pratyabhijñâ*) and Christianity (Byzantine tradition) in an encounter of the personal, of the personal Christ to the world, and between persons (*hypostases*). It is due to the focus on the nature of person and the shared reality of being persons that an encounter with other traditions will be considered from an inter-religious perspective allowing for meaningful reciprocity.

The reasoning behind engaging in comparison and dialogue will be sought by affirming a depth of meaning within the encounters of the personal, not only in the meetings between human persons but in the encounters between the human person and the divine person. But there should be incorporated into attempts at understanding such encounters, elements of what cannot be known or grasped especially when considering how these encounters relate to revelation. It can be affirmed that from a soteriological perspective, encounters on a personal level are to be considered in a way that allows what is concrete and personally real but that through grace the personal life is transformed and so a vision of the personal life rises above the mundane, transformed in the Divine Light and Goodness. Thus dialogue should be sought not only within the context of a shared common experience but through an eschatological vision[9] or a hope of the unity of persons. The place for the eschatological unity of religions, and thus the need for seeking what is common, the shared and hoped for in human beings was also called for in *Nostra Aetate* of Vatican II.[10] Also in new

---

[9] For an example of this approach in relation to dialogue, see Kärkkäinen, *Trinity and Religious Pluralism*, p.87.

[10] 'Declaration on the Relation of Church to Non-Christian Religions', or *Nostra Aetate*, in A. Flannery, *The Basic Sixteen Documents of Vatican Council II: Constitutions, Decrees, Declarations, A Completely Revised Translation* (Dublin: 1995), pp.569-570. See also Gavin D' Costa, *The Meeting of Religions and the Trinity*, pp.101-103.

document 'Meeting *God* in a Friend and Stranger'[11] the Catholic Church has tried for a real attempt at dialogue but I have real concerns in the over inclusivity developed in this booklet which actually starts to denude Christian faith. Thus I look to observe general principles such as relating to being, the soul, salvation, of revelation, the good; points of convergence that aid dialogue rather than looking for specific points of revelation. This is why I chose a comparison with Kashmir *Œaivite* philosophy that deals with general philosophical and theological models of *being* and inner experience where there is considered the meaning behind personal encounters of God through personal experience rather than generating complex models of contrary faith claims concerning humanity that have to be explained. In Kashmir Œaivite philosophy we see models that can be considered in any faith context for it deals with the principles of God's being, will action in the world and philosophical categories that help understand God through personal experience. The ground for dialogue is ultimately sought in the truth of the *eschata*, which becomes the basis for both unity and diversity, helps negotiate, as Kärkkäinen states, "the dynamic and tension between one and many".[12]

The examination of the human person in the context of the Byzantine and *Pratyabhijñâ* traditions will thus be placed within a soteriological and eschatological context in the "universal design of God for the salvation of the human race",[13] who reveals Himself, as Dupuis states, in "many and various ways".[14] The role of divine revelation for the whole of humankind will be viewed as central not only to the discourse of personhood but also to inter-religious dialogue. However the role of Christ as the central salvific figure

---

[11] *Catholic Bishop's Conference of England and Wales* (London, Catholic Truth Society: 2010)

[12] *Nostra Aetate*, p.177.

[13] Pope Paul VI, *Decree on the Mission and Activity of the Church: Ad Gentes* (Boston: 1965).

[14] Jacques Dupuis, *Christianity and the Religions*, p.114.

is underlined for Christ is the central historical figure and pivot of salvation for humanity. God became 'man', not just a principle of revelation, only once to effect change for humanity and to rise up all through His Incarnation, Cross and Resurrection. I again cite Dupuis to support this view in his model of '"one mediator" within "participated mediations"'[15] in which the uniqueness of Christ is upheld while also affirming the place of divine multiple mediations, and multiple revelatory events through the divine revelatory activity. The two positions will be viewed not in conflict, but as complementary.

Thus, this work represents an optimistic view of inter-religious dialogue, as exemplified by Keith Ward in his notion of disclosures,[16] and Ninian Smart's notion of shared experience[17] which also represents an optimistic approach to dialogue.[18]

---

[15] *Ibid.*, p.163.

[16] Keith Ward believes that from such disclosures comparative theology can allow "enquiry into ideas of God and revelation", *Religion and Revelation* (Oxford; Clarendon Press) p.50.

[17] See Ninian Smart, 'Our Shared Experience of the Ultimate', *Religious Studies* 20/1 (1984), pp.19-26. Studies relating to 'shared' experience is also exemplified by, David Brown, *God and the Enchantment of Place: Reclaiming Human Experience* (Oxford: 2006); and Paul M. Collins, *Context, Culture and Worship: The Quest for 'Indian-ness'* (ISPCK: 2006).

[18] Within this context of optimism, and disclosures and truth, the concept of the Absolute will be understood in terms of God who discloses "Himself" and a disclosed truth. I refer to the term "Himself" giving a masculine attribute to God not in a sexist context but because this is utilised in the Greek Patristic tradition, see Pseudo-Dionysius, *DN*, 7.3 (Luibheid), "He is known through knowledge" (PG 3), 872A; and in *Pratyabhijñâ* see *IPK* 4.3, which states "He is taken to be numerous types of finite persons" (Pandit). A notion of truth, through an *Âtmanic* reality, can be correlated to John Hick's concept of the "Real" (see John Hick, *Dialogues in the Philosophy of Religion*, UK: 2001, p.14), which infers a notion of the Absolute divine transcendent, "Ultimate Reality", which, for Ward, is versatile enough to be related to equivalent ideas in Hinduism and Islam (*Ibid*).This line of thought is also taken up by Harold Coward in *The Perfectibility of Human Nature in Eastern and Western Thought* (NY: 2008).

Hence a growing body of theologians have developed and are developing theological models which are not content with underlining the same old barriers of separation, but look to optimism for resolutions and discourse. This work will become part of an ever growing corpus which encourages new ideas, and even new Christologies.[19] It is hoped that ideas relating to the *Âtman-hypostasis* paradigm constructed in this work will add to and aid discourse that invites, what Samartha calls, *"possibilities for Christological developments"*.[20]

Comparative and Convergent Approaches to Theology

While a comparison and convergence of terms will be considered discretely throughout the work, the main emphasis will be upon comparing models of person that relate to the constructs of individuality, modes of existence, relationality and unity. The comparison of such models will represent a wish to develop a convergence of ideas, as exemplified by Brück,[21] and bring such convergence to a point of synthesis.

Developing Theologies through Comparative Studies

The wish to evolve ideas through comparison is not new, and there is a voluminous corpus of material from scholars such as Max Müller[22] to Swami Abhishiktananda,[23] and is exemplified in the

---

[19] Some examples of see: S. J. Samartha, *One Christ many Religions* (NY: 1991); Jacob Parappally, *Emerging Trends in Indian Christology* (Bangalore: 1995); K. P. Aleaz, *A Convergence of Advaita Vedânta and Eastern Christian Thought*; Raimon Panikkar, *Christophany, the Fullness of Man* (NY: 2004); Mathew Vekathanam, *Indian Christology* (Bangalore: 2004).

[20] Samartha, *One Christ many Religions*, p.93.

[21] Michael Von Brück, *The Unity Of Reality: God, God-Experience, and Meditation in the Hindu Christian Dialogue,* trans. James V. Zeitz (Mahwah: 1991). This excellent work by Bruck outlines introductory categories in which *Advaita* and Christian Trinitarian theology can come together.

[22] Max Müller, *Lectures on the Origin and Growth of Religion* (London: 1878).

[23] Abhishiktananda, *Hindu-Christian Meeting Point* (Delhi: 1969, 2005).

contemporary field by Francis X. Clooney[24] and Gavin Flood,[25] who seek to engage in comparative theology to aid dialogue and reciprocity. What this work proposes is to utilise Aleaz's notion of convergence[26] to construct a model of person within a comparison that is workable. To some extent this process could be related to a "re-imagining"[27] of God, as Richard Kearney put it, where we redefine and re-consider the way in which we view God and thus ourselves.

But there are difficulties that confront the inter-religious dialogical theologian such as over confessionalism, which makes the rationale for theological comparison *reductio ad absurdum*. Problems relating to the confusion of theological concepts are highlighted by John Thatamanil, who shows that comparative theologians in their efforts to be comparative may even have become *hyphenated*[28]as a Hindu-Christian or Christian-Hindu. In an inclusivist position the outcome may even become more radical in seeking common ground, as exemplified in Bede Griffiths' promotion of *hybridization*.[29] But while the over-confessional approach represents a stumbling block to comparison and convergence, a model that is too accepting can denude faith claims, and so what should be the approach to inter-religious dialogue?

---

[24] Francis X. Clooney, *Theology After Vedanta: An Experiment in Comparative Theology* (Delhi: 1993). See some other examples of contemporary comparative theology: Ishanand Vempeny, *Krishna and Christ* (Pune: 1988); Catherine Cornille, *The Guru in Indian Catholicism* (Louvain: 1991); Arvind Sharma, *The Philosophy of Religion and Advaita Vedânta* (Delhi: 1995); Hans Torwesten, *Ramakrishna and Christ* (UK: 1997).

[25] Gavin Flood, *The Ascetic Self* (Cambridge:2004).

[26] Aleaz, *A Convergence of Advaita Vedânta and Eastern Christian Thought.*

[27] Richard Kearney, 'Re-imagining God', in John D. Caputo and Michael J. Scanlon (eds.), *Transcendence and Beyond: A Postmodern Inquiry* (Bloomington and Indianapolis: 2007), pp.51-65.

[28] *Ibid.*

[29] Catherine Cornille, *The Guru in Indian Catholicism,* p.177.

Clooney recognises that one way may be to accept "multiple religious identities",[30] in which one enters into partnership and experience with the other faiths, even though he prefers to work through his own tradition. This view is taken up Jacques Dupuis in his inter-religious dialogical approach. Dupuis argues that to engage with the "faith of the other"[31] one must be open to the faith of the other to become a true partner in dialogue,[32] where one enters "into the experience of the other in an effort to grasp the experience from within".[33] But here lies the problem; the term other[34] can imply separateness and distance,[35] and so one solution is either to identify oneself with the other or even become the other, taking on the other's tradition in which one can experience the other's religion and thereby gain respect for other traditions. This has led to the notion of "multiple religious belonging",[36] but there has not been enough work on this side of inter-religious dialogue to see where this line of dialogical theology is going.

Perhaps the notion of otherness in a relational context, of a collective religious belonging could help to support inter-religious

---

[30] Francis X. Clooney, 'God For Us; Multiple Religious Identities as a Human and Divine Prospect', in Catherine Cornille, *Many Mansions* (Maryknoll: 2002), p.44.

[31] See Dupuis, 'Christianity and Religions:Complementarity and Convergence', in Catherine Cornille, *Many Mansions:Multiple Religious Belonging and Christian Identity*, p.63.

[32] *Ibid.*

[33] *Ibid.*

[34] See also Barnes, *Theology and the Dialogue of Religions*, p.45.

[35] Zizioulas argues though, the opposite, where the notion of the other has a relational quality, see *Communion and Otherness*, p.43.

[36] Claude Geffré, 'Double Belonging and the Originality of Christianity as a Religion', in Catherine Cornille, *Many Mansions: Multiple Religious Belonging and Christian Identity*, pp.93-105, and also Phan, 'Multiple Religious Belonging', in *Being Religious Interreligiously: Asian Perspectives on Interfaith Dialogue* (Maryknoll: 2004), pp.60-81.

dialogue when viewed in the context of friendship with the other.[37] This highlights a reciprocal model, where the recognition of what is shared by all persons having the nature of *hypostatic* existence, and the participating in a faith in God, itself brings persons together through the sharing of a common nature and faith.

The theological development of comparativism or comparative theology, has also laid itself open to criticism for its broad generalisations, exampled in Radhakrishnan's comparison of Eastern and Western ideologies.[38] While Radhakrishnan looked to qualify his approach through notions of "self-discovery and self-knowledge",[39] he made broad comparisons between the mysticism and ethics of the West and India and of what is to be understood by the term soul.[40] But he seemed to be mindful of the danger in his approach and underlined that his attempts were but cursory.[41] In addition so often a comparison may wish to accomplish something beneficial but the outcome may be detrimental to dialogue. In this case I am thinking of Hans Torwesten's work *Ramakrishna and Christ,* which compares Ramakrishna with Christ,[42] which denies the uniqueness of Christ, which serves only to repel from a Christian point of view. Another good example of comparison seeking a unity of ideas but actually underlining difference is Bede Griffiths' correlation of the Trinity with *Sat-Cit-Ânanda* or *Satcidânanda.*[43] Bede Griffiths' Hindu-Christian syncretism,[44] though well

---

[37] Thomas Aquinas, *ST,* Q114.1-2 (1670).

[38] S. Radhakrishnan, *Eastern Religions and Western Thought* (Oxford: 1969).

[39] *Ibid.,* p.35.

[40] *Ibid.,* p.145.

[41] *Ibid.,* p.117.

[42] Hans Torwesten's *Ramakrishna and Christ* (UK: 1997), p.21; also see Geoffrey Parrinda, *Avatar and Incarnation* (Oxford: 1997); and R. S. Sugirtharaja, *Asian Faces of Jesus* (Maryknoll: 1993).

[43] Bede Griffiths, *The Marriage of East and West* (Illinois: 1982), also see G. Feuerstein, *Encyclopedic Dictionary of Yoga* (London: 1990).

[44] See also Abhishiktananda, 'The Depth-Dimension of Religious Dialogue', *Vidyajyoti* 45/5 (1981), pp.202-221; Abhishiktananda, 'Notes on Christology

intentioned, actually muddles theological ideas.[45] Hence criticism of the comparativist method thus seems somewhat founded upon real fears. William E. Paden reflects that, "comparativism is not without its problems and critics for it can make superficial parallels, false analogies and misleading associations".[46] Some modern Indian thinkers, such as, Swami Vivekananda and Sri Aurobindo also confused or even blurred theological ideas in their attempts at seeking harmony,[47] and made erroneous correlations between an impersonal divinity and theism,[48] and so it is important to be careful when constructing synthetic models that seek a convergence of ideas.

The theological comparativist has also been accused of developing a non-existent *meta-narrative,* and agenda, and thus, as Paden puts it, comparativism has developed a "kind of conceptual imperialism".[49] However, comparative theology should be used as a tool to push theological boundaries and to promote dialogue through convergence. Perhaps Hindu theological methods could provide a way into convergence, in as much as Hinduism has been *doing* comparison and convergence for a long time. This is exemplified in the *Bhâgavad Gîta,* which incorporated many of the

---

and Trinitarian Theology', *Vidyajyoti* 64/8 (2000), pp.598-612; see also Anthony Kalliath, *The Word in the Cave* (New Delhi:1996); Edward T. Ulrich, 'Swami Abhishiktananda and Comparative Theology', *Horizons* 31/1 (2004), pp.40-63, and R. Yesurathanam, *A Christian Dialogical Theology: The Contribution of Swami Abhishiktananda* (Kolkata: 2006).

[45] These confused models make "superficial identifications" which should not be employed and this problem of "superficial identifications" is beginning to be understood as detrimental to encounter, see David Brown, *God and Enchantment of Place* (Oxford: 2004), p.352.

[46] William E. Paden, 'Comparative Religion', in John R. Hinnells, *The Routledge Companion to the Study of Religion* (London: 2005), p.216.

[47] Vivekananda's Neo-Vedânta, *The Complete Works of Swami Vivekananda* (1-8; Calcutta, 2000) and Sri Aurobindo's *Synthesis of Yoga* (BCL, 20-21).

[48] Swami Vivekananda, *The Complete Works of Swami Vivekananda*, vol.2, pp.175-188; and Sri Aurobindo, *The Life Divine* (BCL, 18-19), pp.338-354;

[49] *Ibid.,* p.217.

philosophical and theological systems of India.[50] In the *Gîtârtha Sangraha*, Abhinavagupta informs us that it is the purpose of the Lord to manifest many paths of knowledge (*Sânkhya*) and action (*Yoga*), and that such a fusion enhances humanity's existence:

> The Lord combines and presents both these paths in one because knowledge (*jnâna*) and action (*kriyâ*) are the very nature of consciousness.[51]

Taking these concerns into consideration we have to be careful when developing comparison and much more careful when converging ideas so that the *why* and the *how* become clear. The *why* is obvious and relates to an ever shrinking world and the need for some form of acceptance and dialogue with the other while keeping the need to proclaim faith ideas in an ever secular world. The *why* relates to understanding God's purpose in the world and correlating His purpose to economic operations: through faith the other is understood to be saved through these operations. By understanding this we can better understand ourselves and God because there can be no other author or divinity, He is the author of true religions for everything comes from Him pertaining to the Good is good. We cannot ignore this other good for that ignores God's activities of goodness, but rather we should try and understand it and especially as Christians we should place it within the larger picture of Christ's unconditional love. Thus on a certain level we seek common ground with other religions as an imperative for fostering mutual understanding and respect. The facing of other religions in inter-religious encounters, is a way to face ourselves and forces us not only to ask the question *why* engage in a comparison at all, but to also ask why have we not engaged in a more meaningful theological dialogue before? Then we have to ask

---

[50] Vedwati Vaidik (ed.), *Úrîmad Bhagavad-Gîtâ* (New Delhi: 2003); and A. C. Bhaktivedanta Swami Prabhupâda, *The Bhagavad-Gîtâ As It Is* (UK: 1986), p.3.

[51] B. Marjanovic (trans.), *Abhinavagupta's Commentary on the Bhagavad Gita, Gîtârtha Sangraha* (New Delhi: 2004), p.82.

to what extent we are prepared to go in comparison and convergence to develop inter-religious dialogue. How far is our dialogue going to extend in developing theologies?

To answer this I really sideline the question to focus on ontological questions to answer the *why* so that to affirm that comparison and convergence should be based not only on an academic need to develop meaning in theological dialogue, or a political will to harmonise cultures and religions, but to look to the deeper consequence of dialogue through a study of person. The engagement with other faith communities should have a deeper significance. Hence I push the answer forward to include an eschatological context. In this the *why* of comparison must have as its centre an ontological and existential quest that seeks a deeper rationale for dialogue. While often the most suitable path to achieve an encounter in the study of religions is found through comparison, so too ontological inquiry is important in informing us of the nature of personhood when asking the questions not only 'who am I' as a person, but also 'who are we' as persons? What is a human person?'[52] In this sense I look to developing a theology of person within the context of converging ideas. Hence comparison and convergence, while serving as a dialogical tool, can also be used to increase our knowledge of who we are as human persons.[53]

Converging Theologies: Theology of Convergence?

The wish to attempt not only at comparison between theologies from different traditions but also a convergence has recently been

---

[52] Rudolf Otto, *Mysticism East and West* (NY: 1932), who was attempted an ontological comparison between Meister Eckhart and Shankaracharya use of *Esse* (*Ibid.*, pp.19-21) and *Âtman* respectively in seeking such answers to these questions.

[53] For this reason Gavin Flood states that "comparisons are not odious but necessary for human understanding", see Gavin Flood, *The Ascetic Self, Subjectivity, Memory and Tradition* (Cambridge: 2004); also see also on this Paul E. Murphy, *Triadic Mysticism, The Mystical Theology of Shaivism of Kashmir* (Delhi: 1999).

adopted by the Indian Oriental Orthodox theologian K. P. Aleaz. He argues that such dialogical approaches can promote a "unitive vision",[54] that is to say a holistic ideal, exemplified in an eschatological vision.[55] He envisions new meanings, and insights gained through convergence[56] of *Advaita Neo-Vedânta*[57] with Christianity, within a category called "Pluralistic Inclusivism".[58] Aleaz structures his approach to theology stressing theological comparison and convergence, and drawing upon *Neo-Vedânta* to develop new Christologies through the incorporation of Hindu philosophies. As with Aleaz, this work will also affirm that isolationist theologies cannot provide new insights into old problems, and that what are needed are new approaches that enrich[59] and bring new dimensions to theology. Aleaz demonstrates that new approaches sought in Indian Christianity,[60] through the incorporation of the term *Âtman,* can be used as an epistemological and metaphysical tool in Christian reformulation[61] theology.

---

[54] Aleaz, *Christian Responses to Indian Philosophy* (Kolkata: 2005), p.120.

[55] K. P. Aleaz, *Jesus in Neo-Vedanta,* p.1.

[56] K. P. Aleaz, *A Convergence of Advaita Vedanta and Eastern Christian Thought,* p.xix.

[57] *Neo-Vedânta* is generally considered as the resurgence of *Vedânta* or *Upanishadic* theology which brought together ideas not only of *Úaivite*, Yogic, and *Vaishnavite* theologies but incorporated the context of other religions and exemplified by Ramakrishna, Swami Vivekananda and Sri Aurobindo.

[58] Aleaz, *A Convergence of Advaita Vedanta and Eastern Christian Thought,* p.xv.

[59] *Ibid.,* p.xix.

[60] It is now can be recognised that there is a distinct Christian approach in India which is called 'Indian Christianity' and which, regardless of the denomination, has a flavour that is distinctly Indian. See R. Boyd, *An Introduction to Indian Christian Theology* (Delhi: 1969, 2005); and M. Vekathanam, *Indian Christology.*

[61] *Vekathanam, Indian Christology* (Bangalore: 2004), p.508.

While many approaches to inter-religious dialogue have, especially over the last forty years, been attempted, what will be considered here is a *space* for theological comparison or seeking the place for developing a *theology of convergence* which enhances inter-religious dialogue and pushes theological boundaries forward towards a goal that contemplates fruitful and harmonious encounters[62] without focusing so much on the *why* of dialogue. A theological *space* for dialogue through comparison and convergence provides a free *space* for academic research without hindrance to investigate theologies on a certain level to explore and experiment so as to properly evaluate the place for real dialogue on a theological level. To that end, this work will not present an overtly confessional or exclusivist approach,[63] nor will it develop a religiously pluralistic model, taken up by Keith Ward and John Hick, which accepts all types of spirituality, but it will seek to explore theological answers to theological problems without detracting the need for dialogue or without making specific faith claims. Thus while this work is a theological exercise it also seeks to use philosophical terms from other faiths such as taken from *Kashmir Shaivism* to better explain, justify, reject or argue modern theological problems that have recently come into Christianity, and to incorporate concepts and terms without denuding Christian faith but so as to allow that incorporation to give better in sight.

In this theological context the necessity to look to new approaches for dialogue through converging ideas and bringing

---

[62] There have in this context, even been some discussion on 'multiple religious belonging' see, Catherine Cornille (ed.), *Many Mansions:* and Peter C. Phan, *Being religious Interreligiously* (Maryknoll: 2004).

[63] Problems relating to confessionalism is highlighted in V. M. Kärkkäinen, *Trinity and Pluralism* and Keith Ward who believes that one cannot hold a "religious view without holding a confessional view", see *Religion and Revelation* (Oxford: 2003), p.108, which is in contradistinction to Hick's interpretation of the "Real", see Hick, *Dialogues in the Philosophy of Religion* (UK: 2001), p.14. D'Costa upholds the view that dialogue is possible but only through exclusivism and "nothing called pluralism really exists" (*Ibid.* p.169).

new terms into Christianity can be theologically justified within in the Early Christian synchronistic use of philosophical terms.[64] In the New Testament itself we see the incorporation of Hellenic terms such as *Logos* to explain Christian theology in convergence of Greek thought and Hebrew based faith. So too, present day Christianity, if it is to respond to pluralism, has to accept the place for the possibilities of inclusion and convergence[65] of theological ideas and terms not traditionally utilised in Christianity. Indeed the task of theology itself when considering an eschatological and a cosmic vision of God must be able to include and not exclude ideas and terms relation to what is good and justified through faith. In this context Keith Ward has stated that, "*theology* is a pluralistic discipline: in it people of differing beliefs can co-operate, discuss, argue and converse".[66] While I would cautiously agree with this, I would state that this is true within a collective faith agreement and assertion of a belief in the One God as a basic platform for discussion.

While previous theological attempts at convergence have not quite fully generating workable theological model, exemplified by S. J. Samartha[67] whose attempts who did not intend to "articulate a systematic fully-fledged Christology" [68] to "indicate possibilities for Christological developments in a religiously plural world",[69] Aleaz goes further. His intention is to try and develop a workable theological convergence between Christian theology and Vedânta through the model of 'Neo-Vedântic Christology'.[70] I intend to use

---

[64] This is highlighted in C. H. Dodd's work, *The Interpretation of the Fourth Gospel* (Cambridge: 1953).

[65] Aleaz, *A Convergence of Advaita Vedânta and Eastern Christian Thought*, p.279.

[66] Ward, *Religion and Revelation*, p.45.

[67] S. J. Samartha, *One Christ Many Religions* (Maryknoll: 1991), p.4.

[68] *Ibid.*, p.93.

[69] *Ibid.*

[70] Aleaz, *Jesus in Neo-Vedanta*, p.1.

this start as a basic model of convergence to investigate how theological ideas can be further converged to push the theological barriers within a *theology of convergence*.

Towards Dialogue: Dialogical Paradigms

There are many problems that confront those wishing to engage in dialogue through experimenting with theologies of convergence such as hostility generated by one's own faith members and in the hardening of religious positions, but while inter-religious dialogue has been affected by the hardening of confessional positions due to the present political problems relating to fundamentalism, this environment itself highlights the importance and necessity of inter-religious dialogue.

Approaches to inter-religious dialogue seem to have been set within certain narratives that reflect a theological stance of faith constructs, developing methodologies that reflect those beliefs, and have been broadly determined within 'exclusivist', 'inclusivist' and 'pluralistic' models.[71] Alan Race in 1983 and Gavin D'Costa in 1986 highlighted these paradigms as being helpful when categorising responses to pluralism,[72] but these are now been superseded. Hence, the ever growing populations and interactions and encounters between religions are forcing theologians to re-think models and narratives through which inter-religious dialogue has been set.

The increasing encounters between peoples of different faiths, although forcing the Western mind to re-address its standards and belief systems, should not be considered as a stumbling block to the Christian mind for many Eastern and Oriental Christians have lived and developed their faith within other faith communities. Also, initially Christianity emerged out of a pluralistic environment

---

[71] Alan Race, *Christians and Religious Pluralism* (London: 1983); see also P. Schmidt-Leukel 'Exclusivism, Inclusivism, Pluralism', in Paul F. Knitter, *The Myth of Religious Superiority*, p.13.

[72] *Ibid.*, p.2.

and was confident enough to engage within a pluralistic culture.[73] This type of Christianity was confessional and yet incorporated non-Christian terms and ideas.[74] The *Letter to Diognetus*[75] highlighted the ability of early Christians to integrate and dialogue with other cultures using Hellenistic words such as *Logos*[76] within a Jewish theological setting yet.[77] But Christianity should not be set merely within a narrative of pluralism, but should confess itself within pluralism and considering that God may manifest through many types of revelations. In the context of multi-revelatory events, religions can be considered as inherently related to each other, but which find fulfilment in Christ.

Responding to Exclusivism

It is because God is God, that His activities come from Him, we cannot reject those works that are obviously divine in origin such as reflected in the religions of Judaism, Islam, Buddhism and Hinduism where names such as Good, Hope, Love, Compassion,

---

[73] 'ÐÑÏÓ ÄÉÏÃÍÇÔÎ Í', in J. B. Lightfoot, *The Apostolic Fathers* (London: 1893).

[74] For example the *Prologue* to John's Gospel is distinctly Platonic, see C. H. Dodd, *The Interpretation of the Fourth Gospel* (Cambridge: 1953).

[75] 'ÐÑÏÓ ÄÉÏÃÍÇÔÎ Í', in J. B. Lightfoot, *The Apostolic Fathers*, pp.490-511.

[76] Gospel of John and C. H. Dodd, *The Interpretation of the Fourth Gospel*, and also see Augustine's admittance that the *Prologue* of John's Gospel has Platonic influences, in *Confessions*, trans. R. S. Pine-Coffin (London: 1961), bk.7.9, p.144.

[77] 'ÐÑÏÓ ÄÉÏÃÍÇÔÎ Í' stated: "For Christians are not distinguished from the rest of mankind either in locality or in speech or in customs. For they dwell not somewhere in cities of their own, neither do they use some different language, nor practice an extraordinary kind of life...But while they dwell in cities of Greeks and barbarians as the lot of each is cast, and follow the native customs in dress and food and the other arrangement of life, yet the constitution of their own citizenship, which they set forth, is marvellous, and confessedly contradicts expectationssee 'Pros Diogneton', 5.1-3, 5.4-6, in J. B. Lightfoot, *The Apostolic Fathers*, pp.493-507.

Unity, God, Bliss, Salvation infer that the activities and revelations of God are being expressed. Consequently the category of dialogical response that is exclusivist is rejected, mainly because of the cosmic vision given by the Byzantine tradition, which affirms that religions and philosophies in some way express parts of the whole truth, but which are revealed totally in Christ.[78] Exclusivism,[79] defined through its rigorous claims, excludes any real attempt at dialogue, and conditions its theology through the term '*extra ecclesiam nulla salus*' (outside of the Church there is no salvation).[80] This axiom is the driving force behind the exclusivist view[81] and it negates any salvation for those perceived not be Christians, however we have to change our understanding of what we mean by Church to include those that believe in God through *faith*. I believe that the word church should in the broadest way include the 'gathering' of all believers in the One God. While theologians of the exclusivist type affirm the erroneous character of other faiths[82] I affirm that this axiom should not be a hindrance. If the word Church indicates the hope of an eschatological fulfilment for humanity, it could be argued that all who are called to God and experience God within another religion apart from Christianity are brought into God's Church through the grace of the *Logos*. Thus the very meaning of the word church or assembly (Ecclesia)[83] has to be examined further,

---

[78] Clement, *Str.*1.13, 756A (Coxe); and Justin Martyr, *Apol.*2.7, 441-471 (Coxe).

[79] Glyn Richards, *Towards a Theology of Religions* (London: 1989), p.14; Allan Race, *Christians and Religious Pluralism* (London: 1981), p.10; K. P. Aleaz *Harmony of Religions: The Relevance of Swami Vivekananda* (Calcutta: 1993), pp.154-173; and Aleaz, *Christian Responses to Indian Philosophy* (Kolkata: 2005).

[80] Cyprian of Carthage, *Epistulae 73.*21 (PL 3), 1169; and *De Unitate* (PL 4), 509-536; on this in relation to inter-religious dialogue see Gavin D' Costa, *The Meeting of Religions and the Trinity,* pp.101-103.

[81] Race, *Christians and Religious Pluralism,* p.11.

[82] Aleaz *Harmony of Religions,* p.154.

[83] Mentioned 114 times in NT, but only 3 in Gospels, all in Mathew, e.g. Mt.16:18; 18:17. There are 46 occurrences in Pauline the corpus.

especially in the context of Christian affirmation in the light of other religions.

Responding to Inclusivism

The next category comes broadly under the term inclusivist which can be said to have evolved out of a response to exclusivist claims. Schleiermacher[84] and Rudolf Otto[85] were forerunners of inclusivism and of the later development of pluralism. The notion of inclusivism, which can be said to define those who work within the acceptance model,[86] belies a reticence to affirm an equal place at the dialogical table. Examples of this type are found in Karl Rahner who argued for an inclusive view through his notion of the "anonymous Christian",[87] and Paul Knitter, whose inclusivism is developed within his fulfilment model.[88] Knitter goes beyond what is to be considered inclusivistic, and seems to develop an *all-inclusive* inclusivism.[89] Aleaz also includes Raimundo Panikkar in the inclusivist category,[90] but Panikkar could perhaps be placed within the pluralist model.

However, the inclusivism narrative is restricted in what it can accomplish, for it does not rely on reciprocity but on metered out generosities. For example Rahner's view, from a Hindu perspective

---

[84] F. Schleiermacher's 'Doctrine of "Original Perfection of Man', in *The Christian Faith*, eds. H. R. Mackintosh, and J. S. Stewart (London: 2005), p.244.

[85] Rudolf Otto, *Mysticism East and West* (NY: 1970).

[86] Aleaz, *Dialogical Theologies: Hartford Papers and Other Essays* (Kolkata: 2004), p.85.

[87] Karl Rahner, *Theological Investigations, Vol. V, Later Writings*, trans. Karl-H. Kruger (London: 1969), p.132.

[88] Aleaz, 'Christian Theologies of Religious Need to Go Global: A Response to Paul F. Knitter', in, *Dialogical Theologies: Hartford Papers and Other Essays*, pp.88-91.

[89] Knitter, *The Myth of Religious Superiority.*

[90] Aleaz *Harmony of Religions: The Relevance of Swami Vivekananda*, p.173.

is innately patronising. Certainly, the increased encounter of Christianity with other religions provoked Panikkar to go further than Rahner, by declaring that the God of Hinduism is the "unknown Christ",[91] and that if Hindus are thereby *anonymous Christians* then "Christians are anonymous Hindus".[92] Panikkar believes that Christians have "no monopoly of truth"[93] and neither do they have a "monopoly of salvation",[94] but that to be a Christian is to work in co-operation with Christ and creation, engaging in a cosmic dialogue. Those subscribing to this view would naturally be inclined to a theology of agreement and inclusion. As Panikkar states, "it is offensive and unacceptable for the so-called non-Christian religions to be described only by a negative feature".[95] He goes on to state, "it leaves a bad taste in the mouth to divide people up in this way".[96] For this reason Wilfred Cantwell Smith asserted that religious separation within self-sufficient[97] positions of any religion cannot legitimately develop a "world theology of religions".[98] Rather, what Wilfred Cantwell Smith purported is a working toward religious dialogue through generic concepts such as *faith*, *God* and the like.[99]

Responding to Pluralism

The last major dialogical category developed has been called pluralism, which called for even greater scope in dialogue between

---

[91] Raimundo Panikkar, *The Unknown Christ of Hinduism* (New Edition; London: 1981), p.13.

[92] *Ibid.*

[93] Panikkar, 'Christians and So-Called Non-Christians', *Cross Currents* 22/3 (1972), pp.281-308.

[94] *Ibid.*

[95] *Ibid.*

[96] *Ibid.*

[97] Wilfred Cantwell Smith, *Towards A World Theology, Faith and the Comparative History of Religion* (UK: 1981).

[98] *Ibid.*

[99] *Ibid.*

religions, but paradoxically, allowing religions and religious type movements their own *space*, discourages dialogue in that static models are generated. Examples of pluralists are Keith Ward, John Hick and Jacques Dupuis. However, this category is at present ambiguous and is muddling models which could be interpreted in any variety of ways. Hence, new categories must be conceived of in which are fruitful, open, and allow optimistic theologies to develop, yet which retain identity and thereby significance. This open approach reflects an optimism to Christian inter-religious dialogue, evidenced in Nicholas Cusa (1401-64), who in *De pace fidei*[100] developed a dialogical approach by recognising the divine in another religion. Cusa considered that each person was a reflection of the divine Person, and thus dialogue gains significance in that encounter with persons of other religions.

The notion of optimism within interreligious dialogue allows for reciprocity and acceptance of other faiths and ideas not possible in comparison,[101] without detracting from personal beliefs. Jacques Dupuis remarks that "affirming the Christian identity is best done in an open dialogue with the other religions".[102] He argues that

---

[100] Willem Dupré, 'Religious Plurality sand Dialogue in the Sermons of Nicholas Cusa', *Studies in Interreligious Dialogue* 15.1 (2005), pp.76-85, see also Nicholas of Cusa, 'De docta ignorantia' and 'Dialogus de Deo abscondito', in *Nicholas of Cusa*, trans. H. L. Bond (The Classics of Western Spirituality; Mahwah: 1997), p.125 and pp.209-213. Troeltsch (1865-1923) too indicated the importance of dialogue with other religions, see Joseph Molleur, 'Troeltsch, Comparative Theology and the Conversation with Hinduism', *Studies in Interreligious Dialogue* 11/2 (2001), pp.133-47. Swami Vivekananda (1863-1902) was one of the first Hindus who argued for inter-religious dialogue at the *Parliament of Religions* (Chicago 11th -27th September 1893); also see Swami Vivekananda, 'Address at the Parliament of Religions, Read at the Parliament on the 19th September 1893', in *The Complete Works of Swami Vivekananda* (1; Calcutta: 2000), p.14.

[101] Richard Schebera, 'Comparative Theology: A New Method of interreligious Dialogue', *Dialogue and Alliance* 17/1 (2003), pp.7-18.

[102] Jacques Dupuis 'Renewal of Christianity Through Interreligious Dialogue', *Bijdragen* 65 (2004), pp.131-145.

Christians should engage in an open dialogue and thereby be "enriched or even renewed".[103] He addresses the question of mutual enrichment, and highlights the importance of convergence in relation to dialogue. So models of convergence and synthesis offer a way to approach dialogue. This approach can be exemplified in early Christianity, and Kippenburg even argues that "early Christianity was a syncretistic religion".[104] In this understanding, new integrations could help to invigorate Christian theology and Aleaz offers such a model with his incorporation of *Vedânta* into Orthodox Christianity.[105] Aleaz calls his model, pluralistic inclusivism,[106] in which, "Inclusivism and Pluralism undergo change in their previous meanings".[107] In this category, he offers the possibility of developing "practical dialogical theology"[108] through convergence exemplified in his Neo-Vedântic Christology.[109] It is my intention to continue along the lines of Aleaz's approach, but I do have reservations about the category of "pluralistic inclusivism" for it is not clear exactly what this means.

Aleaz believes that Indian Christianity, through the incorporation of Indian philosophical terms, could offer new ways of *doing* interreligious dialogue. He points to new types[110] of theology, which are based largely upon *Neo-Vedânta*, in which a "harmony of religions"[111] is substantiated through *Neo-Vedantic*

---

[103] *Ibid.*

[104] Hans. G. Kippenberg, 'In Praise of Syncretism: The Beginnings of Christianity Conceived in the Light of a Diagnosis of Modern Culture', in Anita Maria Leopold, Jeppe Sinding Jensen, eds., *Syncretism in Religion, A Reader, Critical Categories in the Study of Religion* (London: 2004), p.29.

[105] Aleaz, A Convergence of Advaita Vedânta and Eastern Christian Thought.

[106] Aleaz *Harmony of Religions: The Relevance of Swami Vivekananda*, pp.162-176, and Aleaz, *Dimensions of Indian Religion* (Calcutta: 1995), p.262.

[107] Aleaz, *Dimensions of Indian Religion*, p.262.

[108] K.P. Aleaz, *Jesus in Neo-Vedanta* (Delhi: 1995), p.xv.

[109] *Ibid.*

[110] *Ibid.*, p.1, and p.32.

[111] *Ibid.*, p.3

Christology.[112] Concerning the methodological use of convergence, the work will build upon K. P. Aleaz's work, which looks to a convergence of theologies, specifically of *Advaita Vedânta* and the Byzantine tradition.[113] But Aleaz does not consider many of the nuanced debates on the concept of person, such as how a concept of person is related to the term *hypostasis* and the ontological implications when considering the inclusion of *Vedânta* into the Orthodox Christian model. Neither does Aleaz consider *hypostasis* in relation to the contemporary Orthodox existentialist debate. Although Aleaz's general premise of convergence is accepted here, his comparison seems to me to be somewhat flawed in his use of *Advaita Vedânta*. This is because the rigid idealism and *monism* of *Advaita Vedânta*[114] does not allow for any meaningful reciprocity when related to the notion of revelation and divine appearance in Byzantine theology, and especially in relation to personhood. It could be argued that a comparison of the Byzantine tradition and *Dvaita (dualism)*[115] which stresses difference, or *Viúicm âdvaita (qualified non-dualism* or qualified non-difference)[116] might be more fruitful. It is the contention of this work, however, that in both

---

[112] *Ibid.*

[113] Aleaz, A Convergence of Advaita Vedânta and Eastern Christian Thought.

[114] This is exemplified by Shankaracharya who stated that "everything of the nature of the non-Self is negated from the eternally existing Self", in *Upadeshi Sâhasri*, trans. Swami Jagadânanda (Madras), p.218.

[115] The *Dvaita* of Mâdhavâchârya in Indian philosophy indicates a *dualism* is not a Gnostic *dualism* but relates to the concrete realness of the world, which is not negated as unreal. For a synopsis of how these ideas relate to different philosophical systems see Mâdhavâchârya, *The Sarva-Darœana-Sangraha* (London: 1908, 2004).

[116] In Râmânuja affirmed the "reality of the world", Swâmî Tapasyânanda, Úrî Râmânuja, *His Life, Religion and Philosophy* (Madras), p.32; N. Bhashyacharya, *A Catechism of the Vishistadwaita Philosophy of Sri Ramanuja Acharya* (Madras: 1887); see also S. Radhakrishnan, *Indian Philosophy* (2; New Delhi: 1923, 2002). This type of theism comes very close what is accepted by Byzantine theology.

Dvaita and *Viúicm âdvaita,* the ontological outcome is too *dualistic.* Hence, the most useful Indian philosophy from my point of view that provides a fruitful comparison with the Byzantine tradition, in this context, is *Pratyabhijñâ. Pratyabhijñâ,* as with the Byzantine tradition, allows for a mystically completed (perfected) or maximalist notion of *deified* person without negating the place for what is real through the philosophical incorporation of unity-in-diversity or *bhedâbheda.*

When considering an appropriate model on which to focus the comparison, the traditional Hindu openness for dialogue in accepting other faiths can be utilised. This exemplifies a workable dialogical model for the convergence of theologies. This is not to say that the pluralistic landscape in India has always been harmonious and collaborative; on the contrary, in India there have existed historical tensions between its main faiths such as *Shaivism, Vaishnavism,* Buddhism, Jainism, Islam, Sikhism, and Christianity. In the climate of post-Vivekananda Neo-Vedântism, a consensus of an agreed unity-in-diversity[117] came to be evidenced, but this has experienced somewhat of a setback in the contemporary environment in India of political extremism. What is needed is a return to the theological inter-religious vision offered by Ramakrishna (1836-1886). This vision of religious and spiritual harmony which uses synthesis to underpin its dialogical efforts[118] is also shared by contemporary scholars such as Samartha and Aleaz to develop Indian dialogical theologies.[119] Aleaz states:

> The present author's Christian thought in relation to Sankara's Advaitic Vedânta is a practical demonstration of an Indian dialogical theology,

---

[117] Swami Vivekananda, *The Complete Works of Swami Vivekananda,* vol.2, pp.175-188.

[118] This vision was also shared by Sri Aurobindo, see *Synthesis of Yoga* (BCL 20-21).

[119] Aleaz, *Jesus in Neo-Vedânta,* p.121, and footnote 43; also see S. J. Samartha, *One Christ: Many Religions, Towards a Revised Christology* (Bangalore: 1992), pp. 94-104.

> more specifically an Indian dialogical Jesuology in terms of the perspective of Pluralistic Inclusivism for the relational convergence of religions, in this case of Hinduism and Christianity. It is also points to the fact that our hermeneutical context, a major factor of which is Advaita Vedânta decides the content of our theology.[120]

This model of dialogue will be developed through the notion of eschatological fulfilment, where all faith persons dialogue through a shared encounter with the divine. This model safeguards the uniqueness of each religion, yet upholds unity-of-faith, that is to say it allows for faith principles to be safeguarded through the concept the revelatory *event* which allows a faith experience in each person, thus upholding the need to consider what is shared. In this context, categorising is replaced with ideas relating to the experience of what it is to be a human being, the common shared reality of the human person experience. This type of approach has recently been argued by H. Coward in his analysis of human nature and 'perfectibility'[121] in Western Philosophy, Jewish thought, Christianity, Islam, Yoga, Hinduism and Buddhism.

The problem seems to be that inter-religious dialogue has been forced into categories of exclusivism, inclusivism, pluralism, and now the pluralistic-inclusivism of Aleaz. What is needed is a shift in ideas where these categories are replaced within a discussion of theologies on a theological level in a discussion of the convergence of principles. In addition the discussion could be more organic, considering the ways of personal dialogue, the encounter with the personal other, where persons enter into dialogue with other faith persons, because each person as an icon of the divine should be engaged with. In this sense, dialogue becomes not only a spiritual, theological, and dialogical task but also an ontological task. But inter-religious dialogue has to some extent learned ignorance, to

---

[120] *Ibid.*, p.121.

[121] Harold Coward, *The Perfectibility of Human Nature in Eastern and Western Thought* (NY, 2008).

cite the words of Nicholas of Cusa,[122] learnt the language of how not to communicate, not to dialogue and learnt how not to experiment with theologies, but learnt to talk in terms of static paradigms. It has forced categories which are foreign to a notion of sharing and the fulfilment of each person. Inter-religious dialogical theologians have learned ignorance: they have learned how not to dialogue by setting up barriers through these categories. But learned ignorance should be applied to dialogue in such a way where we admit mistakes, our short comings and what we cannot accomplish without divine grace. Through grace we can bring an *apophatic* element to dialogue so that we remain aware of the limits of our endeavours but we come to dialogue with openness with an attitude of humility in the face of truth, for as Nicholas of Cusa stated, "by means of learned ignorance we will ascertain what is the truer".[123] In this context of "learned ignorance", the ignorance that this work shall encourage is convergence through theological synthesis relating to a concept of person within the Byzantine and *Pratyabhijñâ* traditions.

---

[122] *Ibid.*, p.153.

[123] *Ibid.*, p.153.

CHAPTER 2

Types of Convergence

Introduction

We can affirm that there are indeed many theological problems associated with the practical application of *doing* interreligious dialogue and even more problems arising when trying to convergence ideas from different religious traditions, questions arise such as why do it at all, how do you do it and why pick on one specific way of doing it: what are one's motivations? Such questions represent real obstacles and challenges to convergence, nevertheless, I shall continue with this theological experiment because I believe it is valid in that theistic faith based persons have to start dialoguing with each other in a meaningful theological way to overcome false ideas and include notions of the religious *other*, religious faith co-workers. But we should be clear, and re-iterate, that the activity of convergence does throw up many considerable theological challenges. I argue that those challenges in themselves can become the driving force to meet problems head on rather than ignoring them. While dialogue, especially dialogue of the personal, of meeting the other face-to-face, is very important especially when considering the real implication of dialogue, of the meeting with the real other and considering the faith of the other and the very real impact on the other; and so we should approach such meetings without forcefully imposing our ideas or placing upon those meetings conditions or constraints apart from keeping the faith, but we should come to the other within an attitude of listening. Here I would also like change the favoured word 'other', for it just doesn't generate an attitude of acceptance, and use the words co-participators or co-workers in faith which seems to be more appropriate. However, there comes a point in which we have to practically engage in theological dialogue rather than being stuck within static engagement and generate a meaningful engagement with the co-workers in faith. Thus we should seek meaningful engagement and I would define meaningful engagement as an engagement that seeks, rather than procures, a response in the affirmative without forcing the co-workers in faith to respond as we would necessarily like. We cannot say that there is an agenda to dialogue where the co-participator has to respond, but through the offering of an open hand rather than a closed agenda we seek meaningful reciprocity and not just empty smiles. Nowadays however, dialogue seems to be trapped in agenda for there seems to be at the core of dialogical attempts an understated timeline and a sense of urgency that is worrying. Of Course Christians do believe in a timeline which ends with Christ's coming again where all faiths will meet in an ultimate point of engagement. As a consequence we Christians proclaim that any forced agenda is not the way forward but rather by offering an extended hand outwards, the co-workers will join in such a noble task as faith participators to meet each other in a space for dialogue and mutual acceptance. Also given the rise of secularism and fanatical anti-God philosophies we need to converse with our allies. Within the atmosphere of acceptance we can then explain our ideas or models of convergence so that the faith participators are free to accept, reject discuss or improve, but inevitably all things are in the Lord's hands. Just as the Lord stands back until we are ready to come to Him, albeit He is continually sending out His love to us so that we join with Him in that Love, so we follow this model in hope and love so that all faith co-workers can meet with each other in the peace of God.

Vertical Convergences

In the following sub-chapters, I will analyse the place for different models of convergence. The first presented is that of a vertical convergence which represents upward movements from below within an upward-looking growth of convergence. We can use the analogy of a Divine sower who plants seeds of faith in a field manifesting the many different plants growing upwards to God, all vying for the opportunity of healthy life. Fed and watered by the Divine economic grace through the sunshine of the Lord's goodness the plants grow and await to be harvested by the Divine reaper, which is God. This is a good metaphor as it includes the notion of a sower/reaper (the Lord) who plants and then reaps His harvest in abundance, but it does have problems. However, it supposes that all religions are equal, which is not true for there are lesser and greater vehicles of faith. Also dialogue and thus convergence would be constrained and dominated by the inability of these upward growing movements to properly communicate with each other. In this model there is also the problem of a perceived self-reliance of growing to the extent of belief in self-growth that leads to forced types of communication based upon self-willed movements rather than considering movement in the context of Divine purpose. The stalks of faith should be understood as a general harvest to be collected where He wills inter-religious communication as He sees fit as the Creator, where communication and convergence is not to be based on presumed false structures or mere self-willed ideas that force communication. Communication and convergence is dependent on the Lord's will, power and operations to accomplish such a communication.

Multiple Convergences

In the model of multiple convergence we can generate a model of multiple communications and visualise a multitude of equal sized circles all talking and bumping into each other, but dialoguing in a pluralistic secular noisy mumble where no real resolution is made: ideas are being expressed in a sort of chaos, where the circles converge towards each other jostling for a voice to be heard and throw out ideas which other bubbles may feel to be arbitrary and even offensive. To bring order it may be that a larger circle collects other bubbles around it and there is some sort of intercommunion between the large circle and the smaller ones, not between the smaller ones but where dialogue and possible convergence is based upon the hegemonic dominance of the larger. In this model any sort of convergence is not going to be well informed and conclusions will be placed at the expense of truth.

True Convergence

Which leads us to the last type of model expressed here which I perceive to be the truer. Here convergence generates a theology from above through faith inspired ideas that allows a vertical movement to manifest from below to above and from above to below to provide a synergetic meeting of God and world. In this meeting a horizontal perennial flow of wisdom, goodness and truth flow from the Godhead as a mighty river flowing out to mankind. The Lord manifests streams of faith which ultimately flow into the mighty river as it is the mighty river which becomes the visible source of life for the plains below and hence the other rivers join this mighty river to help participate in that nourishment and spiritual growth. The Source of this river is the supreme Godhead and the river eventually flows back to this Godhead, hence all religions can dialogue within this model of convergence in the understanding that such convergences are not for the source but aid the people to whom the mightier river flows. In such a model of convergence ideas of faith communications can be understood in terms of dialogical principles that come from the Divine, which allow us to communicate with each other in peace to further goodness which comes from the Good God. Thus in interreligious dialogue and convergence we co-workers in faith are all really speaking the same kind of language in common terms in describing God as Peace, the Good, and the Merciful, He who saves so that when convergences are made we can decipher what is being said through a common language. Not that we want co-workers to converge at the expense of the loss of their specific *hypostatic* (if we can use this word here) differences, but convergence is a way to generate theological communications. Only the Lord can know where and when all other God-faith based religions will or should communicate with each other and when they will finally and completely be merged in

His Love. But in the outpouring of Himself at the end times all will have to accept His reality as God and thus fully converge into His existence; but for now it is our duty to allow a *space* for convergence. We have to consider ways to develop ideas within a *theology of convergence*, so as to provide a means for co-workers in faith to communicate with us properly, not superficially or to denude the other's practice or manner of faith. The only currency here is faith for as Paul affirmed; Abraham was justified in faith so we all are justified in faith. We will however have no communication or dialogue with those that have corrupted their wills and thus their manner of existence to such an extent so as to worship evil as God or believe that spirits or anything created is God. The fundamental basics for convergence is a faith in God, not a quasi-gnostic acceptance in all faiths, but because God has put His seeds of faith in all true religions, there is a real basis for communication and convergence of theological ideas.

CHAPTER 3

New Ontological Paradigms?

Introduction

This chapter will have two broad aims, to compare terms within the Byzantine and Pratyabhijñâ traditions in order to seek a common ontological ground of becoming in God with a view to entering into meaningful dialogue; and to explore the place for developing new ideas through synthesis and convergence.

Through such convergence I will consider a new model of person, the *Âtman-hypostasis,* within a *space* for convergence or a *theology of convergence* to aid interreligious dialogue[1] within an atmosphere of honesty[2] and openness to dialogue with other religions. Within a premise of openness, it is hoped, that this work will be able to explore terms and ideas from different religious traditions through comparison and convergence without clinging to rigid ways of doing comparative

---

[1] As exemplified in the debate on personhood within an inter-religious dialogue highlighted by Descry, 'Unknowing and Personalism' in Bäumer (ed.), *Mysticism in Shaivism and Christianity* (Delhi: 1997); and K. P. Aleaz, *A Convergence of Advaita Vedânta and Eastern Christian Thought* (Delhi: 2000).

[2] Jacques Dupuis calls for an honest and open approach to inter-religious dialogue, see 'Christianity and Religions: Complementarity and Convergence', in Catherine Cornille, *Many Mansions: Multiple Religious Belonging and Christian Identity* (Maryknoll: 2002), pp.61-75.

theology in an atmosphere of respect for the other's faith and without denuding faith principles of co-workers of faith. Such an approach will affirm the place for multiple divine revelations, which can be considered as the driving force behind inter-religious dialogue. This addresses the problem of one confessionalism within a specific tradition through a focus on what is shared; a confession of the One God who manifests divine *economia* through a multitude of divine operations, through many *events* of the divine *act,* which allows revelation to be upheld within specific faith traditions while at the same time acknowledging the place for a revelatory process that involves the whole of humanity. At the heart of understanding the misunderstandings within the dialogue of world religions is a resolution of the problem of revelation within the context of the accepting of many religions.

The acceptance of the place for many religions impacts on the way we understand the purpose of God and how the divine *act* is related to economic revelations and how the transfer of grace is to be understood. This work will not answer these problems directly, but it will affirm the place for different forms of manifested grace within different traditions through convergence, while affirming the place for many economic revelations of God and restoration of God-centred human persons, which are ultimately to be related to the salvific work of the Christ and the divine principles (*logoi*) of divine operations. This approach goes to the heart of the purpose of God for 'man' and how the divine *economia* relates to human beings in a known or unknown way. While maintaining the right to affirm the place for the salvific work of the incarnate, crucified and resurrected Christ, I also affirm the place for the *economic acts* of the *Logos,* which allow not only the place for many religions but also the exploration of differing ideas and terms to understand revelation within a broad context of understanding the larger revelatory work and purpose of the divine for humankind.

Due to the syncretistic and synthetic nature of this work, it is appropriate here to provide some defence of this approach and to answer detractors that may object to a syncretistic and synthetic model.

We can look to the Early Church Fathers for a defence of this inclusive methodology. Justin Martyr argued the place for considering previous revelatory ideas in terms of the "seed of reason (the *Logos*) implanted in every race of men".[3] Clement of Alexandria also viewed other faiths and philosophies, apart from the Christian, in terms of *Logos-spermatikoi* or the seeds of the *Logos*[4] sowed through time by the *Logos* stating that the "truth, much more powerful than limitless duration, can collect its proper germs (*spermata*), though they have fallen on foreign soil".[5] These seeds of truth[6] represent a context by which multiple revelations can be understood within an inclusive sense and allow the place for fruitful comparison and convergence. This work thus appeals to an early inter-religious dialogical model of the early Church Fathers, which utilised the powerful imagery of the cosmic Christ who sows the seeds of truth in every faith and time to determine that certain philosophies and theologies represent *descents* of truth. Hence philosophies and religions can be said to stem from the perennial flow of truth that flows at all times in history.[7] Inter-religious discourse within this narrative allows for non-hegemonic interpretations and cross-philosophical interpretations within a *philosophia perennis,*[8] as Clement of Alexandria had stated: the "way

---

[3] Justin Martyr, *Apol.*2.8, (PG 6), 441-471 (Coxe).

[4] Clement, *Str.*1.13 (PG 8), 756A (Coxe).

[5] Clement, *Str.*1.13 (PG 8), 756A (Coxe); also see G. L. Prestige, God in Patristic *Thought,* (London: 1959), p.117, who highlights that "logos spermaticos" examples a Christian use of "Stoic conception", or "immanent germinative principle", (*Ibid*).

[6] An interesting contemporary use *Logos-Spermatikos* is exemplified by David Lawrence who sees this type of model as helpful when developing convergence within the philosophical narrative, especially in relation to *Pratyabhijñâ* and Western epistemological models; see David Peter Lawrence, *Rediscovering God with Transcendental Argument* (Delhi: 1999), p.21; 'Aspects of Abhinavagupta's Theory of Scripture', Satya Nilayam; *Chennai Journal of Intercultural Philosophy* 5 (2004), p.22.

[7] Clement, *Str.*1.5 (PG 8), 685-708 (Coxe).

[8] Michael Barnes, *Religious Pluralism* , in, John R. Hinnells ed., *The Routledge Companion to the Study of Religion,* (Oxon: 2005), p.409; Michael

of truth is one, but into it, as into a perennial river, streams flow from all sides".[9]

In Byzantine terms it was the *Logos* that inspired all philosophical endeavours before the *Logos-Sarx* Incarnation, the Christ, who perfectly embodies the culmination of philosophy, and who encourages ascents of truth. In respect of the universal divine work of the *Logos-hypostasis* of the triune deity, the contemporary Byzantine theologian, Philip Sherrard had also criticised concepts of "linear 'salvation history'"[10] that produce negative and exclusive claims, but rather looks to positive or optimistic models that stressed the *economy* of the divine *Logos* and eschatological fulfilment. He stated: "it is the Logos who is received in the spiritual illumination of a Brahmin, a Buddhist, or a Moslem".[11] Thus it is within this sense of cosmic revelation that I wish to explore the place for dialogue through comparison and convergence of ideas and terms of the Byzantine and Pratyabhijñâ traditions through this small study.

A Space for Convergence: A Theology of Convergence

Within the context of openness to dialogue, this work affirms that a theological *space* for convergence and dialogue, or what I call a *theology of convergence,* which could provide a structure by which theological convergence and synthesis could take place, such as an appropriate use of *Satcidânanda* within Trinitarian models. Other correlations could take place, that of comparing the Byzantine use of principles (*logoi*) with *Pratyabhijñâ's* use of the divine principles (*tattvas*). In the forum of a *theology of convergence,* the examination of *Satcidânanda* could be taken out of the discourse of comparativism and analysed more fully in convergence. Likewise

---

Barnes, *Theology and the Dialogue of Religions, Cambridge Studies in Christian Doctrine,* (Cambridge: 2002), p.45; Macquarrie, *Stubborn Theological Questions,* pp.50-51.

[9] Clement, *Str.* 1.5, 713 (Coxe).

[10] Philip Sherrard, *Christianity: Lineaments of a Sacred Tradition* (Brookline: 1998), p.61.

[11] *Ibid.,* p.62.

my new model of person, the *Âtman-hypostasis* also allows for greater exploration of the possibilities of convergence.

A *theology of convergence* would allow fuller theological examinations and open dialogue through synthesis and convergence without concern of recrimination or ridicule but would allow analysis within a *space* of discourse and reciprocation. Given that many theological correlations can exist between Byzantine and *Pratyabhijñâ* traditions,[12] these traditions would not only benefit from a *space* that would allow discourse to take place but may even allow ideas within those traditions to be developed from such comparison and convergence.

Despite obvious dissimilarities between these two traditions, there are many terms that can be equated from the Byzantine and *Pratyabhijñâ* traditions that could be explored more fully through convergence within a *space* for convergence to allow fruitful development, such as the terms: *energeia* and *kriyâ-Shakti*; *Logos* and *Vâc*; *hypostasis/prosopon* (indicating person) and *purusha*; *anthrôpos* (man) as a *zôon logikon* (rational animal) and *pashu* (beast); *nous* (here used in a spiritual, metaphysical *noetic* context indicating the soul) and *Âtman* (indicating the *Self* or soul); *dianoia* (mind) and *manas*; *logismos* (reasoning) and *buddhi* (intellect); *atomos* (indivisible particle) and *anu*; and *guna*(mode of being or existence) and *tropos hyparxeos*.

Logos and Cit

Within a *space* for convergence, correlations between terms, such as *Logos* and *Cit*[13] can be made, where these terms taken from the

---

[12] Some terms have already been examined to manifest a model of convergence dealing with fullness, see Bettina Bäumer (ed.), *Mysticism in Shaivism and Christianity*, and Bettina Bäumer and John R. Dupuche, *Void and Fullness*.

[13] *Cit* = divine consciousness. According to the commentary of Kshemaraja of the *Pratyabhijñâhrdayam*, "Citi (consciousness) used in the singular denotes its non-limitation by space, time, etc., shows the unreality of all theories of dualism. The word *svatantrya* (free will) points out the fact that supreme

Byzantine and Pratyabhijñâ narratives respectively, can be equated with each other to better understand the divine. Both terms allow a shared focus on the Divine will and awareness.[14] But the inclusion of *Cit* within the notion of *Logos* allows the ontological position of the *Logos-sarx* to be made clear, where the divinity of Christ is not only upheld, but through *Cit* is always related to divine unity and never ontological bifurcated although in Christ there is existential differentiation. Conversely, the equating of *Logos* with *Cit,* allows *Cit* to become *hypostasised* and not relegated to a modalist context in relation to the divine act. Within a Christological context the word *Cit* does not imply a mode or principle, but relates to the united Supra shining (*vimarsha*) consciousness of God, which in Trinitarian terms allows *Cit* to be related to each *hypostasis,* upholding unity within the united awareness of the divine nature (*Esse*). This awareness implied in the word *Cit* applies to all aspects of divine *will* (*thelema/icchâ*), which is never divorced from *being* (*ho on/Paramâtman*). In *Pratyabhijñâ Cit* also has an implication of mediating activity (*energeia/kriyâ*) of *Citi-Shakti*[15] between God and the world. This adds an existential dimension of divine *economia* in the Byzantine tradition[16] where both *Cit* and *Logos* become the mediating principle of the divine to the world. Both *Logos* and *Cit* are terms that imply a metaphysical bridge between the transcendent

---

power is of the essence of *Cit,* and thus distinguishes it from the doctrine of Brahman (i.e. *Shankaracharya Vedânta,* where the *Cit* is considered to be non-active). The word *viœva* etc. (in Sûtra 1) declares that *Cit* has unlimited power, can bring about every thing" *Pratyabhijñâhrdayam* (Singh), p.50.

[14] A correlation between these terms is also developed by Vekathanam, *Indian Christology,* p.395, but very superficially.

[15] The *Pratyabhijñâhrdayam* states: "By the power of her own will (alone), she (*Citi*) unfolds the universe upon her own screen (i.e. in herself) as the basis of the universe", *svecchayâ svabhittau vishvam unmîlayati/, Pratyabhijñâhrdayam* (Singh), p.51.

[16] The development of the *Logos* as the mediating principle, especially by the Middle Platonists is highlighted by H. F. Hägg who stated that: "while the concept of Logos has a wide range of applications as a designation of the mediating principle between the transcendent God and the world", *Clement of Alexandria and the beginnings of Christian Apophaticism,* p.230.

and the world through the will (*thelema/icchâ*) of the divine "Egoity", expressed as 'I-Am',[17] in an outward flowing of divine existing through the divine operations (*energeia/kriyâ-Shakti*). The divine revelatory activities can thus be correlated to a *Logos-cit-hypostasis* model,[18] which indicates the ontological relationship of the *Logos* to the divine nature and the supreme awareness of consciousness (*Cit*) of the *Logos* in relation to the divine *act* and the world.

However, the *Logos-cit* model has problems for the two terms are not completely equivalent. *Cit* relates to the consciousness of the Absolute reality that begins to be extrusive and *Citi-Shakti*is an activity of the Supreme *Shiva*.[19] This model does not have (in *Pratyabhijñâ*), a separate ontological existence and identity in itself, which the *Logos* existentially has as one of the *hypostases* of the Trinity. The *Logos* (Word) also implies speech (*Vâc-Shakti*),[20] while

---

[17] As exemplified in *LXX*, Exodus, 3:14.

[18] As it states in Kshemarâja's commentary of Sûtra 4 of the *Pratyabhijñâhrdayam* that: "The magnificent highest Shiva desiring to manifest the universe, which lies in Him as identical with Himself, in the from of SadâShiva and other appropriate forms flashes forth (*prakashamânatayâ sphurati*) at first as non-different from the light of consciousness (*prakashâbhedena*) but not experiencing the unity of consciousness (in which the universe is identified with consciousness) (*cidaikya-akhyâtimaya*), of which state *anâúrita-Shiva* is only another name"; translation by Singh, *Pratyabhijñâhrdayam*, p.55.

[19]*Vâc-Shakt i*is the power of the divine power of speech, see Mishra, *Kashmir Shaivism*, p.159, which is undifferentiated and related to *pashyantî* (3rd person plural, from the verbal root *dristi* to see) or the divine view of the universe, "going forth and 'seeing'", in Tagare, 'Glossary' in *The Pratyabhijñâ Philosophy*, where there is no difference between *vâcya* (object) and *vâcaka* (word).

[20] As used in *Îshvarapratyabhijñâkârikâ*, 1.44, 18, and correlated to *Paramâtman*, the Supreme essence and *Self*, as the highest speech, or '*Parâvâk*'. See also André Padoux, *Vâc: The Concept of the Word in Selected Hindu Tantras* (Delhi; 1990), p.ix; and Lawrence, *Rediscovering God With Transcendental Argument*, p.21; also K. Mishra, *Kashmir Shaivism*, p.158.

Cit relates to the Supreme Consciousness. Perhaps a better term for correlation would be *Vâc*.[21] While *Vâc* would imply a certain modalist quality (in Trinitarian terms) to divine activity, it does come very close to what is conceptually understood by the word *Logos*. In the context of revelation and the ability of the term to convey ontological gravitas, *Vâc* simply does not have the same weight and thus there has to be a return to *Cit*. *Cit* is capable of expressing ontological depth and existential meaning, as a mediating divine activity between that (*tat*) or manifested principles *tattvas*,[22] which indicates the objectified manifestations or *âbhâsas*. *Cit*, as with the *Logos*, allows a bridge between divine 'I-consciousness' and the world and thus an ontological and existential qualification of unity-in-diversity (*bhedâbheda*). The term *Cit* can also be correlated to the *Logos* as the conscious awareness of the divine revelatory activity and how the divine consciousness unites with the world to express a double consciousness, of the world and divine without confusing either.[23]

---

[21] *Îshvarapratyabhijñâkârikâ*, 3.2, p.59.

[22] This represents a double consciousness and will and the uniting of wills and consciousness expressed in Maximus' dyothelite theology. Maximus stated: "let no-one censure the doctrine that forbids a duality of gnomic wills, when they find that nearly all the glorious teachers say that there are two wills...For the divine Fathers do not speak of quantity in relation to gnomic wills, but only in relation to natural wills, rightly calling the essential and natural laws and principles of what has been united wills... so being able to speak always belongs to the nature, but how you speak belongs to the hypostasis. So is it with being disposed by nature to will and willing...Then the Incarnate Word possesses as a human being the natural disposition to will, and this is moved and shaped by his divine will", *Opsc.3*, 45C-48B; translation by Louth, *Maximus the Confessor Maximus the Confessor*, p.193. See also Maximus, *Ep.*19, 592C. As Bathrellos states: "For Maximus, the *Logos* is the same before and after the incarnation, namely God a divine person...Maximus says that the flesh became one with the *Logos* according to *hypostasis*. However, although the *Logos* is identical with the human nature according to *hypostasis*, he is not identical with it according to nature", see 'The Dyothelite Christology of Maximus', in *The Byzantine Christ*, p.111.

[23] On this see, D. Dragas, *Saint Athanasius of Alexandria* (Rollinsford: 2005), p.1.

Principles of Revelation

From the perspective of revelation another important term that can be incorporated in models of convergence, within a Christological context, is the term *Ishvara,* which in *Pratyabhijñâ* represents a divine principle, the fourth *tattva* (principle) of the thirty-six *tattvas* of revelation and relates to the divine *economy.* But Christ is not to be understood merely as a principle of the divine revelation, for that would predicate Christ to a mode of the divine being, which is unacceptable in Byzantine Trinitarian theology. Christ can be considered as the 'One' by whom the *tattvas* become manifest, but not merely a principle of creation. What can be asserted, from a Byzantine point of view, is that Christ (the *enfleshed-Logos*)[24] manifests divine uncreated principles (*logoi*), which come from Him (God) and are non-different[25] to Him, and which could include the "pure" *tattvas* (also the *Ishvara tattva*).[26] The *tattvas* or created principles have to be related to the created world; to that which is *genitos,* and correlated to the natural *physis* of manifested phenomena. In the Christological model, however, the *Logos* becomes identified with the Supreme unmoving 'One' which is the "Highest Reality"[27] or *Shiva,* where the *Logos-activity* could be correlated to divine principles (*tattvas*) or *logoi,* and could be understood as uncreated and "Preexistent"[28] activities of the divine. Here reference is made to Maximus the Confessor's notion of *logoi* or principles of uncreated divine operations in relation to the *Logos*[29] to argue that the *Ishvara* can be understood as an *economic* principle, and as an exterior principle of the divine.[30] As such, the *Ishvara*

---

[24] Maximus, *Ambig.7* (1077C-1081C).

[25] The *"pure tattvas"* belong to the first five *tattvas* and the "pure universe" whilst the remaining *tattvas* belong to the "impure universe".

[26] *Pratyabhijñâhrdayam,* (Singh), p.118.

[27] Pseudo-Dionysius, *DN,* 5.5-5.8, 820A-824A.

[28] Maximus, *Ambig.7,* 1077C-1081C.

[29] *Îshvarapratyabhijñâkârikâ* (Pandit), 3.1.2.

[30] This word is used in *Îshvarapratyabhijñâkârikâ,* 1.44, p.18. According to the *Pratyabhijñâhrdayam,* Shiva is the "Highest Reality...His Self (which

can be understood in terms of a manifested principle of Christ, where the divine principles are considered in relation to the Supreme or unmoving transcendent God (*Paramâtman*),[31] and ontologically non-different from the *Logos-cit* but existentially coming from God. The notion of divine economy also helps to resolve the riddle of whether Christ is to be viewed as another *Avatar*[32] or the only perfect total bodily Incarnation of the divine. To resolve this issue, I utilise *Pratyabhijñâ's* concept of principles (*tattvas*) in conjunction with the Maximus notion of principles (*logoi*) to affirm Christ as the author of the divine principles but not to be ontologically reduced to those principles. I argue that Christ is not to be considered as another *Avatar*, but the source of all principles, including the *Avataric* principle or *Ishvara-tattva*. This principle, related to the term *Ishvara* (God personified in *Pratyabhijñâ*) and the fourth *tattva* of divine manifestation in *Pratyabhijñâ*[33] is to be considered as an extrusive revelatory aspect of the Absolute. The Incarnate Christ as the second person of the *tri-hypostatic* Godhead becomes the source from which *Avataric* forms or divine revelatory principles manifest. As such *Avataric* manifestations can be correlated to the *Ishvara-tattva* and economic manifestations of the Absolute Godhead. While historically the *Avatar* principle or personified divine revelations

---

is also the Real Self of each individual) that is a mass of consciousness and bliss" (Singh), *Pratyabhijñâhrdayam* (*Singh*), p.46.

[31] Which is argued by Torwesten in, *Ramakrishna and Christ*, pp.5-15, 23, 174.

[32] See *Îshvarapratyabhijñâkârikâ*, 3.9, p.62.

[33] The *Bhagavad Gîtâ* states: "Who meditates on Me with his mind controlled by constant practice of Yoga and not wandering astray, O Son of Pritha! He attains to Him, the effulgent self – the Supreme Purusha", *abhyâsa-yoga-yuktena cetasâ nânya-gâminâ paramam purusham divyam yâti pârthânucintayan*, 8.8 (Vaidik). The nature of this Supreme person though is non-different to the reality of that personhood or *Âtmanic* radiance, thus in this context there is no difference between the *Âtman*, Supreme Person or the radiance of the divine *Self*, but in the Byzantine tradition, because of trinitarian theology, there is a need to qualify how divine difference is to be understood in relation to non-difference.

are equated with the *Ishvara-tattva,* it also indicates a type of revelation of the Absolute within the wider Hindu tradition. This is exemplified in the *Bhagavad Gîtâ* where the *Ishvara* is called the "Supreme Purusha (*param purusham*)",[34] which ultimately points to the *Paramâtmanic* reality. Another point that must be raised here relates to the notion of Godhead in *Pratyabhijñâ,* which did not have a precise doctrine of Godhead. Nevertheless, the notion of the unmoving divine essence of *Paramâtman* can be correlated to a Judeo-Christian notion of Godhead, and to a personal sense of *Paramâtman* contained within the term, *Shiva.*[35] But there is again some confusion with regard as to what constitutes the Absolute Reality in *Pratyabhijñâ* for sometimes some terms such as *Maheshvara*[36] and *Pârameshvara* are related to a notion similar to that which is understood by a personal Godhead and at other times in relation to an extrusive principle of the Absolute Reality.[37] In

---

[34] As exemplified by Pandit throughout his translation of the *Îshvarapratyabhijñâkârikâ.* Nevertheless the absolute *being* is described as the "highest Shiva desiring to manifest the universe", *Pratyabhijñâhrdayam,* 4 (Singh).

[35] See *Îshvarapratyabhijñâkârikâ* , 1.2, p.2, which states "Other than the person taking some insentient entity as his Self, who would try to either deny or establish the existence of the eternally existent Almighty God (*Maheœvare*), who has the independent power of doing and knowing, and is, in fact, onne's own (real) Self?" (Pandit), *kartari jñâtari svâtmany âdhi-siddhe maheshvara/ ajadâtma nishedham vâ siddhim vâ vidahîta kah//, Îshvarapratyabhijñâkârikâ,* 1.1.2 .

[36] Utpala states that *Pârameshvara* represented an "exterior aspect" indicating the *Ishvara tattva,* "later, through an emphasis on its exterior aspect, *Pârameshvara* (meaning the *Ishvara-tattva* here) emerges", *bahir-bhâva-paratve tu paratah pârameshvaram//, Îshvarapratyabhijñâkârikâ,* 3.2.

[37] The word or God is used by Pandit not only in his commentary but also in the translation of the text, *Îshvarapratyabhijñâkârikâ,* 2.4.4, (Pandit), p.137, where he refers to the "unknowable Authority (God)" (*Ibid.*). He again refers to God in the translation of the text stating "God has been accepted as the cause" (*Îshvarapratyabhijñâkârikâ,* Pandit, 2.4.8, p.140) when the actual word is *Pârameshvara* (*Îshvarapratyabhijñâkârikâ,* 2.40, p.52), and many times refers to the "Absolute God" in Pandit's commentary, *Îshvarapratyabhij ñâkârikâ, Îshvarapratyabhijñâkârikâ,* Pandit, p.141.

addition, contemporary translations of *Pratyabhijñâ* texts use such words as Godhead,[38] superimposing theological ideas that were not originally present in *Pratyabhijñâ,* but which now have come to indicate a contemporary notion of Godhead. Certainly, in the text of the *Pratyabhijñâhrdayam* the description of the Brahman[39] and words indicating the Absolute Lord[40] do indeed seem to be correlated to an idea of Godhead,[41] and sometimes equated with light of essential *being* (*prakashâtmâ*) of manifestation.[42] But how far this monist reality can be equated with a Judeo-Christian theistic God is still open to question as is how far convergence can help inform Christian theology.

Âtman-hypostasis: A New Model of Person

Nevertheless, to further comparison and convergence I synthesise ideas relating to person from both traditions, within a *space* for convergence, by correlating the term *Âtman* to a notion of personal existing (*hypostasis*) within a single term the *Âtman-hypostasis.* This is to allow person to take on a dimension of fullness within a substantialist context, that is a context in the human condition to include a dynamic of essential unity in a mystical experience that allows for what is concrete and real but also spiritual fulfilment in the recapitulated essence of *being.* But the *Âtman* shall not indicate an affirmation of 'the Self' but a principle of perfection; or that the fundamental condition of *being* cannot be changed for the Lord made *being* and saw that it was 'good', hence *Âtman* becomes the

---

[38] *Pratyabhijñâhrdayam,* 1-2, 'Commentary'; on this also see also *Îshvarapratyabhijñâkârikâ,* (Pandit), p.150.

[39] See *Îshvarapratyabhijñâkârikâ,* 1.1, p.1.

[40] It is also correlated to the human condition, see *Îshvarapratyabhijñâkârikâ,* 1.41, p.17, where Utpala equated the *Âtmanic* experience of the Swâmi with the divine stating "the divine master (*svâmi*) surley has the knowledge of the entire phenomenal existence contained within Himself (in his potency of *Âtman*); otherwise the throb of his will to manifest could not proceed"; *Îshvarapratyabhijñâkârikâ,* (Pandit), 1.5.10, p.59.

[41] *Îshvarapratyabhijñâkârikâ,* 1.34, p.15.

[42] See Nikita Stithatos, 'On the Inner Nature of Things', *Philokalia.*

unchanging principle of perfected *being* experienced in a personal way as *hypostasis* which can be experienced in an *event of Âtman*. In this *deification* experience the *Âtmanic* condition becomes the personal manner of existing fulfilled in a recapitulated context. This allows a dimension of fullness but will not be equated within a natural perfection or *theoria* (contemplation) but is to be equated to a Divine en-gracing which provides a theistic dimension to the *Âtmanic* condition of *re-cognition* when correlated to *deification* within a model of person. The context of *deification*, when taken in the right way, allows the inclusion of the prefix *Âtman* to be included within a Byzantine notion of a restored condition to be included in a concept of person, where through grace (*shaktipata/ charis*) a person comes to live in a *way* that he or she should through divine intentionality and operations. The *Âtman*, when equated with the highest part of the soul, the *noetic* essence,[43] becomes the principle of created life, the principle gained through God's in-breathing, which originally meant a true way of existing. It now means that through an en-graced participation or true union with the divine, union is once again attained through a union of body and soul attained through a union with God. As such the *hypostasis* represents the original condition of the unique concrete person; the 'fallen' state when understood through the limited term of individual and paradoxically the dimension of personal existing in a manner that is perfected or a restoration of the intended way of life meant for us as the condition of *being*. The person attains his/her true 'image' (*imago dei*) of God through 'grace', for all persons were created in the 'image' of God, but this 'image' or true state in both traditions has either been lost or has been corrupted due to 'fallen-ness' or due to a deluded condition and but has to be recovered through grace. This lack of experience of a true condition can be referred to a *fall* or loss of the manner of true *being*: human persons have lost their perfected condition or '*Adamic*' manner of life, but now through Christ or by economia they attain not only the

---

[43] See, Hilarion Alfeyev, *St Symeon the New Theologian and Orthodox Tradition* (Oxford: 2005), p.182.

restored *Adamic* image condition, but also attain the 'likeness' of God in *deification* or recognition. We can call *re-cognition* *deification* by dispensation. In *deification* the Divine ontologically changes the human person to allow for a 'new' type of life as a new self, a 'new' person. This new-ness can be understood through the term *Âtman* which implies the possibilities of an en-graced condition open to human persons in a becoming. Thus the *Âtman-hypostasis* represents both aspects of this en-graced dynamic; the *Âtman* indicates the possibilities or principle of 'likeness' or the possibilities of restoration in human persons and *hypostasis* relates to the personal manner of existing. The personal *hypostasis* represents both the conditions of the 'fallen-ness' and also the possibilities of fullness where human persons are brought back into communion (*koinonia*) with the divine. Thus the possibilities of experiencing a reformulation and the attaining of 'image' and 'likeness' are contained within the *Âtman-hypostasis*.

Another issue concerns the word *Satcidânanda*, which has been correlated to the Trinity by Bede Griffiths and other theologians, but I am suspicious of this for it has modalist implications inherent within such a model. I would rather use *Satcidânanda* to imply a true Trinitarian 'image' state inherent within the human person. Such a correlation of a trinitarian type dynamic has been considered in Christianity by Augustine, Gregory of Nyssa and St Symeon the New Theologian.[44] In the model of this work the human person contains the possibilities of trinitarian 'image' regained through baptism and realised in deified 'likeness' where the soul experiences firstly *being* (*sat*) consciousness, then consciousness (*citta*) and love (*ânanda* or bliss) in a normal way in varying degrees but in the true ontological state of 'likeness' and through the operations and *deifying* activity (*energeia/kriyâ-Shakti*) the condition of *Satcidânanda* is truly experienced as one's own mode of being corresponding to a true state of reformulated *being*.

---

[44] Zizioulas, *Being as Communion*, pp.16-50.

Through the term *Âtman-hypostasis,* the *Âtmanic* monism of *Pratyabhijñâ* is qualified and through an existential stress on *hypostatic* individual existence. This allows a flexible approach to person, so as to allow an individual to rise above the natural or fleshy 'fallen' manner of life, so that through grace the person is able to experience the fullness of personhood through the divine operations. This model is better understood in the theology of person developed by Zizioulas, where he divides person into existential categories of biological mode of *hypostatic* existence as opposed to an ecclesial *hypostatic* existence.[45] As such the latter mode of existence in a true *deified* way allows the different modes of existence to be correlated to higher states of restored *being.* However, unlike Zizioulas' I do not totally rely only on the existential to explain person, but utilise the inner point of *being* to inform the outer, which allows a harmony of both united and perfected through an *event* of *deification* symbolised by the term *Âtman* within the *hypostasis.* I do not only rely on outward looking existential models to explain person, but consider person through a true condition of restored *esse,* where through personal *hypostatic* communion with the divine the lower nature or lower passionate form of life is transformed through the divine to a higher mode of life which we can call *Âtmanic.* Through the *Âtman-hypostasis* the focus comes to be upon both the existential individual and the essential immaterial principle of *being* (*Âtman*) which when unified manifests a state of unity in the person and through grace ultimately a condition of reformed nature in the human person. The *Âtmanic* manner of life represents something different to a natural (fleshy/*sarx*) way of life, but is the principle of *being,* and here we can make a distinction between the principle (*logos*) of nature which is unchangeable and the mode (*tropos*) of personal manner of life which changes, where in a unity in God both are so completely bound to each other to manifest an indissoluble bond. Through grace we are reformulated

---

[45] Albergio et al. (eds.), *Conciliorum Oecumenicorum,* pp.57-63; and Norman Tanner, *Decrees of the Ecumenical Councils,* p.86.

in body and Spirit and experience a new manner of life where the possibilities of *being,* through restoration is fulfilled within an experience of union with the divine. Thus the *Âtman-hypostasis* allows the restoration of individual to be explained in the *hypostasis* within a context of restoration of *being* which correlates to a manner of life. It reveals *how* the specific *hypostatic* life should exist, its type of restored existence intended for a person, and the nature of this existence or *the* ultimate *what* of *being.*

Consequently, the *Âtman-hypostasis* also relates to types of consciousness within the *hypostasis*: one of a mundane condition and another related to a restored condition. The consciousness shifts from the lower condition of *citta* to that of *Cit,* to super-consciousness in the *deified* state. It is because each person can be known as an *Âtman-hypostasis* having an *Âtmanic* potentiality within the *hypostasis,* restored to the human person through grace, the potentiality of *being* is underlined within a specific existence through the prefix, *Âtman*; this potentiality becomes fulfilled within a kinesis of en-graced union. The prefix *Âtman* indicates the principle of immaterial *being* within the existential individual that when fulfilled through the *act* of restoration within an *event* of the soul allows a completed condition to be experienced. In the mundane condition however, a state of disconnection exists, hence a double condition is perceived in 'man', but restored in a unity of existence and *being* in the divine through ontological change. The ontological disconnection in the natural ('fallen') state represents not only existential separation but also an ontological denudation of the soul due to the 'fallen' state, but in the unity of 'man' the (restored) principle of *being* (*Âtman*) is ontologically united to existence in a proper way so that the soul experiences fullness in the body. The individual begins to become of aware of this recapitulated condition and attains a manner of fullness not previously open to the individual. Hence it is through the *Âtman-hypostasis* model that the possibilities of fullness are thus made apparent. While each term independently indicates an aspect of *being* and existence, together they imply a whole condition within the person. The term *Âtman-*

hypostasis also allows ideas of an immaterial nature and material existence to be brought together within a single term (*Âtman-hypostasis*) in the same way the word Christ implied, within a context of the Council of Chalcedon, a uniting of the *Logos* nature and the human nature in the one person of Jesus Christ. In the Council of Chalcedon, the whole Christ was argued where in the one person, two natures were united after the Incarnation and[46] the focus was upon unity through the development of the term *hypostasis* and yet includes a dimension of two natures and a unity of natures. Thus our natures are unified in Christ or rather our principle of *being* is united within a restored manner of life so that we are completed and then raised in Jesus Christ. While in the 'fallen' state of the human person (*hypostasis*) there seems to be evident two conditions of life, one of a life dominated by the biological life which Paul calls the law of sin (Rom.8) and another which is a life in the Spirit, in Christ through His union of natures these two conditions are reconciled. Thus we in God come to live a fulfilled manner of life which is really the true state meant for us at our very beginning. It is not that we have two natures but it appears that way for the two, the principle of *being* and the manner of *being* have been divided through the Divine will in the fall' (for we can do nothing in ourselves, it is the Lord who has all power) and hence it is only through the Divine will that we are healed and restored. These two conditions, the principle of *being* and the manner of life come together within a single property bearer, a single person (*prosopon*) and single subsistent *being* (*hypostasis*).[47] The word *hypostasis,* through the Council of Chalcedon, comes to be synonymous with person but also indicates in the human person perfected condition waiting for us in Christ.

Through the *Âtman-hypostasis* model of person all the conditions of life are contained within a single entity or person and highlights how this perfected state is possible. The word *hypostasis*

---

[46] *Ibid.*

[47] *Ibid.*

denotes an ontological condition within a person that highlights specific characteristics and an underlying spiritual nature restored to the person through grace and the word *Âtman* represents the principle by which perfection is restored to us. The *hypostasis* becomes the personal bearer of properties and it is through this singular existential condition that the notion of person comes to be understood, which contains certain ontological qualities.

The ontological quality of *Âtman* is however, not to be considered as predicated to the existential or outward individual but, as the restored higher spiritual principle which informs person of its true condition. Just as in Christ his unity of natures allows us to consider Him as human and God so we are to become in God both spiritual and bodily beings. Through the unity of *being* and existing within ourselves and to God in a communion of perfection, the *Âtman* implies in us certain qualities of *being* and awareness that indicates the possibilities of 'kinship' with the divine. These possibilities are made real for the Lord has united within us a real and also spiritual way so that each person can experience a manner of personal existence on a mundane level and then a fully manner of life through *deification*. This is accomplished through the restoration of our principle of life to us which is then spiritually perfected through the Divine will, giving a sense firstly of *being* in stasis, then of motion or process of being restored and finally of perfected stasis in the divine intoxicated state. When the divine *hypostatic* model (or specificity) is translated to the human condition the term *hypostasis* can thus be used to denote whole person in a way which underlines the specific properties of a person. Our model copies the Divine pattern so that just as the specific properties of the Trinity where the *Logos-hypostasis* differs to the Father-*hypostasis* and both differ to the Holy Spirit-*hypostasis,* but are united within a single nature, so we experience a unity of *being* and difference in the manner of life through grace, but not in the sense of being *homoousios* with God by nature, but in terms of manner of life.

The equating specificity of *hypostasis* within a sense of unity, as in the Trinity, allows person to be considered through an ontological union but also highlights the importance of specific characteristics. However, while the prefix *Logos* in the *Logos-hypostasis* denotes a particular quality of its *hypostasis* in the Trinity, this correlation cannot be fully ascribed to the human for each proper name of a particular individual would then have to come before the term *hypostasis*. The prefix can be used to ascribe in the human person the species proper to that existence and the possibilities inherent within each individual but opened up and restored to each person through grace: of a unifying ontological condition within the *hypostasis*. As the appellation *Logos,* implies in the Christ that there is a unity with the Father, being *homoousion to Patri,*[48] so human persons (*hypostases*) can be said to become *homoousion* with their own created essential *deified* (*Âtmanic*) nature through the act of the '*hypostatic*-union' so that we experience the manner of life proper to our own (restored) perfection. Consequently, when using *Âtman-hypostasis* the term *Âtman* implies an essential principle of *being* and manner of life intended for the human *hypostasis* and shows how that condition is to be conformed to each person through the divine operations in a state of *deification.*

Through the term *deification* the experience of unity is underlined to show how the manner of life is to be gained through grace within the restored person, whether in a soteriological and eschatological context. The *Âtman-hypostasis* also indicates that reality within *hypostatic* condition where there exists the possibilities of many types of consciousness, pertaining to the mundane and the *Âtmanic* reflecting the two natures within the *Âtman-hypostasis.* In the unified *Âtmanic* condition, the individual becomes aware of his or her *hypostatic* value and *re-cognises* the true nature of that existence through grace. Thus the *Âtman-hypostasis* model represents a qualifying of difference through unity, a unity of the divine within subjective difference representing actuality of existence and the potentiality for fulfilment of the natural *physis* in *deification.*

CHAPTER 4

Considering the Problems:
New Approaches to Person

Introduction

The considering of a synthetic model is not to force comparison[1] into rigid parameters, but to explore the possibilities of theological development through convergence and synthesis because of the ontological implications of restoration or *deification* in God, which is a common feature of all religions where in the highest experience union with God is the highest condition. There is a similarity of the

---

[1] I will build upon the comparative theological attempts exemplified by Francis X. Clooney see, *Theology After Vedanta* (Delhi:1993), p.1, but most especially utilising K. P. Aleaz's model of convergence see, *A Convergence of Advaita Vedânta And Christian Thought* (Delhi: 2000). This type of convergence has also been developed by M. Dhavamony in his, "Indian Christian theological method", see M. Dhavamony, 'Indian Christian Theological Method', *Studia Missionalia* 45 (1996), pp.57, where he outlines how Indian Christian theological method is validated though a correct hermeneutical approach, in which convergence might take place. These hermeneutics are based upon the legitimacy of convergence which is founded upon the primary place of Christ as the ultimate reality who "illumines all people in different ways and in a variety of forms" (*Ibid.*). While I agree with this sentiment, I would question what variety of forms means. Nevertheless I affirm that the notion of cosmic revelation allows the place for convergence though the many activities of divine revelation.

description of this experience in all the main religions. In Hinduism a *deification* type experience is known through the model of *Self*-realisation, which is not the realisation of one's own normative self, but a realisation of 'the *Self*' or *Âtman*. This experience can roughly be equated with *deification* but we can state that affirmation of *Âtman* in Christianity is as a principle of perfection had within a personal experience and fully understood in Christ who gives a Christ context to all realisations which come to fulfilment in Christ who is non different to Paramâtman or Para-Brahman.

As a consequence of an exploration of *Âtman* theological boundaries can be pushed forward. But here lies the problem for how do we truly understand *Âtman* in a Christian context? In *Vedânta* there is only a naked *Âtman* and all forms are false while in *Pratyabhijñâ* 'the *Âtman*' is concrete and the metaphysical Real and the world is also real but through God's shining activities (*prakasha*). Hence in the sense of the Divine activities of revelation in the context of the real world where the Real communes and participates with the world, we can understand *Âtman* as a principle of Divine operations within us, perfecting us and in terms of a principle of our own *being*. It is in this sense we can understand *Âtman* as placed in relation to the Byzantine notion of *deification* where it is correlated to a *deified noetic* (spiritual) essence of the highest part of the restored soul.

When we translate this understanding to the *Âtman-hypostasis* model we can see that through this model the monism of *Pratyabhijñâ* is qualified within a Byzantine sense of concrete person, while utilising the notion of *Âtman* to consider person as including a spiritual dynamic (or substantialist context) through *deification*. This also qualifies any over bearing existentialism that has arisen in contemporary Byzantine studies. By exploring the *Âtman-hypostasis* model I establish a conceptual bridge between *being* and *becoming,* between existence and an essential reality, between mundane individual awareness and relational *hypostasis,* within a concept of *deified/re-cognised* person. The explorations of the theological possibilities inherent within the term *Âtman-hypostasis*, affirms the place for a theological *space* of convergence or a *theology of convergence,* where Christianity (the Byzantine tradition) and Indian Philosophy (*Pratyabhijñâ*) can meet in a fruitful encounter, where ideas from each tradition can inform other faith co-workers.[2]

---

[2] Comparison and convergence in India can correlated to a genealogy of models of convergence (The idea for such a genealogical methodology was taken from Paul M. Collins' use of genealogy in relationality in the development of the term "hermeneutic of relationality", see P. M. Collins in 'The Nature and Mission of the Church Communion: God, Creation and Church'), where the historical development of Indian-Christian ideas have manifested a genealogy and theological evolution of ideas. This represents a type of tradition and Indian Christianity (see A. Mookenthottam, *Indian Theological Tendencies*, p.29). See Robin Boyd, *An Introduction to Indian Christian Theology* (Delhi: 1969, 2005); Anthony Mookenthottam, *Indian Theological Tendencies*; Jacob Parappally, *Emerging Trends in Indian Christology* (Bangalore: 1995); K. P. Aleaz, *Religions in Christian Theology* (Kolkata: 1991); also see Mookenthottam, *Indian Theological Tendencies*. A short genealogy follows: Ram Mohan Roy (1772-1833) who was the founder of the Brâhma Samâj or Brahmo Samaj; Ram Mohan Roy who developed links with Unitarians in England; K. M. Banerjea (1813-1885) who sought a common origin of Hinduism and Judaism. K. C. Sen (1838-1884); Keshab Chandra Sen who was deeply influenced by Christianity and introduced a Christian type of liturgical dimension to the *Brâhma Samâj*; Nehemiah Goreh (1825-1895) refuted Hinduism as a Christian traditionalist; B. Uphâdhâya (1861-1907), who was an important figure in inter-religious dialogue in India, and may be considered the "first Indian Catholic Theologian" (Mookenthottam, *Indian Theological Tendencies,* p.34); M. C. Parekh (1885-1977) also was another important contributor; Swami Abhishiktananda, (1910-1973) developed some of the most significant work in relation to the dialogue between Christianity and Hinduism in modern times see 'The Depth-Dimension of Religious Dialogue', *Vidyajyoti* 45/5; 1981, pp.202-221); Richard De Smet also highlighted important theological points in relation to *Âtman*, see 'Focusing on the Brahman-*Atman*', in Anand Amaladass ed., *Christian Contribution to Indian Philosophy,* Madras: 1995); Bede Griffiths (b.1906) equated *Satcidânanda* with the Trinity; J. N. Farquhar was also an important figure in comparing Hinduism and Christianity, as was Sarah Grant who considered a "world view" as an *Advaitic* Christian.

While the convergence of traditions is placed within a Christian schema, where types of revelatory events will be related to the divine *economy,* to the divine revelatory activity and divine condescension, this allows for an inclusive approach yet upholding the dignity of any given revelatory activity. The model of many types of revelation, considered through the divine economy, permits a synthesis of ideas to relate to the very nature of revelation, in that many types of revelation provides a way to manifest an affirmation that God reveals Himself in many ways but His ultimate revelation *event* was through Christ. But by affirming the place for many economic revelatory events we affirm the place for convergence and synthesis.

Ideas relating to personhood or *hypostatic* difference and unity, are brought together within a focus on unity-in-diversity through the *Âtman-hypostasis* model. This model is constructed to overcome two dilemmas, pertaining to the ontological and the existential. The ontological dilemma relates to a seeming separation of essential *being* and material existing within a context of the 'fall'. This is why the focus is on the *Âtman* in this work to indicate what is essentially real through completeness within *being*, to address the lack of ontological depth in existential models of person. However, this focus on *Âtman* in terms of *esse* or the principle of *being* personally lived in each unique individual is qualified within the personal, the concrete personal character of life, to argue that *Âtman* does not indicate a monist "single changeless entity"[3] or "single monist Self,"[4] but the highest spiritual reality within the human existential person. Both aspects of person, the outward manner of *hypostatic* life and the inner essential nature (recapitulated) is equally stressed and come together within the reformulated person within a model of the whole and the concrete. The focus is on whole person through the *Âtman-hypostasis* to overcome the existential

---

[3] *Îshvarapratyabhijñâkârikâ* 2.50-51, p.56-57; translation by Pandit, *Ishvarapratyabhijñâkârikâ* 2.4.18-19, pp.148-149.

[4] *Ibid.*

dilemma of *individuum*, as highlighted by Zizioulas,[5] and the need to overcome the natural ('fallen)' *physis* or the "ontological necessity"[6] within the naturally biological life.

Thus in the *Âtman-hypostasis* these dilemmas are confronted within a single model that includes the notion of essential *being*, the *what* of *being*, to qualify the existential or the outward looking person, by considering person as a *way* of existing through a *Cid-âtmanic*[7] mode of *hypostatic* existence. Here the stress is on how the essential *being* and awareness (*Âtman*) is experienced within a manner of concrete person. This model includes within it a sense of *deification* and an aspect of conscious awareness of this higher life within the world. However the *tropos* (mode) of existence is not to be considered in isolation as an activity without ontological subsistence, but fundamentally related to the true restored nature or the recapitulated *Âtman* within the *hypostasis*.

Seeking a Common Ground

Thus this work seeks a common ground between the two traditions hence an approach to person are sought by linking substantialist models from both traditions in relation to person and the essential manner of person lived in a *new way*. Consequently, to highlight how this *new way* is to be understood we also underline the concept of the soul in the context of a spiritually lived life. Not to over state the soul at the expense of bodily life but to show that in the 'fallen' state the fullness of the soul is not fully lived but only fully lived through the grace and the reception of the spirit so that a person comes to fully live as body and soul, recapturing the original Adamic state. The soul, or rather the highest part of the soul is to be

---

[5] Zizioulas, *Being as Communion*, p.28.

[6] *Being as Communion*, p.50.

[7] This is to be explained to indicate a mode of existence that shares both the essential nature (*Âtman*) and pure Consciousness and taken from *Îshvarapratyabhijñâkârikâ* (or now *IPK*), 2.51, p.57, which describes *being* in terms of *cid-âtmani* in relation to manifestations (*âbhâsas*).

equated to a principle which we can call *Âtmanic,* while including a *noetic* (reasoning) dynamic within the soul also allows fro a completed dynamic of *deified* perfection. Thus the Byzantine *model* adapts *Pratyabhijñâ* through the inclusion of rational and Spirit based consciousness which so that we can adapt the *Pratyabhijñâ* notion of *Cit* to mean in human personhood a spiritual consciousness. This model mirrors the divine *ousia-hypostasis* model of the Godhead, so that we properly attain 'likeness' with God (*Paramâtman*),[8] but not ontological sameness, by showing how unity and difference are not at odds with each other but complement each other within a model of unity-in-diversity. The equating of *Âtman* with the highest part of the human soul reflects a sense of kinship with the Divine so that we gain participation with God and a manner of existence that is 'like' the Divine indicating a sense of unity of *being* and yet in a context of existential difference. As such we can state that *Âtman* is to be equated with a metaphysical life *akin* to the *Paramâtman* in manner but not according to perfected nature, will and activity, but that it mirrors that perfection and blessedness within us.

However, there are some obvious problems in bringing together ideas from the Byzantine and *Pratyabhijñâ* traditions. One of the most important relates to the notion of ontological separation or the *gulf* between humanity and God in Byzantine theology[9] as compared

---

[8] As stated in the *Îshvarapratyabhijñâkârikâ* 1.44, p.18; and implied by Kshemarâj in the *PBH*, commentary to *Sûtra* 10, referring to the "Exalted One (Shiva)" who is the Highest reality (Jaideva Singh, *Pratyabhijñâhrdayam* (now *PBHs*) p.74. The term is also synonymous with the Absolute personal Godhead or *ParamaShiva,* see *Îshvarapratyabhijñâkârikâ* of Pandit (now *IPKp*), p.65, however the word *Âtman* was also taken to meant the Absolute Reality (*Ibid.*, p.66).

[9] See Staniloae, *Orthodox Spirituality,* pp.32-3. Dumitru Staniloae states that: Christian teaching adopts a middle ground between the mysticism of identity and the irreducible separation between man and God...Christian teaching rejects both identification and absolute separation (*Ibid.*). Nevertheless

to ontological non-difference in *Pratyabhijñâ*. This *gulf* can be seen to be been overcome through the theology of *deification*, but I will always maintain some sort of ontological difference to vouchsafe Trinitarian and Christological theologies. But the Divine *theologia* is not divorced from divine *economia*; the two are intimately related to each other and so when we talk of participation with the Divine we speak of *deifying* the person as far as possible which includes the context of unity understood within the term *Âtmanic* in a *hypostatic* context. The notion of unity or non-difference allows a reference point to understand difference and the two can be brought together in the human condition within the *Âtman-hypostasis*. In this model, simultaneity of difference and unity is argued from a recapitulated perspective, ultimately resolved in a *deification* experience in restoration of the *Âtmanic* condition of *being* in the person in the *event* of *being* within the *hypostasis,* and reflected outwardly in a *Cid-âtmanic* mode of existence. In this mode or *tropos*, the human person can be said to participate with the divine in the *Âtmanic* state, having an awareness of the divine, due to the participating in a manner of perfected *being, akin* or 'like' the Divine manner of existing. While the notion of *deification* is correlated to *re-cognition,* it has to be noted here that *deification* and *re-cognition* are terms that cannot be made totally synonymous. *Re-cognition* implies cognition of a truth of That which already *is*, not a *deifying* of the person who enters into a state of becoming, a becoming of something that was *not,* and now *is*. What can be affirmed is, that both the terms *deification* and *re-cognition* imply the fullness of the human being as far as is possible for a human

Staniloae's views are not an accurate appraisal of Greek Patristic notions of unity, for in the Greek Fathers in the mystical union of *deification*, the lines between anthropological identity and separation, and complete unity with the divine are often blurred (see K. Ware, 'Deification in St Symeon the New Theologian', *Sobornost* 25/2; 2003, pp.7-29).

person. This indicates the *telos* or perfected[10] end of person as an *Âtman-hypostasis* wrought by the perfecter.[11]

Also because *hypostasis* has to be equated with *purusha* this causes problems in relation to what is ontologically meant especially in relation to an already perfected essence of *being* and in terms of how human existence is to be perceived. Nevertheless through *purusha/hypostasis,* human existence is to be understood to be correlated to the individual and limited biological *physis,* but also can be correlated to a higher existence through the restored condition of *hypostasis*. This allows a concept of *purusha/*person to be equated to a category of the common human experience and also to an experience in which the highest mystical condition is given.[12] While *Pratyabhijñâ* did not distinguish ontologically between the divine and the human cases but equated the human condition to a single knowing person or subject-entity (*Âtman*)[13] I do not denude the unique cognitions of individual persons within a suffocating union, but stress ontological difference to the divine, while also focusing on union with the divine as far as possible without destroying the concrete specificity of each person. This model is argued through the Trinitarian model, while utilising the notion of *Âtman* to stress

---

[10] The term "perfect" in the New Testament is better understood as 'completed' for it indicates the end of *being*; from, teleios (perfect, complete), teleiotis (completeness, perfection), teleiô (I perfect, complete), telos (end). Theologically I prefer the translation complete or completed as the word perfect has ethical associations while completed has a fuller ontological implications.

[11] Or the *Paramâtman hypostatic-Purusha*. In Hebrews 12:2 Christ is described in terms as the completer. It is Christ the *Logos* (Jn. 1:1-14) who completes all things which in *Pratyabhijñâ* can be correlated to the activity of God to *Maheshvara* or the Great God, see *IPK*, 1.1, p.1; and in the *Hindi Bible* described as *Parameshvara* or highest God in Genesis 1:1.

[12] As Utpaladeva stated that "a person who sees objects as his own form is called a *pati* (a master), while one lying under the effects of delusion of seeing objects as different from him are called *pashu* (a bound being)", *IPK,* 3.14, p.64, translation by Pandit, *IPKp,* 3.2.3, p.173.

[13] See *IPKp*, p.147.

an essential recapitulated condition within the human person, to affirm an ontological distinction between the *pashu* (beast) and *pati* (Lord) in the human and Divine cases, where ideas relating to both difference and non-difference can be incorporated within the notion of *purusha/ hypostasis,* united through *deification.* In this model, *Pratyabhijñâ's* notion of revelatory activity (*kriyâ-Shakti*) is correlated to the economy of Christ's revelation, where the *Citi-Shakt i*of the divine is equated to the *Logos*-Christ activity. This part of the work will not examine the pneumatological implications in relation to *Shakti* other than to state that there is much scope for examination in this area. The external divine activity, when situated within the term, *Logos,* is to be understood within a synthetic model that includes the conscious awareness within divine activity, or *Cit,* as the *Logos-cit-hypostasis.*[14] This highlights how difference and yet unity is to be understood within a single *hypostatic* model as the *Logos-cit-hypostasis,* which is unified within its *Paramâtmanic* nature, while focusing on awareness to qualify an overt stress on essential substance. When translating this model to a human condition, each person or *hypostasis* can be said to experience individual existence and consciousness or uniqueness, but having an essential condition of *being* correlated to the term *Âtman* and indicating a potentiality for a higher state of *being* or cognition. This correlation of the divine model to the human highlights a pattern by which the human condition can be understood, having at the centre of the *hypostatic* existence and an essential *Âtmanic* principle of *being* experienced as a recapitulated manner of existence in the person.

---

[14] This model is given by Vekathanam (in, *Indian Christology,* p.395, who cites Brahmabandhav use of "Cit-Logos" to argue against a monist interpretation of Brahman in the activity of the *Logos* and equated with *Cit* to give an Indian Christian perspective in Christian theology) as *Cit-Logos,* but I will argue for *Logos-Cit-hypostasis,* where the consciousness of the Logos is highlighted within a hypostatic model. I qualify the awareness of the essential nature (*Paramâtman*) of the *Logos* through *Cit* or consciousness. Hence the notion of *Cit* uncovers the relationship of the unmoving *Paramâtman* to the world through the activity of the *Logos-cit-hypostasis,* which also provides a mode for human persons, made in the image of God, to understand the nature of their own being (*Âtman*) through a *deified* awareness in a *Cid-âtmanic* mode of existence.

Concerning Âtman

What is specifically meant by *Âtman* in the *Âtman-hypostasis* context? The word *Âtman* in *Pratyabhijñâ* indicates a singularity at the expense of specific and concrete persons, hence I affirm *Âtman* to mean a spiritual principle of *being* which is distinguished in the manner of personal *deified* existence. As such I reconsider the very way *Âtman* is understood and defined in Christianity for there can be in a human sense no naked *Âtman.* Thus we have to redefine *Âtman* as a principle, a principle of perfection and so we speak of an *Âtmanic* principle rather than 'the *Âtman*' for in Christianity *Âtman* is not a naked consciously aware reality that has the character and awareness of a divine singularity within which comes to represent another form of divinity other than God, but reflects the Divine will to manifest in the human person a condition of spiritual perfection afforded to the Christ-centred person. It allows for an essential condition as the spiritual *esse* within the personal manner of *being* in diverse and concrete persons. This paradoxical approach mirrors the Trinity, where there is evidenced an equal stress on both specificity and unity in a recapitulated sense.

Through the awareness of a restored manner of *Âtmanic* existing, a dynamic of volition is brought into the equation, where the whole person becomes properly united to the Divine will, overcoming the intentions of the natural *physis*, or the deliberate intentions of lower state through the spiritual or that which has the capability of being deliberately spiritual. Through the restored spiritual nature given to human persons, each person attains the capabilities of deliberately overcoming the natural ('fallen') will or passions through grace, rising above the naturally biological condition through the divine willing of *deification*. Thus there is reciprocity of wills. However, the lower human condition has not the capabilities of restoring itself sentience for the 'fallen' state is due to the Divine will which 'cast' out Adam so that the passionate and fleshy natures dominated the human will. Although wishing to overcome this state could not without grace (Rom.7-8) and so only through His will can we overcome ourselves. The overcoming of this 'fallen' mode of existence is dependent on the Divine will and activity to become restored. This restoration is made accessible through the reciprocal intention of the individual to wish to be restored, but made possible through the Divine will and Divine operations. Restoration is only possible through grace, which also represents Divine intentionality to act out His will for human persons. It is only when we as participators of the divine acts within an awareness and manner in accordance with the divine intention that we live in a full life. The dependency on the divine marks the ontological distinction between the divine and human realities. It allows a sense of the possibilities of human persons as portions of the divine within divine participation, but also marks the limitations of the human person.

The correlation of *Âtman* with as a principle of perfected *being* is defended by equating the *Âtman* within a pneumatological context of spirit and to the divine breath, "God...breathed upon his (man's) face the breath of life (*pnoin zois*) and the man became a living soul (*psyixin zôsan*)",[15] where the human partakes in an economic way the Divine nature (2 Peter 1:4) through that breath. This participation in the Spirit within was opened up to all humanity through the Incarnation and makes accessible the previous perfected Adamic condition which is raised even further so that a future 'fall' is not possible. The partaking of the Divine through a participated *koinonia* through a restoring of what was and now is in Christ allows a focus on the indwelling of a spiritually restored reality to be understood as the true centre of a manner of person within a concrete existence.

The notion of *Âtman* is also to be placed within a substantialist context as the true *Self* as restored *esse* of participated existence. In *Pratyabhijñâ* the *Âtman* was the highest reality of all existence and that human personhood, whether understood in terms of the

---

[15] LXX, Gen. 2:7. In German *atmen* means breaths, which provides a tantalising connection between breath and *being* within the Indo-European languages.

individual or relational *hypostasis*, and has as its centre of existence, the *Âtmanic-cit* nature. The *Âtman* was considered as a single entity as the 'subject of knowing', but in the *Âtman-hypostasis*, this is qualified. Through the accepting of a Divine contextualised willing, there is evident an awareness within the person of God's purpose within the individual acting of the person when restoration is experienced, and unified within the whole person. But in the 'fallen' individual manner of life there is an existential disconnection from the Divine will and participation.

In the *Âtman-hypostasis* model a correlation is made between the *Âtman* and the highest part of the soul or *nous* as already stated. This correlation allows not only a rational element to be considered within the soul, but also the soul within a substantialist context of a principle of *deified being* indicating a manner of *deified* life within the *hypostasis*. I do not, as stated above, equate *Âtman* to an ontological singularity, a notion of a single "knowing subject",[16] but an essential nature in the principle of *being* and as a lived awareness in a type that copies the Divine. The *Âtman* is not to be considered equal to the *Paramâtman,* but allows us to share in a manner of life that copies the Divine pattern. Through a union with God a soul participates with an *Âtmanic* nature, which changes the consciousness of a person, but although the specific subject or person (*hypostasis*) experiences a type of knowing a patter similar to that of the Divine when experiencing union with the divine and divinised as far as possible, but is not God or *homoousios* with the Father.

This correlation of *Âtman* with the soul, which has already been accepted within Indian Christianity and expressed through the term *jîvâtman,*[17] provides a way for *being* to be existentially united

---

[16] *IPK,* 1.67, p.27; translation by Pandit, *IPKp,* 1.7.4, p.84.

[17] See Mathew Vekathanam, *Indian Christology,* p.88. The *jîva* is expressed in *Pratyabhijñâ,* in Kshemaraja's commentary of *Sûtra* 4 of the *PBH,* as "the individual experient" as "Shiva"; translation by Singh, *PBHs,* p.57.

to personal existing through a notion of concrete *jîva* (individual). The indwelling metaphysical portion of the divine or *Âtman* in the human person comes to be personally lived. However, this model has been juxtaposed to a *dualistic* or qualified *non-dualistic* model, which leaves an unsatisfactory resolution between the *jîva* and *Âtman* especially when considering a substantialist type union with the divine. This is why *Pratyabhijñâ* has been utilised to help correlate an essential condition with the soul to a *deified* life, as the metaphysical *stuff* of *being*, through a context of *deification*.

The term *Âtman* while expressing a certain condition of non-difference, is to be contextualised through difference (person) and therefore should not be considered as disconnected from difference. However in a context of difference, phenomenal manifestation appears different to the principle of *Âtman*, but the *Âtman* is not disconnected from the manner of existing individual but the underlying perfected reality of existence is united to the concrete real perfectly through the Divine luminous grace. This luminosity shines in all aspects of creation and is the "very heart of the Supreme".[18] But in *Pratyabhijñâ* this Divine luminosity is "the real essence of all existence"[19] while in the Byzantine tradition, while we can say that God is the Cause there is an ontological *gulf* between created and Creator. But in both instances the particular *hypostasis* indicates the possibilities of a relationship with God implied in the perfected principles of *being* but which is not necessarily existentially available in separated individual but only in an en-graced person. The possibilities of understanding this *Âtmanic* principle in relation to human nature/existing and as *deifying* activities comes to be reflected in a reciprocal movement to the divine within a God-conscious person. It is through *hypostatic* reciprocity that the ability to experience a change of conscious awareness and fulfilment in the *hypostasis* becomes apparent which necessitates the end fulfilment through *Âtmanic* principles.

---

[18] *IPK*, 1.45, p.19; translation by Pandit, *IPKp*, 2.4.13, p.144.

[19] *Ibid.*

Âtmanic Freedom

When correlating *Âtman* to a principle of *being* and principles of *deifying* activities of the Divine for they both have to be considered together for without the one, the other cannot be fulfilled or fulfil. Through the *Âtman-hypostasis* model, this perfecting activity of the Divine to fulfil through the principle of perfection (*Âtman*) represents the freedom of the Divine to act and highlights a corresponding freedom to be acted upon by God in the person. The model of *Âtman-hypostasis* comes to reflect a manner of true freedom, which mirrors the freedom of the divine *Paramâtmanic* God to act and allows the individual to experience total freedom in overcoming the 'fallen' state through the will of God. The human person contains the freedom to *be* and a way of existing which was initially intended by the divine. It is the notion of freedom, the freedom of the Lord to create individuals and allowing the freedom of individuals to *be* that is central to understanding the nature of the *Âtmanic* condition. Freedom is not to be considered a condition dominated by the natural condition but allows the expansion and fullness of human cognition. This full sense of freedom allows human persons to enter into a state of becoming on many levels, firstly of a biological becoming, then of a spiritual becoming and then a fulfilled or *deified* becoming.

Kshemarâja stated that through "His free will, pervasion of non-duality, He assumes duality all around, then His will and other powers though essentially non-limited, assumes limitation".[20] Again we see here a difference of methodologies between the two traditions (Byzantine Christian and *Pratyabhijñâ*) for as Kshemarâja highlights that it is the very Lord who in His nature as Cause becomes creation and difference, in Byzantine theology its is the Lord who is the Cause but does not manifest creation as Himself. Kshemarâja views creation as an aspect of Divine difference which can be correlated to the *Paramâtmanic* causal activity and which becomes localised in a human condition as the *Âtman* having ontological sameness

---

[20] translation by Singh, *PBHs*, pp.71-72

with the Divine and total freedom. This allows for a true sense of God-centred freedom, which within certain constraints can be correlated to a Christian notion of freedom in that a natural (delusional) freedom becomes no freedom at all but true freedom is to be understood in relation to the Divine will and Cause. Also the individual is not an aspect of divine existence or an insentient object but has a real life and freedom in relation to God which for Kshemarâja is the very nature of the *Âtman*. But we can also utilise this condition when relate *Âtman* to a principle of perfected *being* which then becomes a principle of freedom in God. Without the *Âtman*, the human individual would have no capabilities for freedom, bound by its natural *physis* and unable to escape the ontological prison of the biological nature, but the possibilities of *Âtmanic* freedom within the *hypostasis* allows the person to truly *be* free. Freedom is not the ability to do this or that but it is that which allows the person to escape its biological prison and attain perfection.

Through true freedom, the human the person is existentially able to break the bonds of isolation and difference through participation with the divine within or through participated aspects of economic non-difference. But as Kshemarâja considers that if "*Âtman* (Self) has total freedom and greatness, how is it said to be equated with the *anu* (*jîva*) and covered with mala".[21] The answer is provided in *Pratyabhijñâ* in the next *Sûtra*: "in consequence of its limitation of *Shakti*, reality, which is all consciousness, it becomes the mala-covered sâmsarin".[22] It is out of the Lord's own will and freedom, *being* and existence He becomes creation in that it is He that creates and becomes so that creation and individual existence is in truth nothing other than the Lord. This may seem to infer a pantheistic conclusion but what is really being said is that creation cannot be divorced from the Divine will.

---

[21] *PBH.8* (commentary); *PBHs*, p.71.

[22] *PBH.9*, *samsârî*, translation by Singh, *PBHs*, p.71.

Substantialist Implications

Consequently, the *Âtmanic* part (of the *Âtman-hypostasis*) indicates the possibilities of person within a substantialist context as the principle of *being,* that is to say there is an essential dynamic that is perfected in the soul in the most perfect of ways. Each person has at his or her core, or soul, an essential condition within the *hypostasis,* understood as the principle of spiritual perfection within each person that is recapitulated to each person through faith, grace and perfection in the Spirit. The Spirit allows a person to become what he or she should *be* and live in a manner of perfection through the will of God, where persons become and live as something new in God. This becoming can be translated to a process of *deification,* as Rolt stated "God is present in each separate deified soul".[23] The characteristic of this essential condition becomes the *how* of 'likeness' which can be considered as correlated to the deepest parts of the recapitulated person and yet is intrinsically related to way each unique individual lives in a manner that is *deified* but in a context of personal existing, as Gregory of Nyssa stated:

> 'The kingdom of God is within you (Lk.17:21)', by this we should learn that if a man's heart has been purified from every creature and earthly affections, he will see the image of the divine nature in his own beauty...for God imprinted on our nature the likeness of the glories of His own nature.[24]

This implies that at very core of person in the soul, is a principle that allows us to participate with the divine through a metaphysical *Âtmanic* manner of existence, which is the preconceived state for human persons when restored to the human person. The restored state provides a basis for personal existing which allows the person to experience the fullness of *being* within a concrete existence.

---

[23] Rolt, 'Divine Names', *Dionysius the Areopagite* (NY: 1920), p.79, footnote 2.

[24] *The Beatitudes, Sermon 1* (ACW 18:89, 90, 95), in Holy Apostles Convent, *The Orthodox New Testament: The Holy Gospels, Volume 1*, Evangelistarion (Colorado: 2004), pp.84-85.

This *Âtmanic* nature does not imply that there is a negation of the *hypostasis* within a monist reality, but rather both aspects of difference and unity come together in the living person. The *Âtmanic* condition implies essential non-differentiation as a personal experience which has as its attributes of spiritual transcendence, unknowability, and permanence yet also consciousness indicating the total or true *moi*.[25] But in the Christ *hypostasis,* where the two natures of God and human were united in the incarnate *Logos* (or divine reality), Christ unites us to own manner of perfected *being* through His *deifying* theandric activities so that our natural biological *physis* is raised to a new state. The human *hypostasis* when *deified* comes to *re-cognise* its true condition through the activation of the *Âtmanic* principle in an *Âtmanic* event.

However in *Pratyabhijñâ* there seems to be an apparent discontinuity between the *Âtmanic* metaphysical condition and the individualistic distinction of the concrete and unique person, but this situation is resolved in the paradox of *re-cognised* unity and acceptance of difference. But from a Christian perspective there is a need to qualify both the terms: *hypostasis* which cannot stand by itself in its indicating difference or a natural naturally (biologically) caused creature; and *Âtman* which also cannot stand by itself outside of the human condition in a naked state.

Âtman and Paramâtman

The notion of *Âtman* correlates to the essential reality as a principle of *being,* which has been understood in this work as indicating a certain amount of non-difference in relation to a spiritual unified state manifested in the person through the grace of God, but is not equal to the *Paramâtman* (Godhead). While the *Âtman* is similar to the *Paramâtman* in relation to its manner of life, it cannot be in Byzantine terms considered similar ontologically hence we can speak

---

[25] These qualities are described by Pseudo-Dionysius (*DN*, 2.11, 649B; translation by Rolt).

of an *event of Âtman* or and *Âtmanic event* which can be correlated to *deification* in a context of the personal experience or allowing *Âtman* to become a principle of *being* in relation to becoming but we cannot speak of the 'the *Âtman*'. The model of the Godhead in Dionysius provides a pattern to better understand as *Paramâtman* and in terms of *Âtman* in relation to personal existing. In Dionysius the Godhead is expressed in terms of a "Super-Essential Godhead"[26] allowing for Super Essential unity to be juxtaposed to the notion of *tri-hypostatic* difference: there is a paradox of difference and unity which is carried in like manner into the human manner of life. While in Pratyabhiñâ an undifferentiated state of unity in God is carried into the personal existing as *Âtman* we can only state in Byzantine theology that unity expresses a type of life that correlates to a perfecting of personal being established by God. There is not ontological sameness but sameness according the manner of life. Still this is as a result of an ontological reformulation and not because of a mere outward change of life. In the Byzantine tradition the human persons experiences degrees of separateness albeit reformulated and restored to God in Spirit based perfection, but in a personal human way and not a God. Thus when we speak of the *Âtmanic* state and we can correlate this to an event of human *deification*, which becomes a mysterious condition of *being* or a beyond state in the person. Conversely this does not mean that those who do not experience this *deified* state of *being* become non-beings or have non-*being* outside of an *Âtmanic* mode of existence but that *being* is perfected through a restoration of the *Âtmanic* state in the person. The *Âtman* through the *Âtmanic* principle remains the metaphysical bridge of the material to the divine in the context of a manner of participation and yet seems to beyond the normative human condition.

In the case of human personhood, the highest expression of subjective awareness is ultimately expressed as a principle (*Âtman*) lived in a personal manner through the particular *hypostasis*. The

---

[26] Rolt, *Dionysius the Areopagite,* p.4.

Ātman becomes the metaphysical *ousia* of the human soul, the highest reality of unity in human personhood, united completely with the *hypostasis* and not disconnected. Even though humans may believe they experience separation due to the influence of their fallen nature, this separation is reconciled through the fullness of *hypostatic* life wrought through grace.

The difference between the Divine and human cases is an ontological one and yet we can as persons participate with God as far as is possible. It, the Absolute Essence, is Absolute consciousness and awareness and yet it is personally *tri-hypostatic*, united in its unity of *being* in the subject of that *being*, which is the Super Essence, having Super Essential consciousness and yet having differentiation in the characteristics of the Trinity. Thus the paradox of unity and difference in the divine allows for a model to be expressed in a similar way in the human being, where there is difference, individual characteristics, and yet a manner of existence that corresponds to an essential perfected condition, which is *Ātmanic* in nature that is the highest spiritual state. This experience remains unknown until the reception of grace and spiritual fulfilment in the experience of *deification*, but this does not infer that there are ontologically different types of persons but that the fullest states are realised as the *telos* of *being*. The human person can be considered as related to a generic type categorisation and of principles of *being* which becomes to be expressed through the will of God in each individual person having a body and soul where in the highest part of the soul, the soul is to be equated to an *Ātmanic* state restored through Christ. Human specificity thus has ordinary awareness but contains the possibilities of extra-ordinary awareness through developing of a God-centred manner of life for each person is capable of experiencing a true manner of life through Christ who gives to each person this experience of *deification* in many differing ways in an unfathomable *deifying* activity.

In God, the Super Essence when correlated to the *Paramātman*, expresses the highest divine reality (*Shiva*), who in the human

creates in the human person a condition for a way of life a true *koinonia.* Dionysius stated:

> For bestowing upon all things and supernally infusing Its communications unto the goodly universe: It becomes differentiated without loss of undifferentiality and multiplied without loss of unity; from its Oneness it becomes manifold while yet remaining within Itself.[27]

Through the *Paramâtman* there is a correlation of ontological sameness and *Paramâtmanic* unity through an *Âtmanic* life but Christians always have to qualify this. The *Âtman* represents a manner of unity with the divine and yet also expressing difference-in-unity, but this distinction is also made in *Pratyabhijñâ* in the distinguishing of *tattvas* or principles in relation to the divine. This represents a movement from sameness to this-ness (*idam*) and that-ness (*tat*) where it was shown how non-difference comes to be related to difference even in the context of unity with the Divine *being.* From this movement in the Divine *being,* movement comes from God to the created universe through *vimarsha*[28] or the aspect of divine consciousness by which the manifest universe is evident, while simultaneously unity is preserved in the *Paramâtmanic* consciousness (of itself) in the manifested (created) universe. In the Christian model there is no such thing as creation as an emanation, just the Divine will where it is the Lord who creates the universe out of nothing, out of no existing matter or not out of His own nature but by His will alone. Using Byzantine methodology,

---

[27] Pseudo-Dionysius, *DN*, 2.11, 649B, translation by Rolt, *Dionysius the Areopagite*, pp.78-80.

[28] See *IPK*, 1.42, p.18, which states that the divine awareness is the "essential character of consciousness being aware of himself...other wise Prakasha even though bearing the appearance of an object, could almost be compared to some insentient element like crystal" (*IPK*, 1.5.11, Pandit). God's power is not insentient, and thus a movement in the divine awareness becomes related outwardly as an aspect which humans in their ignorant state understand as the created world. The *vimarsha* is the second *tattva* or *Shakti-tattva* (see *IPKp*, p.156) and the existential awareness of the Absolute reality.

unity within difference can be understood, in relation to the human person, as expressed through a unity of *being* through the *Âtman,* as a portion of the divine as the "breath of God"[29] and "mingled in an unseen way"[30] with the divine, within *hypostatic* difference. This mingling represents unity-in-distinctiveness. The person who attains awareness of the highest reality, within the *hypostasis,* experiences an *event* of *Âtman* where the individual consciousness *re-cognises* its true reality of *being* and as such lives in an *Âtmanic* mode of *hypostatic* existence[31] as a *deified* person.

Possibilities of Deified Person

The context of *Âtman,* in relation to a model of *hypostasis, Âtmanic-*person indicates the possibilities of spiritual perfection within a concrete person, and is not be equated with a single entity or metaphysical reality that overwhelms the natural *physis* of the individual or *pashu* but the perfected principle of *being.* It is to be equated to the highest manner of *being* within the personal cognitive experience while allowing for mundane cognitions. In this schema of *Âtman* and *hypostasis* within a single person, there is be affirmed a simultaneous condition of willing, consciousness and *being* of two general types of existing within the unity of human person; of the natural biological and of a *deified* existence but only when the both aspects are united in Christ.

Through a unifying condition the sense of deification in person, person (*purusha/hypostasis*), is altered in the inclusion of the term *Âtman* to indicate the possibilities of a change of awareness and transformation of *being* through the perfection of person through the principle of personal existing which through grace renders in the person and through *deifying* activities of the divine a manner

---

[29] Gregory Nazianzen, 'On the Soul' in *Poemata Arcana,* 447A (Sykes).

[30] *Ibid.,* 453A.

[31] This term is borrowed from Zizioulas' term *mode of hypostatic existence,* see *Being as Communion,* p.50, which will include the term *Âtman* within a context of *deification.*

of existing correlating to a model of *deified* person. This *deifying* activity is perfected through the raising of the human nature to a previous Adamic state in the union of natures in the *hypostatic union* of Christ, which allows for *deification* on a cosmic level and even a further raising so that there cannot exist a new fall. While in the pre-Incarnation era this activity can be said to have been facilitated through the *Logos* activity of the *Parampurusha* after the Incarnation the Christ person personally activates this experience through a reciprocation of faith. Consequently, such activities can be said to be evident in other traditions such as in *Pratyabhijñâ* due to the divine *economy,* where we can qualify such developed theologies evident in these traditions through Byzantine theology of divine *economy* or dispensation. Through the Byzantine model it can be argued that after the Christ *hypostasis* such divine activities were expanded to include not only a few ascetics but all persons of faith. The 'fallen' nature itself is wholly restored in Christ and thus the experience of *deification* is open to all persons of faith and therefore the experience of the *Âtmanic* principle in the *hypostasis* is wrought through the *'hypostatic-union'*. Maximus stated:

> for the incarnation is an effective demonstration of both nature and the economy, I mean of the natural logos of what has been united, confirming the mode of the hypostatic union and 'instituting afresh the natures', without change or confusion.[32]

The *hypostatic Âtmanic* experience has become available to the whole human race, for each person now, has in the *Âtman-hypostasis* the potentiality of experiencing this reality in the Christ. Before the *event* of Christ there was, in the 'fall' a distinction which can be correlated to a distinction between the *pashu* (beast) and the *pati* (the realised master) but now these distinctions have been rectified. This distinction was made in the *IshvaraPratyabhijñâkârikâ,* which argued that someone who experiences non-difference in the enlightened condition is called a *pati,* while the one who is "under

---

[32] Maximus, *Opsc.3,* 48.C (Louth).

the effects of delusion...is called a *pashu* (a bound being)".[33] The biological or natural condition of the *pashu* is distinguished by a covering of *mâyâ* (illusion), or *ânava-mala* (covering of *self*, limitation), or the "defilement of finitude".[34] While the biological condition, equated to Zizioulas' notion of *"hypostasis of biological existence"*,[35] has a mode of existence that is separated from God and contrasts to a relational person or a *"hypostasis of ecclesial existence"*[36] in a true reformulation of *being* persons attain a true mode of life. This can be expressed as a perfected ecclesial existence which represents a soteriological type of life highlighted in the *Âtman-hypostasis*, where grace allows access to the divine life, and where the *Âtman-hypostasis* indicates the potentiality for communion in the relationship with the divine. This is not possible through the natural ('fallen') *physis* of the biological individual alone, but becomes open to all persons through the '*hypostatic-union*'. Inherent in the word *hypostasis*, are the possibilities of *deification* within the human person through the sharing of an underlying stasis (standing) of *being*, where the *Âtmanic* experience becomes open to the *hypostasis* in the experience of this stasis through the Christ-*hypostasis*.

The *Âtman-hypostasis* model clarifies the natural condition and explains that what is happening in the body condition in *deification* is a transformation of mode of existence of the *hypostasis*. There are not two types of *hypostases*, which may be inferred in Zizioulas model[37] one of the biological and another of the ecclesial, but a single *hypostasis* having the possibilities of two types of existences, but I would add there is another type of existence open to persons, that relating to the *deification* experience where the higher transforms the lower through grace opened up to human

---

[33] *IPK*, 3.14, p.64; translation by Pandit, *IPKp*, 3.2.3, p.173.

[34] *IPKp*, p.173.

[35] Zizioulas, *Being as Communion*, p.50.

[36] *Ibid.*

[37] *Ibid.*

persons through the '*hypostatic*-union', the Cross and Resurrection. The '*hypostatic-union*' unites the natural human *physis* to the spiritual because of the *Âtmanic* principle on an individual level and on a cosmic level, for all persons.

The possibilities of *deified* person, allows *deification* to represent a principle of *being* offered up to persons as the true ontological condition of the person, whether through a soteriological/ eschatological context, which informs the person (*hypostasis*) of its true manner of *being*. Within this experience, the individual reality is not to be considered unreal, it is not *mâyic* (illusionary), but real and yet the truest condition of the individual is understood through a *deified* or *Âtmanic* mode of *hypostatic* existence. This position allows for a paradoxical model of person, reconciling *deification/ re-cognition* and concrete material existentiality, of the metaphysical *Âtmanic* reality and the real world. The flexibility of Byzantine and *Pratyabhijñâ* tradition in allowing antinomic models can be appropriated in the development of an *Âtman-hypostasis* model of person in which the human person experiences in the body, an *Âtmanic event* in the soul. This *event*[38] results in the experience of *deification/re-cognition*, which involves human restoration,[39] participation of and within the *hypostatic being* where the *telos* of human personhood is experienced within an *event* of the inner being. This ontological *Âtmanic event* can also be correlated to the inner *eschaton* and to the outer revelatory *eschata* where the final restoration of human personhood is experienced by some persons whilst alive but yet promised for all persons (in a soteriological context) in the eschatological restoration of *all things*. In terms of

---

[38] Related to a Christ event, see Zizioulas, *Being as Communion*, p.130; see also Collins, *Trinitarian Theology West and East*.

[39] Though *Pratyabhijñâ* does not have a theology of restoration to speak of, it does distinguish between what is experienced as a *pashu* (understood to be a bound soul, *jîva/purusha*) a finite experience as compared to a *pati* (lord) who has an infinite experience in the realisation of *aham idam* ("I am this") or "I am *Shiva*", see *IPK*, 4.1-6, pp.70-71.

deification/re-cognition, the *eschaton* or inner *event* can be understood in terms of the completion of *being* in the *now.*

The inner event also relates to the outer *hypostatic* existence and is not only a single experience, but reveals the true cognitive subject, the true 'I am', where the experient (*pramatr*) becomes aware of the true nature of his or her existence in a single *event* revealing a true awareness in an *Âtmanic* consciousness. This *event* flows continuously in time, revealing a unity of *being* throughout time; which also affirms the place for multiple revelations. In the experience of unity with the Divine the *hypostatic* existence in the union with the essential condition of *being* reflects a form of participation (with the Divine) so that a divine type of consciousness is experienced. The conscious subject moves from an ordinary experience to a completed awareness in a perfected ontological manner of life in the *telos* of personhood. Perfection can be called the true state intended for humanity through the fullness (*plerôma/ purna*)[40] of *being* where the fullness of the *Âtman-hypostasis* is *re-cognised* as perfected to a condition of non-difference and *deification* as far as possible in the human person.

The notion of fullness can be considered as a consequence of the divine will (*thelima/icchâ*) and act (or operation, *energeia/kriyâ-Shakti*), and in the Byzantine tradition as already stated, due to the '*hypostatic*-union'.[41] Another way of putting it, is that through *Pratyabhijñâ,* because of the doctrine of *âbhâsavâda,* in which the universe is perceived as the luminous expression of the divine, the person is understood as an outward manifestation of *Cit* (divine consciousness);[42] the human person is perceived as a manifestation of the divine and in the highest way considered in truth nothing other than *Âtmanic* perfection. This divine will to perfect creation, which is understood as perfection in the God intoxicated state but

---

[40] For a good account of the comparison of *plerôma* and *purna* see Bettina Bäumer and John R. Dupuche, *Void and Fullness.*

[41] Example of see Maximus, *Thal.60, 73.*

[42] See *IPK,* 4.1, p.70.

not *re-cognised* as such in mundane awareness, is reflected in the Divine will to perfect creation through the principles (*logoi/tattvas*)[43] of *being*, which makes perfection or fullness (*plerôma/purna*) possible.[44] This notion of perfection of the *hypostasis* (person), becoming aware of his or her true condition, of the recovery of the perfect *telos* of each person is not only an eschatological ideal, but can be considered within the immanent now. All that a *hypostasis* (person) should be is already attained in the fullness of the eternal *Âtmanic* principles but perfected through the Divine will. This represents a simultaneous paradox of *being* and becoming which is to be understood in relation to the fullness of the divine ("One")[45] who has fulfilled all things, fulfils all things, and continues to fulfil all things restoring all things and persons to Himself, to His divine perfection.[46]

In this context, Maximus argued that perfection to be wrought by Christ for everything that is, is by the activity and creating power and will of the *Logos* and thus we can speak of the potentiality of perfection, as there is a *logos* of perfection (perfecting as far as

---

[43] The relating of the notion of *logoi* to principles in the context of *Pratyabhijñâ* has already expressed, but see Pseudo-Dionysius, *DN*, 709D; and Maximus, *Ambig.7*, 1077C-1084D.

[44] This possibility of fullness or perfection is summed up in *Shrî Îúopanishad*, "Om that which is perfect is perfect, the perfect arises from the perfect, when the perfect is taken away from the perfect, the perfect alone remains", *Om pûrnamadah purnam idam, Pûrnât purnam udacyate, Purnasya purnam âdâya, Purnam evâvashishyate*, translation by A. C. Bhaktivedanta Swami Prabhupâda, *Urî Îúopanishad* (UK: 1993), p.1.

[45] Where Pseudo-Dionysius stated that "the name One means that God is uniquely all things through the transcendence of one unity and that he is the cause of all without ever departing from that oneness", *DN*, 13.2, 977C-977D; translation by Luibheid, *Pseudo-Dionysius*, p.128.

[46] "Within its total unity it contains part and whole, and it transcends these too and is antecedent to them. This perfection is found in the imperfect as the source of their perfection. But it also transcends perfection, and in the perfect it is manifest as transcending and anticipating their perfection", Pseudo-Dionysoius, *DN*, 2.10, 646C; translation by Luibheid, *Pseudo-Dionysius*, p.65.

possible) in each *hypostatic*-being. This potentiality or potency (äðíÜìåé)[47] to live in a manner of perfection through grace comes to be fulfilled through the activation of grace through the *hypostatic* condition of the incarnated *Logos,*[48] transforming *being*. In this transformation and perfection, the person attains a state of "likeness" within the human *hypostasis* who, as the "image" of the God, experiences an awareness of the divine within a *Cid-âtmanic mode of existence*. In this experience the *hypostasis* comprehends existence through a cognitive knowledge gained in the experience of *Âtman*, or *jñâna*. This is not mere ordinary or natural awareness or knowledge (*vidyâ*), but a true knowing. In this condition the state of perfection is cognised within oneself as the *Self-Âtmanic* revealed state through a union with God. The principle (*logos*) of perfection is realised in each person through God who allows the individual to enter into a state of becoming as a "portion of God"[49] and live a deified manner of life for bringing the person to a perfected way of life.[50]

The concept of fullness is also exemplified in the works of Gregory of Nyssa who utilised a paradoxical model so that fullness comes to indicate incomprehensibility.[51] The notion of unknowing-knowing[52] allows for an antinomic model through a notion of

---

[47] *Ibid.*

[48] Maximus, *Ambig.7*, 1077B.

[49] *Ibid.*, 1084C-D, translation by Blowers, *On the Cosmic Mystery of Christ*, p.58-59.

[50] Concerning this relationship of the experience of *deification* grace Maximus stated: "By his gracious condescension God became man and is called man for the sake of man and by exchanging his condition for ours revealed that elevates man to God...by this blessed inversion, man is made God by divinization" (*Ibid*).

[51] See Gregory of Nyssa, *V.Mos.*, 376C. For an examination of *plerôma* see L. G. Patterson, '*Pleroma*: The human plenitude, from Irenaeus to Gregory of Nyssa', *SP* (2001), pp.529-540.

[52] See Pseudo-Dionysius *DN*, 7.3, 872A; also see 'Divine Unknowing', in Hans Urs von Balthasar, *Cosmic Liturgy*, p.91.

apophasis[53] in a mystical unknowing-knowing where in that experience epistemological constructs fail. God makes perfect all things even though the world seems imperfect, where God unites all things to this perfection. Another way of considering this position is in terms of love. Dionysius stated that "out of love he has come down to be at our level of nature and has become being".[54] He is also beyond being and human comprehension where his "fullness was unaffected by that inexpressible emptying of self".[55] Dionysius stated:

> He transcends the unity which is in beings. He is indivisible multiplicity, the unfilled overfullness which produces perfects and preserves all unity and all multiplicity. Furthermore, since there are many who are by his gift raised, so far as they can be, to divinization, it would seem that here there is not only differentiation but actual replication of the one God.[56]

In the notion of the perfection of *being* the subject of perfection is not the individual experient but the conscious reality by which union takes place, which when united with the ordinary experient, unites the nature, will and awareness of the divine with the experient.[57] It is the Divine who becomes the reality of the

---

[53] For a contemporary Byzantine correlation of fullness to unknowing, see Yannaras, *On the Absence and Unknowability of God.*

[54] Pseudo-Dionysius, *DN*, 2.10, 646D; translation by Luibheid, *Pseudo-Dionysius*, p.65. Note in Luibheid's translation Chapter 2.10 of the 'Divine Names' has been incorrectly placed at page number 648C-D of *Patrologia Graeca* (PG 3), however the correct page number is 646, and then Chapter 2.11 continues on page 649

[55] *Ibid.*, 2.10 646D; translation by Luibheid, *Pseudo-Dionysius*, p.65.

[56] (*Ibid.*), 2.11, 649C; translation by Luibheid, *Pseudo-Dionysius,* p.67.

[57] Or *pramâtâ* "is the knowing subject which is distinguished from known object (*prameya*), and the Supreme *Pramatr* is *ParamaShiva*, the divine conscious Lord, for whom the entire universe is His subjective Self", See Pandit, *IPKp*, p.226. The *PBH* shows that the nature of the *pramatr* is *mâyâ* in that its consciousness is *citta* or individual consciousness, stating in *Sûtra* 6 of *PBH*: "*The mâyâpramatr consists of it (i.e. Citta)*", *tanmayo mâyâpramâtâ*; translation by Singh, p.62.

experience amid differentiation through His unifying operations as Dionysius stated, "He remains one, nothing less than himself. He remains one amid the plurality, unified throughout the procession, and full amid the emptying act of differentiation".[58]

Concerning Consciousness

The context of *Âtman* within *hypostasis* allows not only for a restored substantiality of the soul but a perfected awareness within this condition. This qualifies the monist implications of *Âtman* through divine consciousness (*Cit*), where the 'knowing person' indicates not just the divine active awareness within the soul but also allows a sense of the rational person to extend within and through the divine awareness. In the Byzantine theology of Gregory of Nyssa, the soul was related to a vital faculty having three varieties; that without perception; perception without the reasoning activity; and the third being rational and extensive throughout the whole faculty.[59] The soul, which is intellectual and rational for Gregory is a "living operation",[60] which allows existing to be expressed through the faculties of reason. This in turn allows for many types of rational expressions, including an awareness of *Âtmanic* operations. The allowing for two types of awareness within the person, one of re-capitulated consciousness and the other a mundane consciousness, both united within a single *deified* person, does not indicate a bipolar person but that through *deification* the whole person experiences both aspects within a united construct. While before *deification* there can be said to be manifest a fracture of cognitive states, in *deification* this fracture is rendered whole through the operations of the Christ.

---

[58] Pseudo-Dionysius, *DN,* 2.11, 649B, translation by Luibheid, *Pseudo-Dionysius,* p.67.

[59] *Hom.Opif.*14, 176A-B; translation by Moore, *On the Making of Man* (NPNF, 5), p.403.

[60] *Hom.Opif.,*15, 177A.

Within the *Âtman-hypostasis,* consciousness is thus expressed through the mundane faculties and the higher faculties, which are united, in varying degrees, within a person. In the highest awareness, the *Âtmanic* faculty unites within the whole person a sense of perfection and completion. Again a way to better understand the human model, can be provided through the Christological, where there was evident a uniting of natures within the whole Christ. The awareness of Christ reflects this unity within a double schema where the rational soul of Christ is expressed through the natural willing of his earthly and human nature (not of sin or gnomic will) but which are also united to His Divine condition. In the same way He unites us to our own promised perfection in a human condition. Thus there is evident in the human person the possibilities of two types of rationality; the natural condition and that of the *Âtmanic* within a single personal awareness, where the higher informs the lower. This informing, for most, is on a level not observed as the *Âtmanic* principle and consciousness can never be divorced from the individual soul in which it resides, but it is reconnected with the person through grace. Thus the Divine wills and activity is continuously present in the individual where the individual comes to experience its perfection through grace. It can even be attested that without the *Âtman* principle mundane consciousness would not be possible for we created as a whole person and not in parts or as bits of *being* and non-*being*. However it is through an out flowing of 'I am' because of a union with the Divine 'I AM' that the unity of being is experienced as a proper manner of life. The finite 'I am' comes to experience a cosmic 'I am' which constitutes a pattern of life mirroring the divine. It is because the *Âtman* is not merely a static metaphysical substance but having pure awareness (*vimarsha*), or true subject awareness, that this awareness implicitly relates to the individual subject and awareness. As such, in the *Âtman-hypostasis* model there is a perfect union of both the particular characteristics of the unique person and particular awareness, and of the principle of *Âtmanic* consciousness in *deification.*[61] But it is the incarnational grace that allows the gulf between the two points of awareness to be unified, and mirroring a pattern of Trinitarian awareness and *being* in specific and unified conditions.

The Âtmanic and the Divine Paramâtmanic: A Model for Spiritual Difference and Non-Difference

The subjective unique and particular characteristics or persons of the Trinity have their set roles, indicating a consciousness that is specific to each in that role[62] and yet they have a united consciousness due to their *Paramâtmanic* nature in relation to the Godhead. This highlights a model in which distinctiveness (or difference) is evidenced in a united *being* (of the Godhead), especially highlighted in the two wills of the Christ.[63] Unity is maintained through the shared nature which is not a static substance or an impersonal mass of *Being*, but is personal, that is, it is the *Self*-aware essential divine reality having its own consciousness (*Cit*). This may seem to affirm that there are two types of consciousness, one relating to each specific divine *hypostasis* and one of the Divine substance, but this is not the case for consciousness in divine *hypostatic* difference is non-different to the united

---

[61] This simultaneity of being and consciousness is expressed in the *Shiva Sûtra*, 1.1, which states *caitanyamâtmâ*, which indicates that the *Âtman* has as its nature, consciousness expressed in the most profound of ways. This profundity indicates that in the individual selves the natural consciousness is an awareness of a deluded or unnatural condition when compared to that of the *Âtman* which is the purest expression of consciousness. This unnatural condition to the human person put upon human beings in Byzantine theology as consequence of the fall, represents a limited consciousness or a consciousness of bondage. This is why in the second *sûtra* of the *SS*, 1.2, it states, *jnñânam bandhah* (knowledge is bondage), that is all knowledge that does not relate to the *Âtman* is bondage. This then leads on to a description of how to gain that experience through the practise of *yoga*. In the Byzantine tradition this practise is called *Hesychasm*.

[62] Of the Unbegotten, the Begotten, and that which comes from the Father; Gregory Nazianzen, *Or.*29, 767C.

[63] Maximus *Opsc.3*, 45C-48B (Louth).

consciousness of the Divine essential nature. The nature of the consciousness of this non-different otherness is expressed, in *Pratyabhijñâ* terms, through the light of its own consciousness (*prakasha*), which is the united consciousness of otherness and becomes the true light of consciousness in human otherness. The understanding of the nature of this sense of unity within the consciousness of *hypostatic* difference or otherness becomes very important when translating this model into the human condition. In the human state there are two consciousnesses within a single person, one pertaining to the mundane consciousness of the deluded state in the natural 'I am', and the other of the inner divine consciousness. In the human state this inner awareness comes to be accessed through the *deified* state where the person comes to *re-cognise* his or her true consciousness in the *Âtmanic* or *deified* condition.

In *deification*, the higher awareness overcomes the sense of separation in the natural *physis* not accomplished by the natural *physis,* through grace, which unifies difference to itself through the principle of *Âtman.* In relation to divine participation through *deification/re-cognition* with the Christ *hypostasis,* the human person attains a true *self*-identity gained within an *Âtmanic* awareness. As Utpala stated:

> For this very reason the Self has been defined as Consciousness as the activity of awareness, in order to express its independent authority with respect to the activity of becoming conscious. This difference accounts for its being different from an insentient entity.[64]

The notions of *deification/ re-cognition* indicate a *noetic* cognition which goes beyond the natural knowing and willing of the human person and allows the person (*hypostasis/purusha*) to understand the nature of his/her true *being* and existence. This cognition reveals a change not only of knowing but of *being* and understood in both traditions through the relationship of *being,* act and consciousness.

---

[64] *IPK*, 1.43, p.18, translation by Pandit, *IPKp*, 1.5.12, p.61.

The Supreme Person,[65] through God's will (*thelima/icchâ*), and power (*dynamis/Shakti*), manifests creation (*âbhâsas*) and then brings creation and human persons (*hypostases/purushas*), through God's activity (energeia/*kriyâ-Shakti*), back to God's own personal being. This return constitutes a change in conscious awareness, which in turn reveals not only the true nature of *being* but a relational context of the divine to the world.

The Self: Self-Awareness

Thus we cannot from a Christian perspective speak of 'the *Self*'(the *Âtman*) of the Divine Reality as the true person within, for that would make us God in total; but of *Âtman* as a principle of perfected *being* lived in a *deified* manner of life and comes to be expressed through a personal consciousness. Consequently, in the *Âtman-hypostasis* the question 'who am I' becomes resolved through a theistic relationality and not because of a natural contemplation of the person as their own personal God within. There is no naturally spiritual consciousness but 'I am' because is. I am relational to Thou (God) are who makes me be and restores to me a deified 'I' because He is. 'I am' who 'I am' but at the same time 'I am' in the sense of becoming in the highest awareness, that becomes aware of 'That' as the truth. There is within the *Âtman-hypostasis* reflected capabilities of perfected awareness but which is perfected through the revelatory awareness of 'I Am That' (*being*). This is expressed in a context of *moi* in relation to the other, to the Divine other who becomes the ground of my own being and the fulfilment of *moi* in Thou. But it has to be stated there is in this sense of union a feeling of becoming Thou but this is due to the reciprocal experience of fullness where there is a feeling of a cross-flow of *being*-ness in participation, but this does not mean we become God but feel that God is I because of the Divine perfecting operations to generate this experience. This true awareness cannot be anything other than,

---

65 In *Neo-Vedântic* models person is indicated in the term *Sat-Purusha,* see Sri Aurobindo, *The Life Divine. Sat* indicates both truth and *being*.

in the highest state, a reflection of the Divine consciousness within an 'I am-Thou' consciousness.

The natural or biological condition comes to be expressed in difference as 'I am' and the other is another; and yet again 'I am' different to the divine to the extent of there can be no participation or true koinonia with God, but through the *deification* these conditions change. Thus my experience changes in relation to the Divine Other and the reception of Christ. If this were not the case, that God was closed to Himself, there would be no expression of the divine 'I Am' within a revealed context but a closed and isolated God 'I', expressed in a close monist context. The declaration to the other of the divine 'I Am', represents not only 'I Am' here whilst you are there, but highlights that the *gulf* between the two is resolved in an outer and inner *event*. Through participation in *deification* the divine 'I Am' is disclosed in an *event* of revelation to the natural 'I am', the lower *self* of the human person. Through this inner *event*, the individual comes to understand his or her true 'I AM' through the *Âtmanic event,* or where the principle of perfection is experienced on a personal level which is as a consequence of the divine commune. The revelatory dynamic of this *event* experienced within the person allows a resolution of the notion of 'the *Âtman*' within *hypostatic* experience. If there were no inner revelation but just the fact of created beings distinct and divorced from the divine, then there could be no condition of *Âtman-hypostasis* available but just isolated individuals. It is because of the divine revelatory activity that the broken ontological condition of the human person is made whole and the principle of perfection experienced in the person.

Through this healing of the human condition the human consciousness becomes intimately related to the divine, otherwise human beings could only attain an awareness of the divine, a knowing about God as phenomena outside of the human condition, which is no disclosure at all and not a personal experience of God. Hence in the *Âtmanic event* there is a disclosure of the true nature of *being* within the manner of life of the *hypostasis*, where the natural mode of existence is transformed into an *Âtmanic* mode of existence.

Cid-âtmanic Mode of Hypostatic Existence

It is because as discussed above, the *Âtmanic* principle has a rational element within the *hypostasis,* that the mode of existence of the perfected *hypostasis* has to include this dynamic through the inclusion of the world *Cit,* here indicating in the human person a spiritual consciousness. This implies that the mundane consciousness, *citta,* becomes transformed into a divine pattern, *Cit-vimarsha.* Hence such a person can be said to live within a *Cid-âtmanic* mode of existence and a true conscious awareness in a personal manner of existing.

The finite individual is moved from a natural mode of existence to a higher mode. The words, the 'individual is moved', implies that movement is not self-caused, but as a consequence of the divine mover. The notion of mode also allows an existential relation to *being,* where the inner ontological dynamic of the *Âtmanic* experience reflects outwardly and allows for a type of existence that reflects an *Âtmanic* condition. In this condition, particular characteristics of the *hypostasis* are not dissolved but perceived through the lens of unity through a Spirit-based *koinonia.* This mode itself, in expressing specificity, also allows the *Âtmanic* condition to be expressed as a manner of existence for without the *hypostatic* condition, the *Âtman* could not be known, for otherwise who would be the knower of the known?

Both conditions of difference and non-difference are needed to express inner being and outer existing, so that the manner of *being,* true being and existing are unified within a mode of deified *being* and existing. It is not the outward changing individual existence that provides stability to an existing person, but the unchangeable Reality which changes us from without and within.[66]

---

[66] As Utpala argued that the "only the interior existence of phenomenon entities is their eternal existence, because they are one with pure Consciousness.

Conversely the *Âtman* principle is experienced throughout the *hypostasis* for without the *hypostasis* experient the Âtman would only be a lump of insentient metaphysical *stuff* of *being*, hence both aspects are needed

The change in the manner of existing is more easily shown to us through Christ, who indicates the *way* a human person should live. This *way* indicates that in the Christian life there is a casting away of the 'old life' (the natural *physis*), which was as consequence of the *fall*,[67] and a unity of existence in the *Âtmanic* condition. In this mode of life, each person becomes "a new creation; the old has gone, the new has come...so that in him we might become the righteousness of God" (2 Cor. 5:17,21), where the lower is transformed in a higher mode of life. The righteousness of God here refers to the restoration[68] of the natural *physis* to its intended condition, which is an *Âtmanic* condition within the *hypostasis*. Irenaeus stated:

> Because the created man was placed upon the earth as one having the divine image and that he might be living, he breathed in his face the breath of life that, both by his creation, man might be like God.[69]

In the restored state of communion with the divine, as previously experienced in paradise,[70] the natural condition and consciousness attains a *type* of existence, where a spiritual life indicates that which is has "likeness" with God, indicating a similar manner and consciousness *akin* to the divine pattern. The previous Adamic

---

Their existence is an exterior phenomenon as well, because they are brought into outward manifestation by mâyâ", *IPK,* 1.84, p.34, translation by Pandit, *IPKp,* 1.8.7, p.84.

[67] As Irenaeus stated, "Adam and his wife eve being expelled from Paradise, fell into much trouble and tribulation, wandering around the earth with much sorrow and hard labour groaning", *P.Ap.*17, 671 (Mekerttschian).

[68] Irenaeus, *P.Ap.*11, 667 (Mekerttschian).

[69] *P.Ap.*11, 667 (Mekerttschian).

[70] Irenaeus, *P.Ap.*16, 671 (Mekerttschian), where Irenaeus refers to a perfected state of "man" who fell from this perfection.

condition of perfection indicates that the perfection has already been given in Paradise by God but was taken away to the human following of its own will. All that is necessary, is a "reconciliation between God and man",[71] between God's will and ours established in Christ. Thus in the *Âtman-hypostasis* model of person a kind of life, or a mode of existence, is indicated which follows the Divine will. To be a true person, is thus to live in *Âtmanic* or perfected consciousness within a *Cid-âtmanic* mode of *hypostatic* existence, which is not only for the few, but afforded to all in the salvific activity of Christ. The question arises, what is the nature of cognition within the *Cid-âtmanic* mode of *hypostatic* existence?

When considering the dynamic activity of the divine reality within the human condition, mundane conceptual knowledge becomes expansive. Whilst having relative consciousness where the subject who knows "this is" and "this is seen by me"[72] and understands the perceptive relative 'I am' awareness in relation to objectified manifestation in a materialistic sense due to a sense of limited 'I-ness', the person comes raised to a new level of awareness. But where does this consciousness originate from? Not from its own natural *physis*, but from a higher awareness shining from the highest part of the soul (*Âtman*) given and restored by God who allows the individual awareness to rise upwards and attain a *Cid-âtmanic* mode of *hypostatic* existence and thereby attain a unified awareness. In this mode of existence the awareness that all subjects and objects are relational to the Divine will. While *Pratyabhiñâ* interprets this awareness as ultimately "non-different from the interior I-consciousness,"[73] we affirm that the *deified* awareness has existential difference in relation to the Divine and yet we attain certain participation with the Divine and thereby raising the mind and soul.

---

[71] Irenaeus, *P.Ap.*6, 664 (Mekerttschian).

[72] This follows the argument of Utpala to identify the true Subject of knowing, see *IPK*, 1.31, p.13; translation by Pandit, *IPKp*, 1.4.8, p.46.

[73] Utpaladeva, *IPK*, 2.24, p.46; translation by Pandit, *IPKp*, 2.3.9, p.127.

In the *Cid-âtmanic* mode of *hypostatic* difference, a person moves away from a limited consciousness to a divine mode of life. While a limited conditioned individual existence experiences lower modes of existence and cannot attain the higher spiritual modes of existence without divine grace, yet the *Cid-âtmanic* mode of existence implies that in difference a unified state is experienced. This unifying state is not divorced from the lower modes even though mundane consciousness in these modes is unable to perceive the innate perfection underlining those modes. Through the perfecting activity of unity of God the differing states of mundane existence, the lower consciousness is raised to a pure (*sattvic*) life, which allows the individual consciousness to experience an awareness of the perfected (*Âtmanic*) state. The *Cid-âtmanic* mode of *hypostatic* existence does not negate the place for the lower consciousness but that through the unity with God both types of consciousness, both pure and impure states, are accepted in a model of unity-in-diversity. But such a unity within a higher consciousness is ultimately inevitable, where the force of theandric *deifying* activities leads the human person to a state of perfection. This inevitability is due to the outward flowing of the consciousness of the *Paramâtman* or the Supreme Godhead which not only accepts manifested phenomena for it is Cause, but through Christ regenerates life.

Concerning Relationality

Throughout this work the notion of relationality within the context of personhood has been considered in relation to Zizioulas' model, but what does relationality truly indicate? In Zizioulas' model relationality is juxtaposed to a sense of communion and a mode of existence which indicates an intimate space between two subjects (persons) or between subject and object (God and human persons). But it is unclear as to what connects the subject-to-subject or subject-to-object by which a bond of relationality is established. Hence Zizioulas' recourse was to diminish the separation between two concrete individuals by stressing that the subjects or persons can have an interrelated mode of existence established through the ontological condition of communion.[74] But I include a proper ontological dimension through restoration where the very condition of personal being is experienced in a new way offering a change in the way we understand relationality. As relational restored persons we truly come to understand the value of the other.

Through restoration the person or *hypostasis* enters into an existential becoming through *a mode,* which allows the *hypostasis* to *re-cognise* his or her true mode of being (through an ecclesial communion) where participation means a fullness of a relational communion. While Zizioulas' model, based upon Byzantine Trinitarian relationality, interprets *being* through a communion of *hypostases* that participates in a certain existential mode of existence[75] through communion, this is really an outward communion providing no real centre of *being.* Through restoration however, a perfected centre of *being* is given to us. Zizioulas' model represents a purely existential approach to relationality through the language of mode or *tropos* of existence, while breaking down the sense of autonomous *self* within the limited consciousness of the human individual revealing a higher communion limits the revelation of the true *self* to an outer act in communion. This reveals not the inner condition of true participation or *koinonia* and thus I propose we have to consider the deeper ontological implication in a relational form of communion which includes a deeper aspect of the manner of existing, through the deifying activities, that implicitly perfects the highest condition of *being.* Thus in the depth of participation with the Divine communion a depth of perfected *being* is experienced in relationality in the context of a restored essential condition (*Âtman*) which provides the basis for a true *mode* by which *being* is lived and fathomed.

---

[74] *Being as Communion,* pp.16-50.
[75] *Ibid.*

Consequently, through the *Âtman-hypostasis,* relationality includes an ontological reformulated dynamic as well as an existential context. *Being* is not only to be interpreted in a materialistic condition or in relation to other persons, but has a metaphysical restored dimension of *being*. The notion of consciousness also adds to the *Âtmanic* principle in regard to *being* relative to the other where I become aware of the relational other in a deeper sense by affirming a true condition of reformulated *being*.

Relationality implies a sense of participation and sharing of a common life, which is correlated not to the outer *hypostatic* life, but also the inner life. The person experiences relationality with the Divine because of the basic nature of the human person reformulated which impacts on how we perceive relationality as a general concept. Just as in the Cappadocian model relational participation can be correlated to a sense of what is shared or a communion through the notion of participation, so relationality can be transferred to how we live as faith God-centred perfected persons. In the same way Basil of Caesarea referred to a "community of substance" to underline the unity within the divine *hypostases* through the common sharing of an essential nature, so too a human communion through *hypostases* can be applied to a shared condition of participated communion, especially in a Liturgical context. This provides the focal point in the relationality of *hypostases*. In this type of relationality, the distinctiveness (or differences) of the individual characteristics of the persons, as in the Trinity, are not diminished or confounded in that unifying experience, but obtain an "inconceivable communion".[76] In this model *hypostatic* difference does not diminish the sense of unity,[77] but allows unity to be

---

[76] See Basil, *Ep.38*, 332D-333A (Deferrari).

[77] Basil stated: "In like manner he who accepts the father virtually accepts along with the Him the Son and the Spirit also. For it is impossible in any manner to conceive of a severance or separation whereby either the Son is thought of apart from the Father or the Spirit is parted from the Son; but there is apprehended among these three a certain ineffable and conceivable

expressed as a perfected manner of life. In the same way that it is impossible to conceive of difference without considering unity in the divine condition, so too human *hypostases* cannot be considered outside of the *Âtmanic* principle which when restored binds human *hypostases* together in that shared participation with the Divine.

Through the *Âtman-hypostasis* model two types of relationality can be identified, which can be expressed in terms of a horizontal movement and that of a vertical movement. Each movement can also be related to the divine and human cases, intimately linking God to the world within that relationality. The horizontal movement takes place in the divine between the divine *hypostases* or *Self*-awareness expressed through 'I Am' and vertically in a circular way through the Divine nature of the awareness of the *ousia* or the *Paramâtmanic* nature in a relationality of the *hypostases* or outward forms of existing. In the human case the horizontal movement exists between each human *hypostasis,* persons-to-persons, while a vertical relational movement exists in relation to our upward movement to God and His downward movement of God to the world is evident through the *deifying* theandric operations. This movement can said to be unceasingly in effect due to the incarnational activity of the Supreme *Purusha* (Christ) and is due to the uniting of natures in the '*hypostatic*-union'.

The relational context between the *hypostatic* existence of the human person and the *Âtmanic* reality indicates that an *event* of perfection takes place within the *hypostasis,* indicating the possibilities of communion within the *Âtman-hypostasis*. Through the *Âtman-hypostasis,* the possibility of union in the human person mirrors the manner of divine perfection and harmonises the outer existential life with the inner reality. The vertical movement relates to the revelation of God to the world and in that descent, how

communion and at the same time distinction, with neither the difference between their persons disintegrating the continuity of their nature, nor this community of substance confounding the individual character of their distinguishing notes" *Ibid.*

human *hypostases* come to ascend to the divine through an inner the horizontal movement. This inner movement or state can be correlated to an ecstatic condition within the *hypostasis*[78] indicating a reality by which the natural mode of individual existence changes to a *Âtman-hypostatic* existence.

However, this mode of existence is not the ontological basis for that existence in itself but rather the *Cid-âtmanic* mode of existence is as a consequence of the ontological principle created and recapitulated by God. It is because of the conscious activity and will of the Divine within the human existence that a mode of *Âtman-hypostatic* existence is possible in which a restoration of the human condition is established which provides the basis for all *deified* relational constructs. Within this understanding the person-to-person relational formula indicates not only my being here in relation to you being there existentially but that the principle of *being* underlines how and why the encounter between persons should take place in its truest context.

Relationality and Otherness

A sense of perfected or restored manner of *being* as relationality includes not only a dynamic of unity but also considers in a notion of difference, concrete existence, where the other as expressed as *hypostatic* participating other, is engaged with through an encounter or an "*event* of otherness".[79] The concrete person meets the other, *face-to-face*[80] which informs the person not only of the 'other' but provides, in an "event of *hypostasis*",[81] a space for participating

---

[78] An example of the use of "ecstasis" can be found in Irenaeus' *P.Ap.* 13, 669 (Mekerttschian), which denoted a deep sleep or mystical state, where Adam was placed into a deep sleep by God.

[79] Zizioulas, *Communion and Otherness*, p.49, which builds upon E. Levinas' otherness see, *Time and the Other* (Pittsburgh: 2000), p.74, in that it considers the relationship of persons in respect of other persons and not just the fact that a person exists with other persons.

[80] E. Levinas, *Time and the Other*, pp.41, 79.

[81] *Ibid.*, p.52.

reciprocity. This space for participating reciprocity becomes implicit to a notion of communion, especially in relation to the divine *hypostases,* which allows God to be considered in a Trinitarian context as "the Other".[82] But where *hypostatic* difference underlines the nature of communion with the other, otherness through specificity, represents not only an outer context of otherness but a participating in a restored inner condition. In this context of the human sharing of the true manner of life (with the other) in and through the true Other (God) participation provide true value of communion and otherness. In this sense of shared participation the value of the other becomes intimately related to the value of *moi* not only because of shared *hypostatic* value, but also because of sharing of a divine *koinonia* which gives a true value of the other and *moi*: we together come to know and experience God in a true and valued way.

Through the model of the principle of participated otherness, otherness becomes intrinsically related to a true manner of *being* and becoming expressed through a mode of existence by which the other also comes to live within. Through this outward sign of *hypostatic* existing as the true other, the participating other is valued as the true Christ-centred person, while at the same time recognising the value of persons who also have the capability of becoming. This perspective gives, within a person, a respect and love for the other as icons of Divine Other.

The outer *hypostatic* other comes to be viewed as the inner reflection of the Divine Other and thus also takes on a dynamic of non-difference through a principle of *Âtmanic* otherness within *hypostatic* difference. This indicates the possibilities of *Âtmanic* otherness through the *Âtman-hypostasis*. When understanding person as the principle of *Âtman-hypostatic* otherness in a relational context, Zizioulas' assumption that in the Greek Fathers, God can be referred

---

[82] This is argued by Zizioulas, see *Communion and Otherness,* p.51, and pp.43-56.

to as the "Other *par excellence*"[83] allows the *Âtman* to be considered as the very manner of the other (person) which is the true ontological value of *moi*. In the encounter of other through *theandric deifying* the individual *self* gains an encounter with the true other (God), where the *self* finds a sense of *being* and becomes informed of itself and otherness.

Being is not objectified but as the pure subject, reveals itself as the true other in the *hypostasis* in an *event* of participation. The event of *Âtman* then becomes an event of otherness within the *hypostasis,* which allows, in a relational encounter with the other, outward events, of *Âtmanic* otherness. Yet this type of otherness is only possible because of the stress on a substantialist context highlighted in the divine context of *ousia/Paramâtman*. Through the *ousia/Paramâtman, hypostatic* otherness is not disconnected from specificity but rather allows otherness to be considered through unity. Consequently otherness comes to be equated with the essential property of *deified hypostasis* as much as the *hypostasis* itself.

When correlating *Paramâtmanic* otherness to human otherness, *Âtmanic* otherness relates to what is unified, where specificity relates to the other within a relational unified context. The sense of unity provided by the *Paramâtman,* on the human level, allows *Âtmanic* otherness to have an extrusive quality in relation to other *hypostases.* As in *Pratyabhijñâ,* through the model of the *Ishvara pramatr*[84] or the extrusive activity of the divine in relation to the phenomenal universe, the extrusive aspect of the principle of *deification* as *Âtman* becomes localised as a particular personal *hypostasis,* but also experiences perfection in relation to other *hypostases.* It is only when through *deification* or *re-cognition* that *Âtmanic* otherness is understood as the true character of the personal other, that the value of other becomes apparent, because the *Âtman* principle and

---

[83] *Ibid.,* p.51.

[84] See *IPK* 3.2-3, pp.59-60, which states that the *Ishvara* Subject is the exterior aspect of the Absolute (*Pârameshvara*).

potentiality comes to be recognised at the very core of those restored *hypostases*. The nature of this *hypostatic* condition is also consciousness (*cid-âtmani*)[85] for in each person the principle of perfection has "the capability of appearing diversely".[86]

Relationality as Movements

The notion of *Âtmanic* otherness when applied to relationality, through the *Âtman-hypostasis* model, shows that there is a movement from non-difference to difference and then back to non-difference. The divine overcomes the distortions of 'fallen' difference through the act of revelation and highlights the paradox of transcendence (*vishvottîrna*) and immanence (*vishvamaya*) in God's own *Being* where there exists the simultaneous contradiction of fullness[87] and the act of God emptying (*kenosis*) Himself out for human persons. The overcoming of this paradox can be understood in Pratyabhijna in terms of a movement from the internal fullness of the *Paramâtmanic* divine state of the introverted *nimesha* (lit., closing of the eye) condition in relation to the divine unfolding (*unmesha*, lit., opening of the eye)[88] of the created universe, as Utpala stated:

> So the *Âtman* coming into the process of creation does not become enmeshed in any sort of diversity, although it is called different names (such as ParamaShiva, God or Paramâtman). This is because these point toward one and the same end, (infinite) I-Consciousness.[89]

---

[85] *IPK*, 2.51, p.57.

[86] *Ibid.*

[87] This is examined by John R. Dupuche 'Themes of Light and Dark in the Greek Fathers', in Bettina Bäumer and John R. Dupuche, *Void and Fullness*, pp.171-185, who argues that the two positions are not incongruous.

[88] See *IPK*, 3.3, p.60, which states that the *Ishvara* is the, "extroversive aspect of the Absolute and *SadâShiva* is the intoversive one, the former being known as *unmesha* and the latter as *nimesha*", translation by Pandit, *IPKp*, 3.1.3, p.159.

[89] *nâhantâdi-parâmarúa-bhedâd asyânyatâtmanah/ aham mrúyatayaivâya srstes tin-vâcya-karmavat//*, *IPK* 1.48, p.20; translation by Pandit, *IPKp* 1.5.17, p.65.

This view is also similar to Maximus' view that the *Logos* nature did not get polluted or confused by the fallen human nature in the '*hypostatic*-union' but that the human nature was *deified* in that becoming.[90] This represents an outpouring of Divine *Being,* in an emptying (*kenosis*) of the Divine for the cosmos, but also represents a relational context in the human becoming through fullness, in the perfecting of the human condition in the experience of Divine-union (*deification*) through a movement of the Divine to the world.

The relational movement from the divine *Paramâtman* to the world indicates that there can be considered movements within a vertical descent, or relational categories of God to the world: firstly, in the creation of the world and secondly, in the bodily condition and encounter with the divine *hypostasis/purusha* in the *Âtmanic-event*. This allows for a relational context on a personal level, where each person experiences a personal encounter with God. Within this relationality a further category can be added where the person experiences, in the highest union, a further movement and union as the experience of *deification/re-cognition.* These movements from divine to the world begin with a movement within itself from the divine unmoving reality (*nimesha*) to the divine outward act (*unmesha*), which can be equated from our perspective to a movement from the Divine Essence to the divine *hypostases.* This movement then continues to manifest created phenomena and the creation of life, which can be correlated to Maximus' notion of the divine "inbreathing"[91]into Adam. This in-breathing was then correlated to the incarnational life of Christ by Maximus, which allows human restoration. Maximus makes a direct correlation to the notion of in-breathing with the human person having the divine likeness and the soteriological activity of Christ stating that Christ himself received "the vital inbreathing of man"[92] and thus receiving

---

[90] Maximus, *Opsc.3* (PG 91), 48A-56B (Louth).

[91] See Maximus, *Ambig.42* (1316C); translation by Blowers, *On the Cosmic Mystery of Jesus Christ,* p.80.

[92] *Ibid.*

as man what was created in the divine image".[93] Through the divine in-breathing the divine imparts the essence of Himself through His operations, which allows a reciprocal inward return where the fullness of *being* is realised. In such a movement the context of relationality in the wish of the divine to engage in a relationship with human persons, becomes revealed, and shows that relationality should not only be considered in terms of outward *hypostatic* meetings but related to the inward *deified* experience.

Relationality and Awareness

Within the notion of the *Âtman-hypostasis,* relationality is not confined only to outward modes of *hypostatic* existences, but can be considered in terms of an inward-outward change of awareness through the relational encounter. This type of relationality is primarily indicated in the I-consciousness of the *hypostasis* which radiates outwards and manifests the outer limited 'I-consciousness' (*aham*), which then becomes transformed in deification. The true 'I' (*aham*) however represents not the individualistic and separated notion of individual but the *deified* 'I' of the *hypostasis* which becomes intrinsically relational to the principle of its own deified perfection restored through *theandric* activities.

Through this radicalisation of 'I' by the will of God the individual experiences a shift in awareness in relation to other individuals, firstly, experienced as relativistic 'I', then as relational *being* as 'I-thou', and then as 'I am-thou'. This corresponds to a movement from individual to *hypostasis* which allows a sense of a deeper *being*. Levinas argues that relationality, in the context of personal *being,* overcomes the dependency on static *being*, of being there (*Dasein*),[94] stating that the "epiphany of exteriority....exposes

---

[93] *Ibid.*

[94] That-being or existence. The notion of *being there* (*Dasein*) of Heidegger should be expanded into, "being here" as argued by Raymond Tallis, see *I Am: A Philosophical Inquiry Into First-Person Being* (Edinburgh: 2004), pp, 142-145, 190-191. *Being there* cannot be considered outside of a sense of the

the deficiency of the sovereign interiority of separated being."[95] However a resolution of this deficiency is not really explored either as Levinas does not fully explore other ontological implications such as in *deification* where *being* becomes 'being as I should *be'* (*sein wie ich soll*). In this context a further movement can be explored in the *Âtman-hypostasis,* which resolves how *being* and existing can come together in allowing for an outer condition to be qualified through the inner reformulation. The inability of the outward individual to convey a sense of what is true was conceded by Levinas in his recognising that the *face* cannot disclose interiority.[96] The relationship and movement from the *face* to the interior condition indicates how *hypostatic* difference is resolved in the unity of the principle of perfection (*Âtman*) while maintaining the concrete existence of the *hypostasis.*

---

personal in which *being* is affirmed in a relational context, but not at the expense of understanding the subject. The cognate or person comes to understand himself/herself through his/her own sense of being which as an embodied existence is in context with other persons. Thus Levinas approach to otherness accepts the place of personal relationality face-to-face, the responsibility for the other and "proximity of neighbour", see Levinas, *Otherwise than Being,* pp.121-129 where *self*-hood is not considered at the expense of the other.

[95] E. Levinas, *Totality and Infinity* (Pittsburgh: 2007), p.180.

[96] *Ibid.* While the Levinas-Zizioulas schema, if we can refer to such a thing, establishes a bridge to overcome the static ontologies in the movement provided in the relationality of personal existing and the consequence of that existing in relation to other persons, the *Âtman-hypostasis* model qualifies this exterior notion of person. The task of Zizioulas is hindered by his inability to accept the role of *physis* in his equation, while Levinas' task is closed in his inability to reach beyond the physics of the metaphysics and death (See, Emmanuel Levinas, *Time and the Other,* p.51). Levinas' works have however helped to somewhat resolve the gulf of otherness by expressing the importance of the personal relationship of persons "face-to-face" (See Emmanuel Levinas, *Time and the Other,* p.79) which overcomes the impersonalism of *Dasein.* Levinas' model then has been transposed by Zizioulas into the Trinity, where otherness expresses an intimate intercommunicative reality. However, Zizioulas model, in bringing otherness into the ontological (trinitarian) debate to revise the existential context of individual through trinitarian personhood, has become a victim of the existentialist debate.

This premise for relationality highlîghted in the *Âtman-hypostasis* and the overcoming of separated exteriority through interiority, allows for simultaneity of both unity and difference, where specific personal existence and the essential reality of that existence are affirmed without negating either. Thus, a relationality of persons is not a relationality of isolated individuals who have something in common, whether in a context of *being* or in an existential context, but fundamentally infers cohesion through an essential participation in God that connects human persons with the Divine, and each other. In this sense relationality is a relationship of difference (otherness) with non-difference or the unity that connects the *hypostatic* others together in a unity of the manner of *being* and awareness through the lived principle afforded in that condition. In this (*Âtmanic*) relational model difference expresses not separation but cohesion through unity and a model of unity-in-difference which shall be the subject of the next area discussed in relation to the *Âtman-hypostasis*.

Concerning Unity-in-Difference

In the last parts of the work the notion of *Âtman* is qualified through the Byzantine model of unity-in-difference[97] or distinction. In the

---

[97] See *IPK*, 2.15, p.42, which states: "In this way the objects of a person desirous of mundane attainments are fulfilled – with the help of entities (in the world) that have (both) unity and diversity as their character. Such a thing is therefore not an illusion", translation by Pandit, *IPKp*, 2.2.7. For an in depth examination of *bhedâbheda* in *Vedânta,* see P. N. Srinivasachari, *The Philosophy of Bhedâbheda* (Madras: 1996). *Pratyabhijñâ* took up this model from *Advaita Vedânta* and incorporated ideas of *Shaivism* of Kashmir, the three aspects of; *abheda* (unity), *bheda* (diversity), and *bhedâbheda* (unity-in-diversity); see also J. C. Chatterji, *Kashmir Shaivism* (Delhi: 2004), p.8. Alexis Sanderson shows that this view of unity and diversity was inherited, in the resurgent monism of the *Trika* of *Kashmir Shaivism* expounded by Vasugupta, Abhinavagupta and Kshemarâja, from the *Mâlinîvijayottaratantra,* see Alexis Sanderson, 'The Doctrine of the Mâlinîvijayottaratantra', in T. Goudriaan (ed.), *In Ritual and Speculation in Early Tantrism: Studies in Honour of Andre Padoux* (Albany: SUNY Press, 1992).

Byzantine tradition the way of viewing unity-in-difference or distinction has come to be understood as M. Törönen describes, within "a principle of simultaneous union and distinction...things united remain distinct and without confusion in an inseparable union".[98] In the Byzantine tradition there is a movement "from above"[99] to the world which allows human persons to be *deified* and a movement to the divine "from below"[100] and then a divine ascent. In the Byzantine tradition unity and distinction were expressed by highlighting an ontological *gulf* between the divine and human conditions, which was resolved through the *hypostatic union* of the Incarnation.[101]

Conversely, in *Pratyabhijñâ* philosophy, the notion of unity and difference or unity-in-difference was developed, not by considering difference (or diversity),[102] but in terms of unity to show that difference was in reality non-different to the divine. This did not negate the notion of difference, for otherwise there would just be the concept of unity, but rather difference was qualified through the light of consciousness (*prakasha*) to relate that sense of difference to a centre of unity. Rather than understanding the

---

[98] See M. Törönen, *Union and Distinction in the Thought of St. Maximus the Confessor.*

[99] See Julius Lipner, *The Face of Truth,* pp.44-45.

[100] *Ibid.*

[101] See Maximus *Ambig. 42*, 73.11, 1325B-C , where he argues that existence, the material and immaterial, is unified in the *hypostatic union* which unifies the world (difference), to the divine in the uniting of Christ's natures, body and soul. This economic *hypostatic union* also represents a model by which union and difference are vouchsafed, Maximus stated "preserving the difference perfectly and in its effects in respect of the natural logos, and again saving union, in the manner of the economy, firmly and hypostatically, so as to confirm the matters that essentially exist in the one and sole Christ God in accordance with the inseparable union", *Opsc.*7, 84B (Louth).

[102] See *IPKp*, p.115.

world from the viewpoint of the world, the world was explained through the Divine Reality.

In both traditions the divine is connected to the world on an intimate level, which manifests a proper relational context to person. The world is "not a thing in itself existing separately from Him",[103] but intimately related to the Divine *Being* and awareness (*Cit*),[104] and therefore difference must always be considered in relation to unity.

In *Pratyabhijñâ*, unity-in-difference (*bhedâbheda*)[105] is fundamental in explaining the paradox of the fullness (unity) of God in relation to the world. This provides a model to understand the nature of *hypostatic* difference in relation to objectified (created) manifestation (*âbhâsas*), of divine revelation in relation to unity or non-difference, of the principle of perfection (*Âtman*) in relation to *hypostasis*. This can be considered through a model of unity-in-difference within the *Âtman-hypostatic* model. Manifestation cannot be self-caused or be responsible for release from its natural condition, or from experiencing difference in relation only to isolated difference. For difference to escape its state of isolated difference, it has to be considered through a reality that can overcome its sense of difference otherwise it is trapped within a gnostic prison. This overcoming of isolated difference in Byzantine theology is paradoxically accomplished through God incarnating as difference.

---

[103] *IPK*, 1.46, p.19; translation by Pandit, *IPKp*, 1.5.15, p.64.

[104] As Utpaladeva stated that: "such light cannot be different from it (world), as the object has consciousness as its very soul" (*âtmârthasya prakashatâ*).*IPK*, 1, 33, p.14; *IPKp*; translation by Pandit, 1.5.2, p.50.

[105] Utpala argues that manifestations cannot be understood from the point diversity because of the "contradiction between unity and diversity", *IPK*, 2.51, p.57; translation by Pandit, *IPKp*, 2.4.19, p.149. , but from the view of Âtman which "consists of pure consciousness with the capability of appearing diversely" (*Ibid.*).

Through divine difference, difference is overcome through the unity inherent within divine difference. But difference (*bheda*) does not have priority over unity, but is dependent on unity, where difference or manifested phenomena (*âbhâsas*) are due to a force creating and acting upon them, the will and reality of God.[106]

Thus, difference (*bheda*) cannot be understood from the viewpoint of difference alone, or that which is from *below,* the phenomenal manifestation (*âbhâsas*), but from a notion of unity through the divine operations where a model of unity-in-difference is juxtaposed to the Christ *hypostasis. Hypostatic* specificity is juxtaposed to divine unity, will and activities and when applied to the human model, *hypostases* come to be understood through a sense of participated perfection. The nature and awareness of a particular existence attains a sense of *self* through participated unity, which allows awareness to exist in a unique and specific way and then in terms of *koinonia.* The notion of specificity or difference is not crushed or dissolved in the unity underpinning that existence but paradoxically, the principle of *being* becomes the basis for that very manner of individual existence. As Christ's existential reality is qualified through the unity with the Father[107] so too human personhood becomes truly significant through an emphasis on participation with the Divine operations.

The importance of juxtaposing the *hypostatic* differences of the Trinity in relation to divine unity is also exemplified by Gregory Nazianzen who argued that:

---

[106] As Utpala stated: "mutual difference is the base on which the sequence of time and space stands. That difference is based on the manifestation and non-manifestation (of particular entities). Such manifestations and non-manifestations are due to the Lord, who brings these wonderful displays into (apparent) existence", *IPK*, 2.4, p.38; translation by Pandit, *IPKp*, 2.1.4, p.109.

[107] As exemplified in Hebrews 1:5, which states, "for which of the angels did God ever say 'you are my Son today I have become your Father'. Or again 'I will be his father and he will be my Son'?"

> We recognise the Father, the Son and the Holy Spirit as God, and
> these as not being mere appellations determining inequalities of ranks
> or powers, but we recognise that as there is one and the same title so
> is there one and the same nature, substance and power of Godhead.[108]

This unity does not to undermine the specific characteristics of the
each *hypostasis* but highlights that unity within the divine nature
does not denude a notion of difference, so that the notion of
difference can exist simultaneously within unity. When this model
is translated into the human case, *hypostatic* difference also allows
the underlying principle of personal participation attaining unity
through gaining 'likeness' with God.

Consequently, difference can only be properly understood from
a viewpoint of unity and unity through difference. Difference cannot
understand itself or be informed of itself in a total way for in a self-
informing perception of nature only the subject exists in relation to
the subject in objectified world ; it cannot objectify itself and no
where apart from 'man' in nature is the perception of world in a
abstract way evident. Consciousness in a natural model only pertains
to a limited self-informing position and cannot experience itself
outside of its own context. In such a self-oriented consciousness
objectified perception of itself in the world would be impossible,
for how would separated difference communicate its sense of reality
to anything outside of its reality. The answer lies in a notion of
unity within difference or a divine consciousness that allows
difference within the human person to experience its own reality
and others through unity, but which is not immediately experienced
in a limited condition. In this context it is possible to understand
the how unity in the incarnate *Logos* rose up human nature "like
by like"[109] so that the lower might attain the higher.[110] In this

---

[108] Gregory Nazianzen, *Ep.101*.14, (Wickham).

[109] *Ibid. Ep.101*.9.

[110] As Gregory stated that the "meaner element has been assumed so that
it may be hallowed...leavened and blended anew with God, deified by the
Godhead", *Ibid, Ep.101*.8.

situation the natural sense of difference is displaced by a divine notion of difference. This is not to state that human *hypostatic* difference is identical to divine *hypostatic* difference, but that human *hypostatic* difference is not only transformed but fully participates with the divine through a unity in the *deified* experience, but attains its very mundane awareness through the divine activity. In both traditions, in a human context, the lower cannot properly comprehend itself or experience a higher reality within itself but the limited *self* is transformed. Consequently, in the term *Âtman-hypostasis,* the word *Âtman* is prefixed to qualify *hypostatic* difference, which allows the term *hypostasis* to be understood in relation to a principle of perfection which restores *hypostasis* to a higher state. As Utpala argued that "the interior Reality is only one and that One alone develops multiplicity".[111]

The what of Existence

The model of unity-in-difference affirms not only the outer existential difference but highlights the principles underlying that existence or the *deified* manner which underpins all categories of difference through the Christ centred promises. This manner of true life in a Christian context is to be viewed in terms of ontological reformulation within a faith based and en-graced condition. Under such terms the recapitulated *what* of *being* as the true state meant for all persons becomes the metaphysical *what* of existence, this something (the ôüåå æ), or the spiritual *what* of the *hypostasis,* which informs the *hypostasis* of its true value and thus conforms the person to a true mode of existence. The metaphysical *what* of existence indicates a deeper context to the *how* of the outer life and through the conscious awareness of itself in relation to the world, reveals *how* to attain a depth of existence through the principled *what.* The metaphysical recapitulated *what* informs the *how* of existence, as its true manner of life by establishing a bridge between the outer and inner life through the reformulating activity of Divine

---

[111] *IPK*, 2.10, p.40; translation by Pandit, *IPKp*, 2.2.2, p.116.

consciousness (or *Cit*) and will within the human *hypostatic* existence. This consciousness reveals itself, not only through the mystical state, but also in mundane life through revelatory events, and in the person conforms the individual to an *Âtman-hypostatic* mode of existence through *theandric deifying* activities and as such indicates the possibilities of a *Cid-âtmanic* mode of life. The unity expressed in the *Âtmanic* reality through a *Cid-âtmanic* mode of life allows the sense of difference, within mundane existence, to gain significance in the possibilities of the higher mode without denuding the dignity of the lower mode, which too becomes an expression of the Divine will. The affirmation of the recapitulation does not mean that before this state non-being was experienced but that the fullness of *being* lies with the reception of grace and living in this true state of *being*.

The intimate relationship of living in a mode on non-fullness as compared to fullness can be explained in terms of difference in relation to non-difference which can be understood as an act of revelation in a movement from the awareness of the Absolute subject to this-ness (*idam*) and then to the objectified world or that-ness (*tattvas*). In that-ness the loss of perfection is experienced but through grace a new movement is developed upwards back to the original condition so that human beings begin to experience fullness. The movement from *Cit-aham* to *tattva*,[112] from Supreme Consciousness to the world shows how the true I-consciousness relates to objectified manifestation or difference and how the individual experients can attain unity, through the divine manifestation and unity-in-difference as an *Âtman-hypostasis*. Unity

---

[112] As Utpala states in *IPK* that the nature of *Cit* (infinite I consciousness) under the seeming effect of *mâyâ* as *cit-tattvam*, is not revealed and seems to be identical to "deha (physical body or with prana (the animating life-force or with vacuous individual consciousness; and is taken to be the (individual knowing and acting) subject", *IPK*, 1.56-57, p.23-24; *IPKp* 1.6.4-5 (Pandit). This individual subjective existence has been correlated to the notion of the natural *physis* of human existence in this work.

is vouchsafed through the conscious activity of the manner of recapitulated *being* (*Âtman*).

It is in the *Âtman-hypostasis* model, that unity of awareness is experienced as the *what* of existence, or the nature behind *hypostasis* within the *Âtman-hypostasis,* allowing specificity to be experienced. This model highlights perfect unity and the divine presence experienced in the *Âtman-hypostasis* and at the same time mundane existence. Hence, there is expressed a paradox of form and beyond form; of mind and beyond mind; of imperfection and beyond imperfection; of part and whole; and of nature and beyond nature, where impurity, delusion and ignorance are qualified in the unified activity of the *Âtman*. As Utpaladeva stated "the Lord by virtue of His infinite divine power manifests this apparent phenomenon, through the power of his divine will".[113] Here all types of phenomena exist in relation to the unity of divine awareness, will and power and not by their own existence.

Difference through Unity

Existence then comes to be expressed perfectly through a condition of difference, where a sense of differentiation does not indicate separation or even some sort of outward relational belonging wrought through a common sense of existing, but indicates that at creations very core, even in difference, there is expressed the essential reality of that existence. The reality of personal difference, or created persons, even to gain an awareness different to others and specific to a unique individual consciousness is only possible due to the will and activity of divine. At the very centre of personal difference, and the core of mundane existence, is an awareness that focuses outwards in such a way as to indicate that such a limited and isolated consciousness should not be able to even conceive of itself within the phenomenal existence. How could a conscious force in itself establish a conscious awareness of itself in an unconscious universe? The answer is found in that both the

---

[113] *IPK*, 2.33, p.50; translation by Pandit, *IPKp*, 2.4.1, p.135.

Byzantine and *Pratyabhijñâ* traditions there is an intimate relationship between manifested or created phenomena and the Cause by which creation is made manifest. The divine comes to express itself in a revelatory way through the very nature of difference as an expression of the luminous activity of *Citi-Shakti*, allowing individual consciousness to be expressed and to express itself. This luminosity brings into creation a consciousness out of non-form and awareness where even the lowest forms of consciousness come to be understood as expressions of the supreme consciousness having as the very nature of that consciousness the divine awareness. Of course this has to be qualified in Byzantine theology to manifest a difference between the created and Creator. Form and expression of that form through consciousness attains awareness of itself because of the very nature of the divine presence and activity within phenomena. This conscious activity of the divine within mundane consciousness allows the very concept of difference to be expressed as non-different to the One who has manifested that very difference. The basic expressions of consciousness can then be understood as developing within phenomena, which become more complex until awareness encompasses all levels of *being* where a consciousness, which sprung from the divine, experiences itself in a unified condition while experiencing the conscious awareness of difference. The experience of unity while in difference is paramount, for without this condition the divine would be unable to break the bonds of its own reality in relation to the phenomenal universe being an impotent force.

Hence, the divine will and power to manifest creation and then to let creation *be*, experiences firstly: as a conscious awareness of itself through human persons; and secondly where difference becomes aware of the divine. This affirms the complete authority and perfection of God to overcome the bonds of difference, which has been set into place by God in the first place. To negate difference would then be a negation of the divine will and power. Difference within the human consciousness cannot be divorced from the individual experience, in which consciousness is expressed or the divine reality, which creates that consciousness and allows it to *be* what it is and to become what it should *be*. This becoming is to be linked to a movement within the individual who moves into a true awareness within the *hypostatic* condition where the person *re-cognises* his or her *Âtman-hypostasis* and perceives that difference is to be understood as intrinsically related to divine unity. Thus implicit to the term *Âtman-hypostasis* are the possibilities of *being* in difference and becoming within difference through the inherent unity implied in the ontological condition of the *Âtman-hypostasis*. This unity, expressed through the *Âtmanic* principle, does not negate the place for *hypostatic* difference but rather rejoices in it, for that difference is viewed as a luminous manifestation of the *Cit-Shakti* or divine operations (*prakasha*).[114]

Unity-in-difference implies a movement from God to the world and a reciprocal movement from the human individuals (world) to the divine, for it is the Lord who is the Cause of both difference and unity. Dionysius argued that God is the cause of the movements of what is perceived and preserved[115] indicating a simultaneity of the "One and the many".[116] In the context of the *Âtman-hypostasis,*

---

[114] As Abhinavagupta stated: The pure consciousness, having adopted *Mâyâ* as a part and parcel of its self becomes impure but is pure and appears as the finite subject known as *Purusha* who is bound like a beast with (the chains of bondage consisting) of *kâla*, the sense of time, *kalâ*, the limited capacity to do just a little, *niyati*, the law of natural causation, *râga*, the limited interest in particular something and *Avidyâ*, the limited capacity to know just a little. *Abhinavagupta, PSA,* 16 (Pandit).

[115] Pseudo-Dionysius, *DN*, 4.10, 705B-C; translation by Luibheid, *Pseudo-Dionysius*, p.79. Dionysius goes on to say that; "it is the source, the origin, the preserver, the goal, and the objective of rest and of motion. The being and the life of the mind and of the soul derive from it. Also from it come the small, the equal, and the great in nature, the measure and the proportion of all things, the mixtures, the totalities, and the parts of things, the universal one and the many, the links between parts, the unity underlying everything, the perfection of wholes", (*Ibid.*).

[116] *Ibid.*

unity is vouchsafed in the *Âtmanic* experience within *hypostatic* difference. This notion of difference is not to be considered in relation to a self-informing natural condition, but related to the divine, who "remains One in the act of Self-multiplication; undifferentiated throughout the process of emanation and fullness in the emptying process of differentiation".[117] So too in the *Âtman-hypostasis*, it is the divine itself that reveals a specific existence of the true nature of that unique existence,[118] of both distinctiveness and union due to the character of the *Âtmanic* principle in the human *hypostasis,* which can attain its true 'image' and 'likeness' of the Super Essential Godhead.

Conclusion

Through the *Âtman-hypostasis* model, a synthesis of ideas, developed from the two traditions allowed the human person to be considered in both terms of a concrete person (*hypostasis*) and yet intimately related to the divine through the context of the principle of perfection of that existence. When the individual nature (what is *below*) is raised to a higher level of *being* the consciousness of the person changes and so reflects the divine consciousness within an *Âtmanic* mode of *hypostatic* existence. The synthesis of terms from both traditions allowed an evolution of the Cappadocian and contemporary ideas which has led to an over emphasis on the existential negating a focus on the *physis* of personhood. The re-addressing of these ideas in this work underlined the importance of stressing the notion of difference to retain the notion of concrete personhood in relation to the higher (*deified*) *physis* of the *hypostasis* through the *Âtmanic* principles of *being*.

---

[117] Pseudo-Dionysius, *DN*, 2.11, 649B; translation by Rolt, *Dionysius the Areopagite*, p.79.

[118] As Dionysius stated: "He is nothing less than the archetypal God, the supra-divine transcendentally one God who dwells indivisibly in every individual and who is in himself undifferentiated unity with no commixture and no multiplication arising out of his presence among the many", Pseudo-Dionysius, 2.11, 649C-D; translation by Luibheid, *Pseudo-Dionysius*, p.67.

Conversely, the notion of *Âtman* was taken out of a purely monist category related to a principle of *hypostasis* that allows a sense of difference within a sense of perfected *deification*. Thus in the *Âtman-hypostasis* model there is the movement from *above* (God) to the world, to that which is below, while at the same time a movement from below to God. However all movements are ultimately considered in relation to the Divine will and activity for without this context, all movement is self-informing and thus trapped within a prison of its own lower or 'fallen' nature. Thus *being* and existing are not dislocated or separated into diverging categories, but are considered together within a single model. The model of *Âtman-hypostasis* successfully juxtaposes *being,* within a context of restoration of the natural *physis* of humans, and the existential manner that includes a sense of restored existence and consciousness expressed in the *Cid-âtmanic* mode of *hypostatic* existence. This provides answers to the question 'who am I' from a view of absolute *being* (or *Âtman*) and consciousness within the existence of concrete personhood.

In this part of the work, the *Âtman-hypostasis* model has indicated something more than the ordinary condition or the natural human *physis*, where human being-ness is restored and elevated, body and soul, to a state of *becoming* of "everything that was".[119] Hence, in the experience of union with the divine through the *Âtman* principle the person/*purusha* achieves the fulfilment of *being,* as an *Âtman-hypostasis*. While in *Pratyabhijñâ* in this cognitive experience the individual *pramatr* experiences either delusion (as *pashu*) or enlightenment (as *pati*) leaving no room for a simultaneity of both, the *Âtman-hypostasis* incorporated ideas of both. This allowed for a flexibility of recognising both conditions without negating either. In such a model, unique characteristics are affirmed as is the possibility of *deification*. However, unlike the Byzantine

---

[119] Dumitru Staniloae, 'Deification', in *Orthodox Spirituality*, p.269.

model of *deified hypostases* this is not confined to an existential mode, even though it is expressed through a mode of *Âtmanic* existence, but affirms the place for an essential restored and *deified* condition in the *hypostasis*. The notion of *hypostasis* is not confined only to an outward activity, but includes the notion of *deification* implied in the term *Âtman-hypostasis,* where the person understands that his or her own manner of life in a restored state is intimately related to the supreme *Self.*[120]

---

[120] *IPK,* 4.1, p.70.

PART 2

Personhood in Pratyabhijñâ
(of Kashmir Shaivism)

CHAPTER 5

Introduction

In this part of the work I want to redirect ideas so that I approach a model of person from a *Pratyabhijñâ* perspective, but within framework of converging ideas that have already been discussed. This part of the work provides the research framework of such convergences but where *Pratyabhijñâ* ultimately converges into Christian faith doctrine.

I will consider whether *Pratyabhijñâ* had a notion of person and whether ideas revolving around such terms in *Pratyabhijñâ* could be related to a concept of person that can be placed within the contemporary debate. The study of person will centre on an answer to a notion of individual in relation to *re-cognition*. The notion of *re-cognition* allows the focus in person to centre on consciousness or *Cit*.[1] Through the use of consciousness the very way we understand person is changed where through the activity (*kriyâ*) and will (*icchâ*) of divine consciousness changes the nature of individual (*pashu*) from a *self*-orientation perspective to a *Self-*

---

[1] *Cit* or *Citi* is the Universal consciousness, which as Kshemarâja stated is "the form of the limited subject, descending from its stage of *Cetana* (universal consciousness) disposed to comprehending objects...becomes *citta* (individual consciousness)" *PBH* commentary on Sûtra 5; translation by Singh, *PBHs*, pp.60-61.

Âtman-realised[2] condition of a yogi. Here *re-cognition* will be considered through the notion of person (*hypostasis*) and equated with *purusha* to include not only a sense of difference, but also unity. The relationship of *Âtman* with *purusha* (person), within the *Pratyabhijñâ* tradition, through consciousness (*Cit*) will qualify separation or difference, through the divine activity, but also the very notion of *Âtman,* where *Âtman* and consciousness will be intimately related to each other. The examination of person will thus be placed in relation to an experience of the unity-of-*being,* where unity is thus qualified through unity-in-difference which will be fundamental to the development of a concrete notion of person.

In both the Byzantine and *Pratyabhijñâ* traditions much of the theological rhetoric was directed to resolving the problem of reconciling God to the world, without diminishing the truth of either, and so the examination of person will be placed within this context. However, this leads to another important issue, that of how *Pratyabhijñâ* itself, understood the nature of the divine reality, what constitutes divine existence and the relationship of that existence to the human condition. While the Byzantine tradition came to adopt an *apophatic* (that which is hidden) approach in relation to understanding the absolute God, highlighting the ontological difference between the human and divine conditions,

---

[2] The *Âtman* is the metaphysical reality of everything: it is the principle that transcends the phenomenal universe yet immanent in the universe. Kshemarâja stated that the *Âtman* is "both immanent in the universe and transcends it", *PBHs*, p.68. Kshemarâja qualifies a total non-dual stance by stating that while the followers of *tantra* believe the *Âtman* to transcend the universe and the texts of the Kula to believe that *Âtman* to be in the universe, the *Trika* followers (including *Pratyabhijñâ*) believe that the *Âtman* is both transcendent and immanent (*Ibid.*). The *Âtman* is the metaphysical reality of everything: it is the principle that transcends the phenomenal universe yet immanent in the universe. Kshemarâja stated that the *Âtman* is "both immanent in the universe and transcends it", *PBHs*, p.68. Kshemarâja qualifies a total non-dual stance by stating that while the followers of *tantra* believe the *Âtman* to transcend the universe and the texts of the Kula to believe that *Âtman* to be in the universe, the *Trika* followers (including *Pratyabhijñâ*) believe that the *Âtman* is both transcendent and immanent (*Ibid.*)

Pratyabhijñā's approach focused on unity and consciousness and a singular "knowing subject".[3] One could know of God, not through mundane consciousness, but through an experience of an awareness of divine *being* through *re-cognition*. It is through this experience that the individual comes to understand that the nature of everything, including one's own limited condition, is nothing other than the divine reality. This experience highlighted unity rather than difference, but also accepted the simultaneity of both.

Due to the theistic implications in *Pratyabhijñâ*, the human condition was recognised as not self-caused or self-contained but so completely related to the divine, that non-difference is *re-cognised* as the ultimate ontological condition. When considering person, the starting point is not a focus of finite individuality or separation but from the perspective of unity, which has apparently been lost through false identification and has resulted in delusion. Consequently, both traditions tried to overcome the notion of separation in different ways, and it is through the overcoming of this notion of separation that an examination of person in *Pratyabhijñâ* will be placed.

Pratyabhijñâ philosophy emphasised unity or non-difference to explain difference and was not concerned with ignorance, but an emphasis was paradoxically placed on difference as the *Âtmanic* experience was not considered in isolation. Its monism was placed in relation to the world and thus a focus on the divine activity or *Citi*[4] also became important, where its monist position was qualified through the term *Citi*. Notions of separation and ignorance consequently became important aspects of *Pratyabhijñâ*. This was

---

[3] *IPK*, 2.64, p.26,; translation by Pandit, *IPKp*, 2.7.1, p.81.

[4] Although *Citi* was, in *Pratyabhijñâ*, generally considered as an aspect or extrusive power emanating from the divine monist reality, (*PBHs* 3 and 4, pp55-.59) it was sometimes personalised as 'she', as the *PBH* states "by the power of her own will, she unfolds the universe as a screen (consciousness)" *svecchayâ svabhittau vishvam unmîlayati* (translation by Singh, *PBHs*, 2, p.51), where the power of God has this feminine aspect. This was common in the *Tantric* and *Âgamic* traditions.

due to an affirmation that separation and ignorance are not considered unreal, but in which the higher truths come to be revealed and ultimately viewed as the divine itself. Within this qualifying of the mundane, *Citi* becomes the mediating activity by which revelation is made possible and by which human persons attain unity with the divine consciousness. *Pratyabhijñâ* equated the differing states of existing with the modes of existence or *gunas*.[5] Here the Byzantine notion of mode or *tropos* will be utilised and equated with the *Pratyabhijñâ* use of the *gunas*, which highlight the importance of *being* in relation to a *way* of existing in relation to the unity of *being*. The model of *tropos hyparxeos,* taken from the Cappadocians and Maximus the Confessor and adapted by Zizioulas to indicate an existential outcome will be qualified to show how the essential underlying condition of perfection relates to the existential character of a particular concrete individual.[6] The notion of modes of existing will be contextualised through *Pratyabhijñâ's* model of *re-cognition* and the admittance of what is real which affirms the place of mundane existence as a mode and the highest level of personal *being* to be considered as a mode of *Âtmanic* existing. This type of existence experienced within the spiritual condition will also be equated with a *Cid-âtmanic*[7] mode of *hypostatic* existence, or a mode of existence that relates to an *Âtmanic* consciousness within the *hypostasis,* without negating the place of ordinary existence.

---

[5] Utpala stated in the *IPK*, 4.4, p.71, that the "knowledge and action of a *pati* or enlightened master are aimed towards objects taken by him as his own, as well as his power to manifest the viewpoint of diversity and become respectively (the three *gunas*) *sattva rajas* and *tamas* of a bound being", translation by Pandit, IPKp, 4.4, p.194.

[6] This context in *Pratyabhijñâ* is explored through such terms as *purusha, jîva, anu, pashu,* and *nara,* concerning *purusha* see *IPK*, 2.19-20, p.44; concerning *jîva, anu* see *IPKp*, p.168, but not directly mentioned in the text; concerning *pashu* see *IPK*, 3.7, p.61, and 4.4, p.71; also see Sanderson, 'The Doctrine of the Mâlinîvijayottaratantra', p.297.

[7] This is taken from the *IPK* which argues that all manifestation and existence is due to *Âtman*-consciousness (*cid-âtmani*) which is responsible for the world "appearing diversely", *IPK*, 2.51, p.57; translation by Pandit, *IPKp*, 2.4.19, p.149.

CHAPTER 6

Pratyabhijñâ

Introduction

What is *Pratyabhijñâ*, what does it mean, where did this philosophy arise and how does that meaning relate to human personhood? The word *Pratyabhijñâ* means *re-cognition*,[1] the *re-cognising* of who one is, and the philosophy of *Pratyabhijñâ* was intimately related to an epistemological and ontological quest to uncover the truth of *being*, emerging out of the *Trika Shaivism* of Kashmir in the ninth to the twelfth/thirteenth centuries in Kashmir.

Pratyabhijñâ refers to a *self-recognition*, to an experiential *event* where the person discovers who he or she is, by grasping the

---

[1] *Pratyabhijñâ*, Jaideva Singh defines as, "Prati + abhi + jña = *Pratyabhijñâ*...though known, now appearing as forgotten through delusion 'Abhi' means facing i.e. close at hand. 'Jña' means illumination or knowledge. So *Pratyabhijñâ* means re-cognition of the real self" (*PBHs*, p.117. For a similar definition see Tagare, *The Pratyabhijñâ Philosophy*, p.46). See *A Descriptive Analysis of the Kashmir Series of Texts and Studies*, p.5.The word *Pratyabhijñâ* according to Gopinath Kaviraj, "literally means a flash of light, - a revelation, is usually found in literature in the sense of wisdom characterised by an immediacy and freshness", see 'The Doctrine of Pratyabhijñâ in Indian Philosophy', *Annals of the Bhandakar Oriental Research Institute*, 5, 1921, pp.1-18, 133-132. Pratyabhijñâ is also stated as meaning "intuitive light" (see *PBKt*, 1.7.1, p.136).

essential reality of *being* (or *Âtman*); through knowledge or awareness that one's *self* is the true *Self*.[2] *Re-cognition* thus infers *Âtma-Pratyabhijñâ* (the *re-cognition* of *Self*) or *Âtma-jñâna* (knowledge of *Self*),[3] but the word also implies a remembering (*smriti*) of things and a knowledge of *being* already known by the true knower or true subject, as Utpala stated;

> A memory although risen out of the impression of a past experience, is essentially limited to its own self. It is therefore not the knower of that previous experience.[4]

This is not mere memory but a flash, a throb (*spanda*)[5] of an inward metaphysical reality (or *Âtman*) within the individual *purusha*. In this context two natures and cognitions are evident, that belonging to the lower natural *physis* and that of the higher in which true participation takes place. Hence, the whole philosophical system of *Pratyabhijñâ* can be understood to be dedicated to understanding how the highest spiritual experience relates to the concrete individual. While *Pratyabhijñâ* viewed the notion of separated individual within a negative context through the terms *purusha, jîva, anu, pashu,* indicating a bound, limited ignorant and finite existence, the experience of *re-cognition* unites the mundane with the highest reality. To develop a notion of person in

---

[2] Abhinavagupta stated that: "*Recognition* means shining (*Jñâ-jñâna*) as facing oneself (*âbhimukhyena*) of what was forgotten...not that the consciousness of the Self has never before been a fact of experience, because it always shines; but that...through His own power, it appears as though cut off, or limited. Recognition consists in the unification of what appeared once with what appears now", *IPV,*1.1 (commentary); translation from Pandey *IPVp,* p.6.

[3] *Pratyabhijñâ* is not only a theological system and school but also a philosophical term, see K. Mishra *Kashmir Shaivism* (Delhi: 1999), p.80 and pp.253-6.

[4] *IPK,* 1.17, p.7; translation by Pandit, *IPKp,* 1.2.3, p.27.

[5] The *Spanda* theory forms an integral part of Non-dual Kashmir Shaivism, see *Spanda Kârikâ* (KSTS 5). Also see: Jaideva Singh, *Spanda Kârikâs* (Delhi:1980); S. Mukhopadhyaya (ed.), *Spandanirnyâya by Kishemaraj* (Delhi: 1986); Mark S. G. Dyczkowski, *The Stanzas on Vibration* (Varanasi: 1994).

Pratyabhijñâ both the metaphysical and the concrete have to be considered within a unity of both. This is achieved through the construction of a model of *purusha* (as an *Âtman-hypostasis*) that considers personhood in terms of modes of existence that are informed by the essential condition of that existence, where the mode of that natural existence becomes transformed through divine participation within a *Cid-âtmanic* mode of *hypostatic* existence. In this context, relationality is not only to be considered in terms of intercommunicative *hypostases,* but through an essential reality that binds and informs *hypostases* of their true nature and mode of existence. The notion of *hypostatic* existing through modes of existence will also be correlated to types of awareness, that of the mundane consciousness (*citta*) and that of the divine consciousness or *Cit.*[6] Within a concept of person, a unity of both is to be attained where the focus is ultimately the highest conscious experience of *re-cognition,* which is related to the highest experience and knowledge of God.[7]

Did Pratyabhijñâ have a Notion of Person?

The question then has to be asked whether *Pratyabhijñâ* had a notion of person in relation to a modern understanding. The answer to this question is probably no, but this does not negate the quest

---

[6] In using the word *Cit* here, I am incorporating ideas relating to the whole of the *Pratyabhijñâ* corpus and accepting the influences of Abhinavagupta and Kshemarâja on such terms, considering in particular the influences of Kshemarâja on many of the *Kashmir Œaivite* works. Sanderson has been critical of academic research that has not considered such nuances, see Sanderson's book review of Lillian Silburn's work *Shivasûtra et Vimarshinî de* Kshemarâja, in *Bulletin of the School of Oriental and African Studies, University of London* 46/1 (1983), 160-161, *http://alexissanderson.com/ aboutus.aspx.*

[7] Sanderson makes the point that such an experience of enlightenment in *Œaiva* practise have not been related to liturgical and cultural norms as, "for most will occur only at death" (see Sanderson, 'The Doctrine of the Mâlinîvijayottaratantra', who cites Abhinavagupta's *Tantrâloka,* 1.43). However in the *IPK* this is not what generally being expressed, but it points to an existential attainment while alive (see *IPK,* 4).

to relate *Pratyabhijñâ's* notion of individual to a person, developed through the term *purusha.* The notion of person will also be qualified through types of existing and consciousness, where the type of existence that a person experiences mirrors a type of consciousness that comes to define the individual. This approach to person will ultimately be considered as juxtaposed to unity. The concept of person will not be confined to a specific type of consciousness but will indicate that many levels of person are possible within personal existing, culminating in an *Âtmanic* awareness.

The notion of individual in *Pratyabhijñâ* was situated within a complex philosophical system, which underlined non-duality and yet accepted the world as real, through a complex cosmological system of *tattvas* (principles). This places a notion of person, as the *purusha-tattva,*[8] firmly within its system and allows person to be considered through its acceptance of concrete phenomena as manifestations (*âbhâsas*).[9]

Through the *purusha-tattva,* the notion of person, which has already been established as synonymous with *hypostasis* will also, be equated to the term *purusha.* The term has been historically accepted as equated with person within Indian Christian approaches to personhood.[10]

Purusha in *Pratyabhijñâ* was an existential determination indicating the outward individual (*jîva*) and as such, inferred: limitation, egoistic 'I' (*ahamkâra*); finite-ness (*anu/nara*); and

---

[8] Implied in *IPK*, 3.9, p.62.

[9] Utpala stated that the world's activities "whether pure or impure are experienced within the Lord, who shines, decorated by the manifestations of various different phenomena, *ittam aty-artha-bhinnârthâvabhâsa-khacite vibhau/ samalo vimalo vâpi vyavahâro 'nubhûyate//, IPK,* 1.77, p.32; translation by Pandit, *IPKp,* 1.7.14, p.92.

[10] As exemplified by Bede Griffiths, 'The Advaitic Experience and the Personal God in the Upanishads and the Bhagavad Gita', *Theological Studies* 15/1 (1978), p.80.

bound-ness (*pashu*/ beast).[11] As such, *purusha,* when understood as separate, finite individual and beast seemed to be used in a pejorative context, especially when considered in relation to *Pratyabhijñâ's* non-dual ideal, for it implied a sense of distinction or difference and thus separation rather than unity or non-difference. This is exemplified in the word *pashu,* which denoted a bound animal. Utpala stated: those under "delusion and seeing objects as different from him is called a *pashu* or a bound being".[12] Abhinavagupta had also argued that the *pashu* has to be considered as a reflection of the Lord, stating that: just as "a pure and colourless crystal takes up the appearance of different types of hues reflected in it, so does the Lord also take up the different types of gods, human beings, animals, and plants".[13] However, Abhinavagupta overplays his non-dualism, which is not so much the case in Utpaladeva, who allowed for a concrete sense of person but which attains fullness in the context of the Absolute awareness who "feels like this 'I am He'...all this is my own being".[14] Utpala shows that the individual person is not negated but has a concrete sense of existence, where the *pashu* attains a higher condition through the divine and comes to understand a true reality. This higher condition is attained through the reception of grace or *Shaktipâta,* which allows for a full sense of person to be developed. Abhinavagupta stated that:

> Just as one's face appears clearly in a clean mirror, so does this *Âtman* shine as pure consciousness in a mind purified by the bestowal of grace (*Shaktipâta*) of Lord Shiva.[15]

Hence the terms *jîva, pashu* and *purusha,* while indicating a sense of isolation, do affirm what is existentially real and imply the same as a notion of person when viewed from an ontological perspective

---

[11] See *IPK,* 4.4, p.71.

[12] *IPK,* 3.14, p.64; translation from Pandit, *IPK,* 3.2.3, p.173.

[13] *PSA,* 6 (Pandit).

[14] *IPK,* 4.12; translation by Pandit, *IPKp,* p.201.

[15] *Âdarshe mala-rahite yadvad vadanam vibhâti tadvadayam/ Shiva-Shaktipâta-vimale dhî-tattve bhâti bhârûpah, PSA,* 9 (Pandit), p.24.

and so allow for a sense of person to be explored through these terms. However this notion of concrete existing, in *Pratyabhijñâ*, was qualified through an experience of unity. This sense of unity in *Pratyabhijñâ*, implied through the term *pati* (lord),[16] can also be correlated to person because the differences between *purusha* and *pati* do not imply ontological difference, but a change in consciousness. The word *pati* indicates that the *pashu* is transformed through a relationship with the divine and hence the term person can include ideas relating to both the terms *purusha* and *pati*, where person indicates the whole human *being*. It is in this context of whole person that I argue that *Pratyabhijñâ* developed a model of human existing and *being* that can be equated to a concept of person.

Person and Âtman

A concept of person, however, is not to be considered in the same way as in the Byzantine tradition where the focus was on specificity, but has to be developed by focusing on unity, which does not displace difference but rather qualifies it through the *Âtmanic* experience. In *Pratyabhijñâ* models of existing were considered through the *Âtmanic* reality, but this reality was not situated within a closed monist isolation, but in relation to the world through *Cit.*[17] Nevertheless *Pratyabhijñâ* argued that any models of individual (person) hinged on how one understands cognition in relation to specific existing, who is the true "knowing person".[18] *Pratyabhijñâ* argued that since the individual is completely dependent on some other reality, for plainly no human can cause themselves or another's existence or consciousness due to mere will: human existence and cognition is a condition of dependence[19] and this dependency allows for a focus on the cause of existence. This distinction between

---

[16] *IPK*, 3.14, p.64.

[17] *PBH*, 1.

[18] *IPK*, 1.5, p.3; translation by Pandit, *IPKp*, 1.1.5, p.11.

[19] *IPK*, 1.4-5, p.2-3.

dependency and non-dependency, non-eternality and eternality in *Pratyabhijñâ* is important, for it highlights the superiority of the one as compared to the other. If knowledge or consciousness were related to non-eternality then it would be correlated to an unconsciousness nature and as Utpala stated, if consciousness was "unconscious by nature, then how can it illumine anything".[20] It could also be argued that the faculties of person such as *buddhi,*[21] "bears in it the consciousness of the *Âtman*".[22] But this is refuted by Utpala, as such an outcome would necessitate that *Âtman* would become sentient, that is bound to material nature, or to be understood as insentient not having existence in itself, but in either case "it cannot illuminate anything".[23] For both *Âtman* and person to gain significance, the characteristics of each must be preserved, where the former brings meaning to the latter.

Hence, the focus on cause is not from a position of ignorance but of knowledge, for while certain knowledge of the body and other bodily existences may allow "a means to infer the existence of knowing"[24] this knowing is conditional, where "the real significance of the *Self* is not usually grasped because of delusion (*moha*)".[25] The divine Cause is continually illuminating through its divine powers to raise or restore the consciousness through *re-cognition*[26] and it is in this context that a notion of person will be sought through the *Âtmanic* experience.

This experience is possible because of two factors, firstly because of the *Âtmanic* condition within each person, and secondly because of the ability to cognise such an experience within the human condition, which is due to the activity of the divine

---

[20] *IPK,* 1.12, p.5; translation by Pandit, *IPKp,* 1.2.7, p.20.

[21] *IPK,* 1.13, p.6.

[22] *IPK,* 1.13, p.6; translation by Pandit, *IPKp,* 1.2.8, p.21.

[23] *Ibid.*

[24] *IPK,* 1.5, p.3; translation by Pandit, *IPKp,* 1.1.5, p.11.

[25] *IPK,* 1.3, p.2; translation by Pandit, *IPKp,* 1.1.3, p.9.

[26] *Ibid.*

consciousness or *Cit*. Without consciousness, the *Âtman* would be a "useless lump"[27] of immaterial substance having no connection with material phenomena and generating a gnostic outcome. So it could be argued that through person the significance of *Âtman* is really appreciated in the conscious awareness to perceive such a condition within the human experience, which reflects how the *Âtmanic* reality experiences consciousness as an out flowing of divine will and purpose. The activity of *Cit* allows consciousness to be considered as an outward movement of the divine, where the rational element within the human person mirrors equivalent dynamics within the divine. This rational element will be equated with the soul within a substantialist model through *Âtman*.

The focus on rationality shows that material existence reflects types of consciousness that become aware of a harmony of individual existence through a unity with the *Âtmanic* nature. The highest mode of person expresses a freedom to *be*, not only in an existential context but in relation to the essential nature not dominated by the natural *physis* or the bound nature. A defence of this model is provided by emphasising the Christ model which shows how in divine unity, the lower natures are transformed through the higher within the human person. The Christ model emphasises the importance of considering three points in relation to person; firstly that there is possible within the existential person both unity and yet distinctiveness; secondly, unity in the higher manner of life does not detract from a complete union with the lower; and lastly the unity of the lower ('fallen') nature with the higher infers a simultaneity of a higher awareness within the lower.

Within the human person the unity of consciousness can be considered as expressing an awareness of the essential condition of *being,* or *Âtman* through the faculties of the individual. Although the *Âtman* can be experienced through these faculties, the faculties are not to be viewed as the *Âtman*; otherwise *Âtman* becomes

---

[27] Also as Pandit argues, *IPKp*, p18.

reduced to thing of nature. There is a continual stress on the concept of doer, who is the real doer, and dependency. Hence, through the perception of the divine, through the faculties of perception, the *Âtman* is eventually understood to be the very subject of existence and a substratum of person. This allows a unifying condition, through those faculties, to be expressed and thus intimately related to a process of transformation, where the faculties change and are transformed within that process.

The faculties of person can be equated with the mind (*manas*), intellect (*buddhi*) and the senses of perception (*jnânendriyas*) in *Pratyabhijñâ*,[28] and to the *tattvas* of manifestation. The faculties of a person can also be related, within the highest sense, to the highest part of the soul or *Âtman*. In *Pratyabhijñâ* the highest spiritual nature, in the human condition, is correlated to the *Âtman* and also to a *Paramâtmanic* nature. But in Christianity we affirm ontological difference, where ontological distinction is made between the divine *ousia* as *Paramâtman* and the *Âtmanic* nature of human *beings*. The latter will be recognised as different according to the manner of the former, but allows for participation according to the fulfilment of the *stuff* of *being*.

Even though such an ontological distinction is not immediately obvious in *Pratyabhijñâ* philosophy, such distinctions between the Supreme and the human can be discerned in *Pratyabhijñâ's tattvic* categorisations and the differing experiences of the *pramatrs* (cognitive subjects) according to their experiences.[29] In other words, the relationship of the *Âtman* to the cognitive subject is *re-cognised* as being the same as the divine but in addition there is some level

---

[28] As inferred in *IPKp*, pp.167-170; see also Tagare, *The Pratyabhijñâ Philosophy*, (Delhi: 2002), pp.24-32.

[29] This is evident in Kshemarâja's commentary of *PBH* where he describes the levels of experiences of *pramâtâs* in relation to 'I am' (*aham*), 'that' (*tat*) and 'this' (*idam*), which shall be examined also later; see also *PBHs*, pp.52-53.

of difference in that the "highest Shiva"[30] is differentiated[31] in the *tattvic* manifestations. Such distinctions are also apparent in the theistic devotional salutation to *Maheshvara* by Utpala[32] stating that:

> having somehow attained the position of a servant of the Great Lord Maheshvara, and now being desirest to do good to other people as well, I am presently expounding the doctrine of His recognition.

This devotional context of some measure of ontological difference is highlighted by Pandit's translation, where the term *Maheshvara* is understood as "the great Almighty Lord".[33] While there is this sense of difference, which is highlighted through the *tattvic* manifestations, the phenomenal universe is ultimately related to the divine as the "different states of the Lord Shiva in His universal aspect" (*paramâtmanah Shambhoh*).[34]

The nature of the divine Godhead as distinguished as a Supreme condition is exemplified in that it was correlated to the *Brahman*. This reality was for Abhinavagupta the transcendental unmoving reality beyond everything, which reveals itself through its *Shakti*.[35] However the lines between this non-different reality and difference, of the nature of *Âtmanic* will and activity in relation to the human condition are often blurred. While sometimes the *Âtman* is equated

---

[30] See *PBHs*, p.55. Also Abhinavagupta in his *Vimarúinî* of the *IPK*, the *IPV*, 4.7, which states that while the "pati is identical to Ishvara...there can possibly be no talk of object in relation to the Highest Lord, ParamaShiva", translation by Pandey, *IPVp*, p.224. Though this is stated in the context of pure non-dualism, it also provides a distinction between the Absolute and human conditions.

[31] The power of differentiation as a manifestation of the Lord to create difference was called *Apohana Shakti* in Abhinavagupta's *IPV*, 1.4; *IPVp*, p.40.

[32] *IPK*, 1.1-2, p.1; translation by Pandit, *IPKp*, 1.1.1, p.5.

[33] *Ibid*.

[34] Which will be correlated to the Absolute God (*ParamaShiva*), *PSA*, 26 (Pandit), p.37.

[35] *PSA*, p.43.

with the divine condition, and indicated an unchanging reality,[36] at other times it seemed to be conditioned (through the human context) to the difference between the higher *Self* and the individual *self*. Yet ontological difference seemed to be conveyed in *Pratyabhijñâ's* use of such words as *Maheshvara*.[37] This term (*Maheshvara*) implies a Divine condition that indicates a notion of God and that stands independent and outside of the human reality as Cause. Terms such as *Maheshvara* and *ParamaShiva* come to indicate points of Divine Absolute and yet imply points of encounters of divine and the world, as Abhinavagupta stated:

> Sometimes the Lord may Himself unbound and reveal His real nature by means of yoga that illumines the infinite luxury of one's self-knowledge. ParamaShiva, the Absolute God, plays thus His wonderful game of bondage and liberation.[38]

These points of encounter are made possible because the human nature shares a pattern similar to the divine, which becomes the real nature of humans and is indicated through the term *Âtman*. It is through the encounter with the divine that persons come to experience their true nature and understand the true condition of person.

Person as a Point of Revelation and Encounter

In *Pratyabhijñâ*, through an encounter with the divine within the individual, an ensuing change of consciousness takes place in *re-cognition*,[39] where revelation and individual consciousness meet. Through this meeting a restoration takes place where human awareness recognises that it is the Lord that has appeared "as one's finite Self",[40] within a "renewed understanding", which is called

---

[36] The *IPK* stated that the Âtman "does not change at all during its different functional activities", 1.11, p.5; translation by Pandit, *IPKp*, 1.2.6, p.19.

[37] See *IPK* 1.1, p.1.

[38] *Sva-jñâna-vibhava-bhâsana-yogenodvestayennijâtmânam/ iti bhanda-moksha-citrâm kridam pratanoti ParamaShivah*, *PSA*. 33 (Pandit), p.40.

[39] See *IPKp*, p.133.

[40] *Ibid*.

Pratyabhijñâ or "the recognition of the divine nature as the Self".[41] This allows for a change in the understanding of individual through that encounter as person. This flexibility in the notion of person allows for a change of what it means to be a person. But the notion of divine revelation was not confined to an inner experience but considered in terms of an outer revelation where divine scripture was given to humanity and in this sense the singular experience is expanded to include all humanity, to all persons, which is exemplified in the *Shiva Sûtras* being revealed to Vasugupta on a rock. Also Utpala stated that the *Ishvara Pratyabhijñâ Karika* was composed "for the purpose that people attain perfection".[42]

While in the Byzantine tradition, this encounter with the divine was expressed through a downward movement from the divine to the world, where participation with God was afforded through grace, which allowed an ascent to the divine, in *Pratyabhijñâ* there is no real movement but a perceived movement in that the human person is viewed as nothing other than the highest reality. This perception of movement also reflects shifts of awareness in the divine within the transcendent *being* and is considered in terms of fluctuations of consciousness, from the pure 'I Am' to 'I am this' and then 'I Am that',[43] to allow the appearance of manifestation through the *tattvas* or principles.

These perceived movements of consciousness reflected the will of the divine to create manifested phenomena and thus individual persons. But this creativity also allowed a reciprocal movement where human persons through the power of cognition come to understand their true nature and in this experience the notion of isolated individual comes to be understood through the term person or *purusha* within a relational context. The different levels of cognition, of 'I see' allow awareness and knowledge to be

---

[41] *Ibid.*

[42] *IPK*, 4.18, p.74; translation by Pandit, *IPKp*, p.207

[43] *IPK*, 3.1-30, pp.59-68.

become related to the subject of perception. But what is the subject of perception? In *Pratyabhijñâ* it is the Self that is the true Subject of cognition, which allows for all types of knowing, and does not negate those differing perceptions. Utpala stated that the many cognitions, although "arising at different times, do have mutual unity... unity is actually the single subject (the *Self*), shining as both 'this' and 'that'".[44] Hence, phenomena are not self caused but it is the divine that manifests subjects, the relative finite individuals, and objects. This allows for the awareness of 'I am' a limited person and of 'this is' the world; and also a united field of consciousness, where both perceptions come to be understood as having as their cause the divine awareness. This divine awareness allows for a sense of person in a limited and expanded context.

The personal is not negated but finds meaning through the higher awareness.

The implications of the relationship of the divine with human persons, allows the non-dualism of *Pratyabhijñâ* to be viewed as qualified through the light of consciousness (*prakasha*).[45] In this context of the activity of *prakasha* the notion of individual attains meaning through this activity or perceived movement from the transcendent God to the world. The world is not viewed *"from below"*, where the lower nature can never understand its true reality, but is understood *from above*, from the highest viewpoint or consciousness or *Citi* which is the cause (*hetu*)[46] of the world. As Abhinavagupta argued, all phenomena including individual finite beings are "none other than Lord *Shiva* Himself, having taken up such a form of the bounded being".[47]

---

[44] *IPK*, 1.26, p.11; translation by Pandit, *IPKp*, 1.4.3, p.40.

[45] *PSA*, p.30.

[46] See Kshemarâja's commentary of *Sûtra* 1 of *PBH*.

[47] *PSA*, 5 (Pandit), p.22.

When considering the implications of the *Pratyabhijñâ* understanding of divine revelation and activity, the notion of person has to be considered through both a sense of difference, or an awareness of concrete mundane reality, and non-difference or an awareness of the highest reality. The awareness of a higher reality experienced through mundane consciousness allows an apparent movement from *citta* (the mundane mind) to *Cit* (supreme consciousness), from the deluded cognitive subject (*mâyâpramatr*)[48] to the personal God (*Mahâpramatr*). This indicates not only a change or shift of consciousness and thus a shift in how the terms are to be considered but a reciprocation, which allows the human person (*hypostasis/purusha*) to be considered within the context of relationality. Within this relationality a person can be said to exist within a mode that experiences its own sense of difference, within the *hypostasis/ purusha,* while at the same time *re-cognising* non-difference through the experience of unity with the divine nature, or essential reality, within the human person.

Thus a notion of person is approached by incorporating aspects of difference, through the terms *hypostasis/ purusha,* in relation to the highest reality, or non-difference, which leads to the construction of a single model of person, the *Âtman-hypostasis* as already discussed. This single model adapts a notion of concrete existence (or *hypostasis*), to consider person through relationality as a mode of existence, that explains how *re-cognition* or the *deification* experience relates to the transformation of the natural *physis* and to a model of whole person.

Philosophical Background

While the model of person accepts a notion of concrete personhood, qualified through the essential reality of being (or *Âtman*), it is also accepts that *Pratyabhijñâ* philosophy is ultimately *non-dual*. But this stance is in itself qualified in that it accepts both the *Âtmanic*

---

[48] As the *PBH, Sûtra* 6, stated that the "*mâyâpramâtâ* consists of it (*citta*)"; translation by Singh, *PBHs*, p.62.

reality and the world as the "Highest Real, (i.e. Shiva)",[49] where the that-ness (*tat*) of manifestation (the world) is accepted as real.[50] The tension between the metaphysical reality (*Âtman*) and what is real, in *Pratyabhijñâ,* is related to the philosophical tension between *non-dualistic* and *dualistic* influences respectively.

Although the philosophy of *Pratyabhijñâ* is thought to be predominantly *non-dual*, especially in the works of Abhinavagupta, exemplified in the *Vimarshinî* of Utpala's *IshvaraPratyabhijñ âkârikâ,* it is also considered in *dualistic* terms as having relational elements.[51] This *dualism* was exemplified in its inclusion of the *Trika Ûâstra,* or the "threefold science",[52] where the resurgent *Trika,* having its roots in the older *Tryambaka* School, put an emphasis on triadic (thus *dualistic*) archetypes, concepts and iconography. From this triadism the term *Trika*[53] evolved, which was religious and philosophical in character, developing constructs of *parâ* (supreme), *aparâ* (lowest) and *parâparâ* (combination of highest and lowest), and which related to deities and also to philosophical divisions.[54] This followed the schema of the *Mâlinîvijayottaratantra,* which developed into the theological distinctions of; *non-dualism;* the world (indicating *dualism*); and revelation or the qualifying *dualism* in unity. The term itself, *Trika,*

---

[49] See *PBHs*, p.61.

[50] See also *Descriptive Analysis of the Kashmir Series and Texts and Studies,* p.2.

[51] As highlighted in *Pratyabhijñâ's* philosophy of dependency, where phenomena are dependent on *Âtman,* and come to be realised as *Âtman,* see *IPK,* 1.7, p.5. This relationality is not a relationality within difference or of mutual relational entities but relationality that is ultimately expressed through unity or non-difference.

[52] See *A Descriptive Analysis of the Kashmir Series of Texts and Studies,* p.1.

[53] Peter David Lawrence, *Rediscovering God within Transcendental Argument* (Delhi: 1999), p.29.

[54] See Sanderson, 'Shaivism and the Tantric Traditions', p.673; and Lakshmanjoo, *Kashmir Shaivism,* p.129.

indicating three-ness, can hardly said to have come from a monist imperative, and must therefore have had ancient roots that pre-date the later pure monism with which it is usually associated.

Thus, the new *Trika* philosophically reflected *Âgamic* influences[55] in its incorporation of a qualified monism which continued the divisions extant in *Mâlinîvijayottaratantra,* of the three classes pertaining to *Shiva, Rudra* and *Bhairava.*[56] This also reflected a conceptual three-fold division of duality (*bheda*), duality-unity (*bhedâbheda*) and non-dual monism (*abheda*).[57] *Trika* established triadic conceptual models and even the ontological triadism of, God, activities and the world. In *Trika* or *Trika-ûâsana, Trika-Ûâstra,* or *Rahasya-Sampradâya*[58] (secret lineage) philosophical approaches were expressed to suit certain philosophical or theological problems and established a basis and methodology of revelation, philosophy and faith through triadic (and thus *dualistic*) archetypes, which the new *Trika* used within a *non-dual* context.

The triadism of *Trika* was also reflected in triadic methods of praxis (*upâyas*), evidenced in Kshemarâja's *Vimarœinî* of the *Shiva Sûtra* of: *Œmbhavopâya* (way of the divine); *Ûaktopâya* (energetic way); and *anavopaya* (way of the individual).[59] So even in the

---

[55] *Ibid.* However these influences are shown by Abhinavagupta to relate to non-dualism stating, "non-duality is based upon the authority of Âgama" *IPVp,* p.186.

[56] *MT,* p.vii.

[57] *Ibid.* and Chatterji, *Kashmir Shaivism,* pp.8-9; see also Hanneder, *Abhinavagupta's Philosophy of Revelation,* p.193.

[58] Chatterji, *Kashmir Shaivism,* p.3.

[59] *SSVs,* pp.1, 82, 126 and Pandit, *The Trika Shaivism of Kashmir.* The qualifying of *non-dualism* is extant in the influences of the *Shiva Sûtra* in the new *Trika* schema, in the inclusion of the *anavopaya* in Kshemarâja's Vimarûinî, *SSVs,* pp.126-127. This reflects the acceptance of the concept of individual *self* or *anu,* which has *citta* or human consciousness and *buddhi* (intellect), *manas* (mind), and ('I-ness'), but which in truth is *Cit.*

non-dual text of the *Shiva Sûtra,* in Kshemarâja's *Vimaraiñî, dualistic* teachings are evident. This teaching emphasised spiritual practice and thus echoed the teachings of *Mâlinîvijayottaratantra.* But as Abhinavagupta argued, there cannot be total *duality* due to the monist nature of the Absolute, and neither can there be *non-duality* due to *duality,* but rather both shine in effulgent consciousness, the *Cidrûpa* of the Lord.[60]

The Contemporary Debate

The tension between *dualism* and *non-dualism* in Kashmir Shaivism has raised consequent problems in contemporary scholastic interpretation, as highlighted by Alexis Sanderson.[61] The *dualistic* tendencies in *Kashmir Shaivism,* as Sanderson argues,[62] have been ignored in contemporary interpretations and have consequently led to *non-dualistic* approaches. This has also led to interpreting human individuality through pure *Advaitic* models.[63] *Pratyabhijñâ,* not with-standing the *non-dualistic* influences of Abhinavagupta who as Sanderson shows superimposed his ideas onto the *Mâlinîvijayottaratantra,*[64] expresses *dualistic* notions through the admittance of manifested *tattvas.* The *Mâlinîvijayottaratantra*[65] was simply for Abhinavagupta, as Sanderson states, the "core-text of

---

[60] *IPV,* 2.4.20-21.

[61] See Sanderson, 'The Doctrine of the Mâlinîvijayottaratantra'. See also Jürgen Hanneder, *Abhinavagupta's Philosophy of Revelation, Mâlinîûlokavârttika 1, 1-399* (Groningen: 1998) who shows that it was far from clear whether the resurgent *Trika* of the 8th- 12th centuries was *non-dualistic* in that, and he cites Somânanda who seems to condemn pure *non-dualists* (*Ibid.* p.5, footnote 9).

[62] *Ibid.*

[63] As exemplified by Kamalakar Mishra, *Kashmir Shaivism* (Delhi: 1999).

[64] Sanderson, 'The Doctrine of the Mâlinîvijayottaratantra', p.306.

[65] Sanderson clearly makes a connection between the *dualism* of the *MT* and the impact upon the *Trika* tradition including *Pratyabhijñâ,* see 'The Doctrine of the Mâlinîvijayottaratantra', p.282, footnote 7; also see Koshalya Walli, *A Peep into the Tantrâloka and Our Cultural Heritage* (Delhi: 1998).

the Trika Tantras...embodying the very essence of the *non-dualistic* tradition".[66] However, as Sanderson demonstrates, the *Mâlinîvijayottaratantra* was also *dualistic,*[67] which points to the *dualistic* influences on the new *Trika* [68] and is exemplified in *Pratyabhijñâ.*[69]

Hence, these influences have to be considered when constructing a model of person in *Pratyabhijñâ.* While the *Mâlinîvijayottaratantra* had clear *dualistic* implications in its philosophy, its conclusions were ultimately *non-dualistic* in accepting *Shiva* to be the ultimate monist reality,[70] which allows the incorporation of ideas of difference within non-difference in a concept of person (*purusha*). This paradoxical model was continued in the *Shiva Sûtra* and in the later resurgent *Pratyabhijñâ,* which was a theistically *non-dualistic* polemical text composed to refute *dualism* and other "erroneous' doctrines".[71] Despite this, Sanderson shows that *dualistic* influences of the *Mâlinîvijayottaratantra* were apparent in Abhinavagupta's work and thus in the resurgent *Trika.* This refutes the claim that the new *Trika* was completely *non-dualistic.* Sanderson concludes that *non-dualism* has thus been superimposed upon *Kashmir Shaivism,*[72] or *Trika,* but both the *Shiva Sûtra* and *Pratyabhijñâ* were clearly *non-dual.* What has to be concluded is that the new *Trika,* as exemplified in *Pratyabhijñâ,*

---

[66] Sanderson, 'The Doctrine of the Mâlinîvijayottaratantra', p.282.

[67] *Ibid.,* p.293, see also Hanneder, *Abhinavagupta's Philosophy of Revelation,* pp.5, 89, 172, where Hanneder states that *MT* shared the "basic dualism of many other Âgamas" (*Ibid.* p.172).

[68] I will refer to the resurgent *Trika* of the 8th- to 12th centuries as the new *Trika.*

[69] This can also be corroborated by Hanneder, see *Abhinavagupta's Philosophy of Revelation,* p.5.

[70] See Madhusudan Kaul's introduction of *MT,* in *MT* pp.i-xxxvi.

[71] Chatterji, *Kashmir Shaivism,* p.11; and Pandit, *IPKp,* p.xxiii.

[72] Sanderson, 'The Doctrine of the Mâlinîvijayottaratantra'.

represented a stronger emphasis on a *non-dual* interpretation than the older *Trika.*[73]

Because of the theological implications to personhood pertaining to the *non-dualism* of the resurgent *Trika,* in the context of the older *dualistic* systems,[74] the need to refer to the resurgent *Trika* as new is underlined, for where did this new *non-dualism* arise? The answer is that the new *Trika* was not as *non-dualistic* as it first seems and that the older *dualism* was not as *dualistic* as Sanderson maintains. Conversely, although Chatterji dates the *Trika-sasana* to the eighth or ninth centuries in Kashmir,[75] confusing the older *dualistic Trika* with the new monist *Trika* to underline the *non-dual* association, he also admits that *Úivâgama* on which *Trika* is based is far older,[76] which was more *dualistic.* But he never

---

[73] Sanderson argues that consequently there were three phases to *Trika,* the "cult of the three goddesses" (see Sanderson, 'Shaivism and the Tantric Traditions', p.696) the '*Kâlî*' phase and then the philosophical phase of the "*Pratyabhijñâ*-based *Trika* of Abhinavagupta" (*Ibid.*). This last phase also had various developments, that of the *Shiva Sûtra;* the *Pratyabhijñâ* non-dualism of Somânanda and Utpala; and then the *Trika* of Abhinavagupta (*Ibid.*, pp.694-696). The last phase did not negate *dualistic* praxis and ritual, but clearly had at its core the theological belief that the ultimate reality, though expressed as a theistic personal *pramatr* (*Shiva*), was *non-dual.* Tthis is evident in the *MT* where in the categorisation of the *pramatrs,* the highest is *Shiva* who is undifferentiated (see *MT,* p.xxiii) and in *IPK* where this idea is extant.

[74] See Sanderson, 'The Doctrine of the Mâlinîvijayottaratantra'.

[75] Chatterji, *Kashmir Shaivism,* pp.3-5.

[76] *Ibid.,* p.5. When trying to clarify ideas within the two different types of *Trikas* in relation to a model of person, what has to be considered relevant are the influences on both types of *Trika* and the consequent philosophical stress. Both *Trikas* drew from *Âgama* and *Tantra,* see Flood, 'Shared Realities and Symbolic Forms in Kashmir Shaivism', p.226. But as Flood shows, the *non-dual* focus becomes underlined in the "Trika theologians" (see Flood, *An Introduction to Hinduism,* p.168) such as Abhinavagupta and Kshemarâja. He clearly links the *Trika* to what I call the new *Trika* schema and yet also he highlights that *Trika* is a generalistic term that indicated a philosophical ideal, and the "ritual system or basis of Kashmir Shaivism" (*Ibid.,* p.167) the former being *non-dual* and the later *dualistic.* This contradictory position was also emphasised by B. N. Pandit who argued that the philosophy of Somânanda

explains how this new *non-dualism* sits within the older *dualistic* corpus.

Hence, *Trika* seems to have evolved, emerging out of the landscape of *dualistic Shaivism*,[77] and the philosophy-theology has also evolved, gaining a non-dual emphasis especially in relation to Abhinavagupta and his superimposing a non-dual stress on to *Mâlinîvijayottaratantra*.[78] Hence there are not only two notions of *Trika* but various philosophical models being applied simultaneously. While one could refer to a collective tradition, as Singh does under the umbrella of *Trika*,[79] where a synthesis of all systems is developed,[80] the philosophical landscape is made clearer if a new schema is offered, that of a new *Trika*. This is also supported by the evidence given by Mark Dyczkowski, who informs us that the form of *Trika* learnt by Abhinavagupta did not even originate in Kashmir,[81] so it is not even clear if *Trika* can be stated as being exclusively Kashmiri. Dyczkowski also argues that the landscape of *Tantric* literature had another dimension in which the *Kula* and *Krama* schools played an important part.[82] In Dyczkowski's in-depth study, he highlights that the lines between each school were blurred, and in many instances *Trika, Kula* and *Krama*, though remaining distinct, shared "common roots".[83] Abhinavagupta also

---

was both monist and theistic, where the 'Lord' has a "theistic nature" and "transcendental unity", see B. N. Pandit, *A History of Kashmir Shaivism* (Srinagar: 1990), p.31.

[77] Chatterji, *Kashmir Shaivism*, p.13.

[78] See Gavin Flood, 'Shared Realities and Symbolic Forms in Kashmir Shaivism', *Numen*, 36/2 (1989), pp.225-247; and Vasudeva, *The Yoga of the Mâlinîvijayottaratantra*, p.xi.

[79] See *SSVs*, p.xv.

[80] As argued in the *A Descriptive Analysis of the Kashmir Series of Text and Studies*, p.1,

[81] see Mark S.G. Dyczkowski, *The Doctrine of Vibration: An Analysis of the Doctrines and Practices of Kashmir Shaivism* (NY: 1987), p.12.

[82] *Ibid.*

[83] *Ibid.*

seemed to have brought these systems together within a collective basket in a unifying and encompassing system.

Consequently, the new *Trika* schema can be understood conceptually as a monist-cum-theistic doctrine in the post *Shiva Sûtra* age that applies to the doctrines put forward by the new *Trika* theologians, but which utilised *dualistic* ideas from the older *Trika*. The re-introduced form of *Pratyabhijñâ* from the resurgent new *Trika* of the eighth to eleventh-twelfth centuries, developed within this sphere of many influences including that of the *Shiva Sûtra* which along with *Spanda,* form a part of the new *Trika* doctrine, as Lakshmanjoo argued, thus forming "one thought", which was non-dual.[84] While Sanderson does not accept this, in that for him the older *Trika* was not completely *non-dual,*[85] he does agree that the resurgent *Trika,* culminating in Abhinavagupta and Kshemarâja, was essentially *non-dualistic.*[86] The vast majority of scholars[87] argue that the resurgent *non-dualism* was not to be considered in isolation but as a continuation of the *non-dualism* inherent in *Trika,* and therefore it would be incongruent to refer to different types of *Trika.* Moti Lal Pandit also states that the "Trika Shaivism of Kashmir, whose philosophic content and orientation is characterised by a non-dualistic mode of thinking, and has its basic source in such primary revelatory texts that are known as the Âgamas or Tantras".[88] This echoes the views of Chatterji, who stated that *Trika* was a system that was idealistically monist,[89] but this is not

---

[84] See Lakshmanjoo, *Kashmir Shaivism,* p.129.

[85] Sanderson, *'Shaivism and the Tantric Traditions',* p.703.

[86] Sanderson, *'The Doctrine of the Mâlinîvijayottaratantra',* pp.281-309; and *'Shaivism and the Tantric Traditions',* p.695.

[87] For examples see: J. C. Chatterji, *Kashmir Shaivism,* Delhi: 1914, 2004; J. Rudrappa, *Kashmir Shaivism,* Mysore: 1969; Jaideva Singh, *SSVs,* p.xv; P. E. Muller-Ortega, *The Triadic Heart of Shiva,* Delhi: 1989; B. N. Pandit, *A History of Kashmir Shaivism*; Kamalakar Mishra, *Kashmir Shaivism,* Delhi: 1999; Moti Lal Pandit, *The Trika Shaivism of Kasmir,* New Delhi: 2003.

[88] Moti Lal Pandit, *The Trika Shaivism of Kashmir,* p.ix.

[89] J. C. Chatterji, *Kashmir Shaivism,* p.4.

the full consensus for example J. Rudrappa had stated that in the resurgent *Trika* (*Pratyabhijñâ*), there was a "synthesis of monist and dualistic approaches".[90]

Double Cognition

Consequently, the experience of the non-dual state of *re-cognition* can be said to qualify the apparent *dualism* of the new *Trika*, where the human *dualistic* consciousness was corrected within the experience of *re-cognition*. This evidenced a development of a double cognition schema, one of the divine and another of the mundane, where "several cognitions although arising at different times, do have mutual unity".[91] Through unity, true *self*-awareness arises, which is not the result of an impersonal force or due to a natural consciousness or *physis,* in *Pratyabhijñâ* is viewed as "impure"[92] and cannot reveal the truth. The distinction between what is 'pure' and that which is 'impure' reveals differing levels of cognitions, or a double cognition, one of purity and another of impurity in relation to phenomenal existence[93] As Utpala stated that:

> Phenomenon, in such a state (of *vidyâ*), seem imperfect and inferior because they appear a non-Self (non-Âtman). These are at the same time perfect and superior by virtue of their being invested with I-Consciousness. Such a state of vidyâ is thus superior and perfect, on one hand, and inferior and imperfect on the other hand since it is a state of unity in diversity, indicating both purity and impurity.[94]

The condition of many levels of perception and cognition is reflected in the acceptance of many levels of knowledge, where the double

---

[90] J. Rudrappa, *Kashmir Shaivism*, p.9.

[91] *IPK*, 1.26, p.11; translation by Pandit, *IPKp,* 1.4.3, p.40.

[92] See *IPK,* 1.77, p.32; translation by Pandit, *IPKp,* 1.7.14, p.92.

[93] As Utpala stated that the activities of the world which reflect differing levels of cognition, "whether pure or impure, are experienced within the Lord" (*Ibid.*).

[94] *atrâparatvam bhâvânâm anâtmatvena bhâsanât/ paratâhantayâccâdât parâpara-daúa hisâ//, IPK*, 3.5, p.60; translation by Pandit, *IPKp,* 3.1.5, p.161.

cognition schema of *Pratyabhijñâ* can be viewed as an epistemological basis by which to approach person. It is because mundane knowledge, though revealing some aspects of truth, cannot reveal the whole truth. Hence, another awareness apart from the mundane becomes observable as acting upon ordinary consciousness. This higher cognition reflects a higher willing and acting in person through a unity, which also represents a single cognition in a completed context. Only in the highest condition of *Shiva* there is total perfection, but due to the relationship of the divine will (*icchâ*) and activity (*Shakti*) the individual comes to ultimately realise that one's *self* is non-different to the divine *Self*. While initially a double cognition is apparent and is expressed in the difference between the willing and activity between divine and human conditions, these cognitive differences are overcome through unity in the divine *Self*. This distinction is also apparent in the outward cognition of manifested phenomena as Utpala stated:

> It is thus established that two types of phenomena, the relative finite subject and the object, appear within one basic subject while considering: 'This is' and 'this is being seen by me' or 'that was' and 'that was seen by me'.[95]

Through the awareness of 'I am' in relation to 'this is', the finite subject comes to reflect a way of cognising and *being* of the divine who manifests diversity through his own subjective reality. While the cognition 'this is', seems to affirm objectivity and thus the separation of individual subjects, it actually reflects a cognitive ability to experience 'I-ness', which later comes to be realised as conditional to the divine 'I'.

It is in this understanding that the term person is placed, within the context of divine movement (or revelation) to the world and how this movement is understood and then correlated to reciprocation and unity, through the experience of *re-cognition*.

---

[95] *IPK*, 1.31, p.13; translation by Pandit, *IPKp*, 1.4.8, p.46.

The external objects or manifestation (*âbhâsa*), through "appearing in one's perception",[96] come to be *re-cognised* as part of the divine activity firstly through mundane perception, through the 'I' condition and secondly in *re-cognition*. In *re-cognition* the pure 'I' replaces the impure 'I' and as such person attains the fullest mystical condition and the vision of God[97] within a concrete existential context.

Consequently, in *Pratyabhijñâ* it can be stated that two types of knowing were developed, the ordinary knowledge (*vidyâ*), and *jñâna* or a deeper level of knowledge and consciousness which qualifies the natural *physis*. The lower natural *physis* is not capable of self-revelation (through its own nature) but is understood through a modified form of knowing in which the individual comes to slowly understand a higher experience through the *Vidyâ-Shakti*[98] of the Lord through the Lord's power of differentiation or *apohana-Shakti*.[99] In other words, through the Lord's power creation understands itself as different but comes to the divine through modified forms of difference in a movement from *mâyâ* (illusion indicating delusion) to *vidyâ* (knowledge), and then to pure knowledge *jñâna* and "pure consciousness".[100] There are not many ontological types of persons, but depending on different types of

---

[96] *IPK*, 1.32, p.14; translation by Pandit, *IPKp*, 1.5.1, p.50.

[97] Utpala refers to *Shivahood*, becoming *Shiva*, and the vision of *Shiva*, making reference to Somamanda's work *Shiva-drsti*, see *IPK*, 4.16, p.73. In fact Utpala states that the whole the *Pratyabhijñâ* system was created to enlighten an aspirant "about his real character" (*IPK*, 4.15, p.73; translation from Pandit *IPKp*, 4.15, p.204), and "for the purpose that people attain perfection without ant arduous effort" (*IPK*, 4.18, p.74; translation by Pandit, *IPKp*, p.207.

[98] *IPK*, 3.6-7, p.61.

[99] Utpala argued that it is the Lord who manifests the "powers to know, to recollect and differentiate", *IPK*, 1.23, p.10; translation by Pandit, *IPKp*, 1.3.7, p.34.

[100] *IPK*, 3.6, p.61; translation by Pandit, *IPKp*, 3.1.6, p.163.

knowing, the modes or types of existence change according to a specific experience or a specific level of consciousness or knowing. The varying forms of differentiation in *Pratyabhijñâ* allow for types of existing that comes to reflect a deeper reality of *being,* both existing simultaneously within the *purusha* (*hypostasis*) and allowing for a sense of difference and non-difference.

The ability to *re-cognise* objects in relation to true *being* and the relationship of divine activity with past actions, present actions and future actions, which consists of affirming a double consciousness. Within this double awareness of the lower and the higher, free will, activity and consciousness of the individual subject depends on the will and power to do so, which ultimately rests in the will and consciousness of the Absolute Reality. As a consequence, when an "object shines"[101] the cognition to perceive the object, and the power of being the object, is due to the will, activity and *being* of the Absolute Subject or *Âtman.* The relation of the subject to the object, manifests not a negation of the objects for if that were so, how is duality recognised? Thus two cognitions are accepted, the ordinary and the Absolute where both are considered equal for both are manifestations of the Lord.

The paradox of difference and non-difference existing simultaneously reflects a continuous movement of consciousness from the pure 'I Consciousness' (*ahamkâra*) to this-ness (*idantâ*), and then to that-ness (*tat*)[102] or the phenomenal universe (object). This movement also constitutes a reciprocal movement back to the pure 'I' (Subject) and manifests a relationality between the objects of perception (*grâhya*) and the subject perceiver (*grâhaka*),[103]

---

[101] *IPVp,* p.136.

[102] *PBH, Sûtra* 3, describes *tat* (that) as the universe or differentiation, where "that is manifold because of the differentiation of reciprocally adapted (*anurûpa*) objects (*grâhya*) and subjects (*grâhaka*)", *tannânâ anurûpa-grâhya-grâhaka-bhedât*; translation by Singh, *PBHs,* p.52.

[103] *Ibid.*

between the relative 'I' and the Supreme 'I'.[104] Through the knowledge and experience of God the object of that knowledge or the individual, comes to know the true subject or divine "Egoity",[105] the divine 'I Am'. This becomes related on an intimate level to the human 'I-am' within the concrete human experience.

Âtmanic Unity

At the centre of this paradoxical dynamic is the unmoving supreme reality, which allows a sense of unity to be grasped through the term *Âtman,* which has to be considered at the centre of any model of person developed in *Pratyabhijñâ*. While *Pratyabhijñâ* understood *Âtman* within a monist sense and a naked condition of being, I qualify this for never was there a time when a person experienced this condition of *being* without the concrete and real experience. The real experience provides the condition by which the metaphysical Real can be experienced as the metaphysical backdrop to all philosophical considerations.[106] In this work the notion of *Âtman* taken from the *Pratyabhijñâ* tradition, indicates the essential nature of the *purusha* (*hypostasis*), by which the specific individual

---

[104] Mark Dyczkowski argues that the influence of *Pratyabhijñâ* on Râjânaka Rama in his development of Spanda, was apparent in the emphasis on "two types of egoity", *A Journey in the World of the Tantras,* p.36. Dyczkowski also highlights the problems of understanding the texts which referred the term "*âtmâ*" when referring to the relative *self* (*âtman*) and the divine Self (*Âtman* or the essential nature of *self*). I make the distinction between *self* and the *Self* to make a distinction between the natural *physis* and the divine nature (also within the *Âtman-hypostasis* model), but which also affirms the place of both natures. However, as understood in *Pratyabhijñâ* the relative 'I' rests or is completed in the Absolute 'I'.

[105] See Mark Dyczkowski, *A Journey in the World of the Tantras,* p.36.

[106] This is evident in Utpala's countering erroneous doctrines in *IPK,* 1.2, p.2, where he argues that the "Godhead" is the independent authority, whose nature is the "pure Consciousness" is the *Self* of every human person, giving "every person the power to know"; translation by Pandit, *IPKp,* 1.1.2, p.7. It is the ability of each individual to cognise that shows the reality of *Âtman* shining through as the true nature of that cognition.

characteristics are unified within an essential reality of (restored) *being* and consciousness.

In *Pratyabhijñâ* the notion of *Âtman* becomes the reality of *being,* providing a sense of unity within human persons, but this raises issues of how to overcome the ontological dilemma of bridging the *gulf* between the monist essential Transcendental One, the Divine *Being,* which is done so by changing the term to mean a principle of *being*. It also provides a platform to overcome the existential dilemma of the relativist individual but at the same time it infers that person is not denuded in a total absorption with the divine. The isolation of the individual is not overcome at the expense of destroying any real sense of person. The *Pratyabhijñâ* solution was to affirm that the mundane consciousness is not denied, even when experienced in a *pati* context, but is viewed as a manifestation of the divine and thus intimately related to the divine. Utpala stated:

> The Lord, being all powerful, manifests spatial sequence by creating wonderful variety in the forms of creation, and He also brings about time sequence by manifesting variations in action.[107]

The individual person is thus not denied but affirmed as a manifestation of the divine. Difference and non-difference were not disconnected, where the former is dissolved in the latter, but accepted for it is the Lord Himself who assumes forms and at the same time does not deny those forms. As Abhinavagupta stated that, "the act of assuming or entering into different forms"[108] becomes possible due to the freedom of the divine whose essential nature is *Parâmaraa* or the "will in the form of desire to do so".[109] In this condition (of unity) the individual lives "within the Lord"[110] and not in separation.

---

[107] *mûrti-vaicitry ato deaa-kramam âbhâsayaty asau/ kriyâ-vaicitrya-nirbhâsât kâla-kramam apIshvarah//, IPK,* 2.5, p.38; translation by Pandit *IPKp,* 2.1.5, p.110.

[108] *IPV,* 2.4.20-21 (commentary); translation by Pandey, *IPVp,* pp.186-187.

[109] *Ibid.*

[110] *Ibid.*

This model is due to an accepting that creation is a manifestation (*âbhâsa*) of the Lord is not disconnected from the divine reality. Utpala stated that difference, which is the base of time, is based upon manifestation and non-manifestation and "such manifestations and non-manifestations are due to the Lord".[111] Therefore person cannot be rejected within a context of non-*being* through total absorption, but created by the Lord, and thus has to be accepted as real.

Unity as Conditional Relationality

Through the concept of unity in *Pratyabhijñâ*, difference is established as dependent on the subject of manifestation, or the doer (*Âtman*).[112] This doer relates the differing substances as a single substance "residing simultaneously in more than one substance"[113] and is essentially one, where phenomena attain a relational condition through "a single real fact".[114] The dependence of difference indicates that difference gains a relational context, between subjects and objects and between impure and pure realities, within a condition of unity. The condition of existing as a subject in relation to objects and the divine reality is made apparent by Utpala, who refutes *Vijnñânavâdins* (Buddhists) and cites their objections to a concept of *Âtman*[115] to highlight how phenomena are dependent and relational to the divine within the condition of the *Âtman*. This condition allowed *Pratyabhijñâ* to accept that *âbhâsas* are real, which qualified its non-dualism through a model

---

[111] *IPK*, 2.4, p.38; translation by Pandit, *IPKp*, 2.1.4, p.109.

[112] See *IPK*, 1.16, p.7.

[113] *IPK*, 1.16, p.7; translation by Pandit, *IPKp*, 1.2.11, p.25.

[114] *Ibid.*

[115] Utpala states that the *Vijnñânavâdins* believed "what is seen is the rise of some particular objects...and nothing beyond that. Only such is the relation between cause and effect...The concept of doer is imagination", *IPK*, 1.15-16, p.7; translation by Pandit, *IPKp*, 1.2.10-11, pp.24-25.

of unity-in-diversity (*bhedâbheda*).[116] In this model, the focus is on the relationships between subject and object highlighted in the medium by which this relationality[117] was to be achieved.

Pratyabhijñā worked within a double philosophical schema, allowing for elements of the *dualistic,* such as accepting the world, within a non-dual context. This non-dual context was not divorced from mundane existence and awareness, where "determinate cognitions"[118] of individuals, perceiving the universe and themselves in differentiation and multiplicity, ultimately rested on unity. Without the "right consciousness"[119] only difference or multiplicity is seen. The relative position (*dik*), where objects are cognised as external to the Absolute subject and thus separate, is considered firstly in relation to unity, then diversity and then unity-in-diversity.

The relationship of the Lord in respect to objects evidences the concrete reality of objects, not their non-reality, and points to the unity inherent in the relation between subject and object. In this context this relationality is conditional to unity and understood in terms of the "manifestation of the universal power of action".[120]

Within *Pratyabhijñā* philosophy, a relational approach was also evident in its philosophic categories: *non-dualistic*; *dualistic-cum-non-dualistic*; and *dualistic* divisions within the different

---

[116] See *IPV*, 2.2.5-7.

[117] *IPV*, 2.2.6; translation by Pandey, *IPVp*, p.135.

[118] *IPV*, 2.2.5; translation by Pandey, *IPVp*, p.134.

[119] *IPV*, 2.2.6 (commentary); translation by Pandey, *IPVp*, p.135.

[120] *Ibid*. As stated in the *IPK*, 2.17, p.42, that "attainment of purpose by means of an object that has both unity and multiplicity, is possible for a subject, who seeks causal efficiency, only according to the view that has been stated above. Therefore, ideas of revelation etc. are not erroneous", *evam evârtha-siddhih syân mâtur artha-kriyârthinah/ bhedâbhedavatârthena tena na bhrântir îdrshi//*; *IPV*, 2.2.7; translation by Pandey, *IPVp*, p.136.

schools.[121] Again the triadic divisions of I, you, he/she/it (*aham, tvam, sah*)[122] affirmed a philosophical relationship of the transcendent subject with divine manifestation, but qualified in the unity of *being*. This relationality was evident in the relationship between the divine subject and objects, where the objects were fulfilled through the essential reality of *being* and not only in an existential dynamic. This contradictory approach led to the Tantric dictum: "*sarvam sarvâtmakam*, everything relates to everything else".[123] Hence *Pratyabhijñâ* did not view the dichotomy of *dualism* and *non-dualism* as necessarily presenting a philosophical problem, but rather representing different levels of consciousness which are ultimately expressed as the divine reality.

Pratyabhijñâ, while using *dualistic* philosophical constructs, viewed the relationship of subject-to-objects as real, confirming the real-ness of human existence and the place for the totality of *being*. Hence *Pratyabhijñâ* accepted the notion of concrete person but through a non-dual context. This model reconciles notions of transcendence (*vishvottîrna*) and revelation or immanency (*vishvâtmaka*) in a model that incorporated the metaphysical and the concrete person within a single model. This was accomplished by the re-addressing of how *Self-realisation* or knowledge of *Self* was to be attained by admitting the place for *âbhâsas* or manifestations,[124] but which are ultimately *re-cognised* as non-

---

[121] Of *Shiva, Shakti,* and *Nara* in *SSVs*, p.xv; also *para* (Supreme), *parâpara* (Supreme-non-Supreme), and *apara* (non-Supreme); and *abheda* (non-difference), and *bhedâbheda* (diversity-in-unity) and *bheda* (difference). See Chatterji, *Kashmir Shaivism* p.8; see also Gavin Flood, *Body and Cosmology in Kashmir Shaivism* (San Francisco: 1993), p.12; also see Pandit, *Aspects of Kashmir Shaivism,* p.18. This philosophy is outlined in *IPKp*, pp.116-120.

[122] Jaideva Singh, *Abhinavagupta, Parâ-Trîûikâ-Vivagraha, The Secret of Tantric Mysticism,* ed. Bettina Bäumer (Delhi: 2005), p.xvi.

[123] *Ibid.,* p.xvii.

[124] See *IPK*: 1.32; 1.35; 1.40; 1.54; 1.60-61; 1.78-81; 2.4; 2.6; 2.8; 2.35.

different to *Maheshvara* or the Supreme.[125] In this respect *Pratyabhijñâ* was both the path and the goal where "self-re-cognition"[126] is the means and the end in determining the value of both existence and *being*.

---

[125] *Ibid.*, 1.1.; and see *IPV,* 1.1.1.

[126] *IPV,* 1.1.1. The reality of becoming in *re-cognition* could be had in a "flash", *SK* (KSTS 5), as stated in the *Spanda* philosophy or as a process of awakening (*IPK,* 4.11-12; *IPKt,* chp.1, 1.1, p.85; and *IPKp,* pp.200-210), which allows a correlation to be made to the concept of *becoming* in *deification,* see Moti Lal Pandit, *The Trika Shaivism of Kashmir,* (New Delhi: 2003), pp.108-9. The notion of *deification* in relation to *re-cognition* is also broached by Motilal Pandit who argues that the state of the perfected one (the *Siddha*) lives in the state of perfection (*deification*) in which the body too is *deified.* In the *deified* or *re-cognised* condition, life becomes a "divine wonder" (*Ibid.,* p.114) in which the cosmos is seen (*drishti*) as a vision of the play of the Lord, a, "play of consciousness", see Swami Muktananda, *Play of Consciousness, A Spiritual Autobiography* (South Fallsburg: 2002). *Deification* and *re-cognition* are both words that can conceptually expresses ontological fullness of *being* and exemplified by Utpala who referred to an awakening in the form of grace through *Shaktipâta,* see *PSA,* 9, p.24 (Pandit); *Tantrâloka,* 5.1, pp.52-53, citation taken from N. Rastogi, *Introduction to the Tantrâloka* (Delhi: 1987), p.13. This awakening culminates in the *telos* of human existence, in an experience of fullness or rather an ontological *re-cognition* of union with the Lord, and this experience of *re-cognition* represents the fullness of *being,* of what it is to be a person.

CHAPTER 7

Developing a Concept of Person in *Pratyabhijñâ*

Introduction

It is due to the *Pratyabhijñâ* double schema, of accepting both *dualistic* and *non-dualistic* models, that a concept of person can be developed. This double schema did not however indicate a bipolar philosophy, a bipolar approach to personhood. Such a schema highlights unity in the face of multiplicity where the "ordinary every day life"[1] is not negated, but accepted and raised to the divine level. The *deification* or transformation of the thought processes within a *re-cognition* of the truth of divine unity is very similar to those ideas already expressed in my work, *Deified Person*, in relation to the Byzantine model of *deification*, where what is *above* raises up that which is *below*. *Pratyabhijñâ* in *re-cognition* also accepted that which is *below* by allowing for a transformation

---

[1] *IPV,* 1.7, 13-14; translation by Pandey, *IPVp*, p.110. As Abhinavagupta stated: "Not only relations of cause and effect, of remembrance and of contraries, which characterise all the general transaction of ordinary every day life, but the particular transactions also such as purchase and sale, which are impure, and relation of teacher and taught etc., which are pure, depend upon one subject, because transactions depend upon some kind of unification" (*Ibid*).

of consciousness. In this context both that which is pure or impure is accepted, as Utpala stated:

> Thus the whole world's activities, whether pure or impure, are experienced within the Lord, who shines, decorated by the (reflective) manifestations of various different phenomena.[2]

Thus as Abhinavagupta argued, "practical life is experienced as resting on the omnipresent Lord"[3] whose "essential nature"[4] is not changed by manifested phenomena. In the experience of *re-cognition* the ordinary life is not dismissed but *re-cognised* to be "identical with the level of *Shiva*, which is characterised by the realisation of the essential nature of the subject".[5] As a consequence, difference is in itself impossible, as argued by Abhinavagupta, "unless there be one substratum of all these",[6] whereby difference when intimately related to non-difference, which is accepted as having both concrete existence and meaning.

When considering a notion of person or *purusha* in *Pratyabhijñâ* this simultaneous accepting of two natures, pertaining to the divine and the objectified world, indicates that in the human person there exists a double nature of essential *being* and outward existence. There must also be affirmed a double consciousness of willing and acting, where the two are unified in the experience of re-*cognition*. This is very similar to Maximus the Confessor's *dyothelite* Christology,[7] which argues that in Christ there is a natural

---

[2] *ittham aty-artha-bhinnârthâvabhâsa-khacite vibau/ samalo vimal vâpi vyavahâro 'nabhûyate//*, IPK, 1.77, p.32; translation by Pandit, *IPKp*, 1.7.14, p.92. Pandey's translation of the verse in Abhinavagupta's *IPV* (*IPVp*, p.110) is: "Thus experience shows that all transactions, whether pure or impure depend upon the omnipresent Loed, in whom all the objective manifestations, so very different from one another, are reflected".

[3] *IPV,* 1.7.14 (commentary); translation by Pandey, *IPVp*, p.110.

[4] *Ibid.*

[5] *Ibid.*

[6] *IPV,* 1. 8. (commentary); translation by Pandey, *IPVp*, p.111.

[7] *Opsc.*7, 80D-84D, and *Opsc.*345B-56D; also see Bathrellos, The Byzantine Christ, pp.99-174, who significantly highlights the strengths and shortcomings of Maximus' Christology.

human will and an "essential divine will".[8] Both are simultaneously united in Christ without separation or change to the divine nature. In the same way in the human individual there are two conditions in *Pratyabhijñâ*, which are united through the divine activity in *Âtman*. In the natural *physis,* a feeling of bound-ness (*pashu*) exists which is overcome when united to the essential divine nature or the *Âtman* within the human person (*hypostasis/purusha*), through divine grace. However, the distinction between the divine and human although remaining in Byzantine theology, is dissolved in *Pratyabhijñâ,* as Abhinavagupta explains that *Bhagavân* (God) is both the "knower and doer",[9] and continues:

> Although in reality there is only one Samvid, which is nothing else than pure light of consciousness and free consciousness, yet this difference has been brought about by Himself in order to make others understand (true nature of Shiva).[10]

Personhood through Means of Knowledge

The single entity or individual subject (*pramatr*) reflects a person's ability to cognize the essential reality, from which self-shinning, self-awareness (*vimarsha*) extends and from which comes *jñâna* (knowledge) and *kriyâ* (act). The individual subject (*pramatr*) experiences his or her personhood because of the Supreme Person, the absolute Subject (*pramatr*), who manifests persons through His own personal existence. Utpala explained:

> It is only He (*pramâtr*, the Absolute Subject) who is almighty God (*Maheshvarah*), by virtue of His constant Self-awareness (*vimarsha*), because Self-awareness is the pure knowledge (*jñâna*) as well as the pure action (*kriyâ*) of the Lord.[11]

Human personhood, therefore, is a reflection of the divine personhood, having *self*-awareness and the ability to *be* and act,

---

[8] *Opsc.7,* 80C (Louth).

[9] *IPV,* 1.8 (commentary); translation by Pandey, *IPVp*, p.111.

[10] *Ibid.*

[11] *IPK,* 1.88, p.36.

having also freedom, volition and power. This awareness, *being*, freedom and action though limited in the individual and bound by the lower nature indicates the possibilities inherent through the higher or divine awareness, *being*, freedom, and action. The ability to act and be acted upon, reflected through the ontological condition of *being* a human person, affirms that the bodily existence is manifestly real but does not exist in isolation. It exists in relation to the divine reality where the higher ultimately informs that condition of its truth, as Utpala stated: "exterior existence of such entities is the eternal Truth".[12] Consequently, an individual entity has to be considered in terms of material existence or "determinate consciousness",[13] which relates to the attainment of exterior knowledge. This exterior knowledge is attained through *pramânas* (means of valid knowledge), whereby knowledge indicates not only the nature of subjective cognition, but also the limitations to this knowledge and awareness. But there are limitations to *pramâna* and Pandit relates the term to "mundane activities"[14] not capable of revealing God. However, as Abhinavagupta argues that *pramânas* although they express certain exterior qualities, "shine determinately as dependent upon another...having the nature of Samvid",[15] and are not separate from *Cit. Pramânas* are not independent in that they do not shine independently but are fundamentally dependent on the divine, and related to that which allows them to shine. This Dependence on the divine indicates the nature of the cognition of the limited subject, and to that to which it is related. Thus the *pramânas* are related to the relative consciousness; as Abhinavagupta goes on to state that:

> If this *pramâna* be not related to the limited subject, the consciousness 'I who had consciousness of Nila, am now having that of Pita' will not be possible. But such personal experience is undeniable and is never contradicted. This the Âbhâsa (extrovert light) which shines as

---

[12] *IPK,* 1.5, p.34; translation by Pandit, *IPKp,* 1.8.5, p.95.

[13] *IPV,* 2.3.1-2 (commentary); translation by Pandey, *IPVp,* p.142.

[14] *IPKp,* p.121.

[15] *IPV,* 2.3.1-2 (commentary); translation by Pandey, *IPVp,* p.140.

related to the limited subject and appears every moment in a new form, because of its facing object, is called pramâna because it operates to bring about cognition.[16]

While *pramânas* indicate exterior knowledge, they also relate to self-determinate consciousness, which has as its characteristic the ability to "produce the determinate knowledge",[17] to determine "this" (*idam*).[18] The ability to allow an external recognition of another condition outside of the initial cognitive awareness, infers an ability to attain other types of consciousness in relation to individual awareness and the attaining of higher knowledge. The relationship of knowledge to manifestation (*tat* or *âbhâsa*) and the relationship of such *âbhâsa* (that-ness) to cognitive subject will be examined later, but it is the determination of such objectification, which consequently leads to an awareness of something other than "this" (*idam*), a reality by which "this" comes into *being*. The relationship of individual conscious awareness to manifestation (*âbhâsa*), or that-ness, indicates a movement of exteriority, which through a means of valid knowledge, allows an inward movement and awareness to 'this-ness' (*idam*) and 'I-consciousness' (*aham*) or 'I am', confirming a sense of personal awareness. In this personal awareness a sense of difference is attained through the power of differentiation or *apohana-Shakti.*[19] It is because this difference is

---

[16] *Ibid.*, p.141.

[17] *Ibid.*, p.142.

[18] Utpala stated: "The means of right knowledge (*pramâna*) is that because of whose power the object shines determinately as "this" (*idam*) and "of such nature". That is also self-luminous and rises afresh every moment. That (*tat* or *pramâna*) as determinately cognising within itself (this light, whose essence is the inner reflective awareness, *vimarshâtamâ*) an object, for which a single expression stands and which is free from temporal and spatial limitations, is the cognition (*miti*), provided that it is uncontradicted or invalidated (not an illusion)", *IPK*, 2.16-17, p.43; translations from: Pandey, *IPVp*, p.140; Torrela, *IPKt*, p.161; Pandit, *IPKp*, pp.121-122.

[19] *Ibid.*, and *IPKp*, pp.27-35; Rudrappa observes that in *Kashmir Shaivism*, *being* seems to be "bifurcated as Brahman and Jîva" (Rudrappa, *Kashmir Shaivism* p.69). However this bifurcation represents a unity-in-manifestation,

the *Self*-luminous principle (*Samvedana*),[20] a notion of personal difference comes to indicate a sense of non-difference, in that, difference cannot stand independently outside of unity, but is dependent on the divine.

Person as a Mode of Existence

The reality of being a person, having a sense of difference, and the consciousness of a particular individual on a particular level, in *Pratyabhijñâ*, depends on the mode of existence (*guna*)[21] of that individual. Thus the type of existence of a person reflects the *guna* in which that person exists.[22] In the higher *guna* (mode of existence) of *sattva*, pureness through knowledge (*jñâna*) is attributed, even

---

a unity in the nature of differentiation, for all cognitions are the shining luminosity of divine consciousness (*IPV,* 1.4.8). Rudrappa notes, in *Kashmir Shaivism,* "everything is the manifestation of the Godhead ParamaShiva" (Rudrappa, *Kashmir Shaivism* p.19) hence the unity of person is also safeguarded. The "individual self is none other than the Lord Himself with limited powers" (*Ibid.*112).

[20] *IPVp,* p.41.

[21] The philosophy of the three *gunas* are accepted and developed in *Pratyabhijâ,* see *IPK,* 4.4-5, p.71.

[22] Utpala stated "the knowledge and action of a *pati* (liberated one) aimed toward objects taken as his own, as well as his power to manifest the viewpoint of diversity, become respectively (these *gunas*), sattva, rajas and tamas of a bound being. These *gunas,* becoming transformed into instrumental and objective elements, are not spoken of as the powers of the powerful One (*purusha*) because (as *tattvas*) they are separate from *purusha*" IPK, 4.4-5, p.71; *IPKp,* pp.194-195. Because of this sense of the personal, Mishra concludes that the "whole *Pratyabhijñâ* system centres round the concept of person", see Kamalakar Mishra, 'Person in the Light of Pratyabhijñâ Philosophy', *Indian Philosophical Annual,* 8 (1972), 206-214. However, Mishra never quite states what this means other than developing a broad notion of person. In my opinion he uses general philosophical and psychological terms to establish that, in *Pratyabhijñâ,* God should be understood in an Absolute, theistic, personalist sense, having a personal consciousness, which significantly reflects the need for a personhood category (*Ibid.,* pp.207-208).

in differentiation. In the lower modes of *rajas* and *tamas*[23] existence is related to action (*kriyâ*) and bound-ness or illusion (*mâyâ*) and to impurity, implying negative attributes to these types of existences. While the Supreme Person (*purusha*) remains beyond the *gunas,* the human person can be expressed through types or modes of human existence in which the highest existence, as already stated, can be called a *Cid-âtmanic* mode (*tropos*) of *hypostatic* existence.

This mode expresses the freedom to overcome the natural *physis* or lower *guna* in a *tropos* which relates to the subject of pure consciousness (*cid-âtmanah*),[24] where a person (*pati*) experiences divine consciousness. This model utilises *Cit* to develop a link between *being* and existence within an *event* of *Citi,* where the *hypostatic tropos* cannot be divorced from the essential reality of *Âtman. Cit* or the *Citi-Shakti* thus establishes an existential and ontological link between the divine *being,* having will (*icchâ*) and the power of action (*kriyâ*), in relation to the world. In a mode of essential *being* this infers a relational context of essential subject to object, of God to the world through the activity of *Cit,* where the "common" manifestation comes to understand the "uncommon"[25] through the activity of *Citi* in a mode of divine existence. This represents a model of unity within diversity, of *being* within a mode of existing, where the "light of consciousness (*prakashah*)"[26] becomes existentially available to the individual (*narah*)[27] who attains an awareness of non-difference, and thus can relate to a *Cid-âtmanic* mode of existence.[28]

---

[23] *IPV,* 4.4-6.

[24] *IPK,* 3.23, p.67.

[25] *IPV,* 4.11.

[26] Within this mode an experience is had as Sanderson states where: "the result is said to be the state of duality within nonduality (*dvaitâdvaitam, bhedâbheda*). Shiva consciousness arises when the objective universe...dissolves entirely into non-dualistic self-representation (*aham vimarshani*)", see Sanderson, 'The Doctrine of the Mâlinîvijayottaratantra', p.295.

[27] *Ibid.,* p.295.

[28] *Ibid.*

Through existing as a mode, a person comes to know the nature of his or her personhood, through the dynamic activity of *Cit*, which reveals the true nature to the person. *Citi*, the conscious activity of *Âtman*,[29] the luminous being-ness (*Prakashah*) of the Absolute as *Para-Samvit* (supreme consciousness),[30] or *vimarsha* (shinning free-consciousness),[31] purifies the lower modes of existence or *gunas*, raising up the consciousness, while at the same time *being* all levels of consciousness and *gunas*. Utpala explains that *Cit* is non-different to His own *Self*-awareness as the Absolute *Pramatr*[32] (divine experient or *Maha-Pramatr*) and this fundamentally relates to how to understand human personhood, *being* and conscious existing. *Cit* has a revelatory function in informing relative consciousness and modes of existence of its true nature in the individual *pramatrs* (experients), it also has the ability to cognise divine unfoldment (*unmesha*)[33] or manifestation (*âbhâsa*)[34] of the universe, which highlights the relationship of divine activity to revelation. Through transcending "modes"[35] of existence, the divine exists as these modes as a "mass of *prakasha* (light of consciousness)"[36] for the states or "modes" are only "the form of *prakasha*".[37] The revelatory or extrusive aspect of the divine (*unmesha*) as compared to intrusive (*unmesha*) divine inwardness[38] indicates how *Pratyabhijñâ* overcame the problem of *being* and act through the notion of *prakasha*, by including the revelatory medium of *Cit* to overcome any ontological *gulf.*

---

29 *PSA*, 7, p.23; and Chatterji, *Kashmir Shaivism*, p.47

30 Tagare, *The Pratyabhijñâ Philosophy*, p.75.

31 *IPV*, 1.5.14-15; translation by Pandey *IPVp*, pp.74-76.

32 *IPK*, 1.88, p.36.

33 *IPK*, 3.3, p.60.

34 *IPK*, 1.83, p.34.

35 *PBH*, *Sûtra* 4 (commentary); translation by Singh, *IPKs*, p54.

36 *Ibid.*

37 *Ibid.*

38 *IPK*, 3.3, p.60. Unmesha means "opening of the eye" and nimesha indicates "closing of the eyes" (*Ibid*).

The overcoming of this ontological *gulf* within the human person can be correlated to a consciousness, as stated above, to a *Cid-âtmanic* mode of personal, or *hypostatic,* existence which lives in the divine consciousness. This existence can be said to relate to a bodily existence through the term *purusha,* where the *purusha* attains the highest level of consciousness.

Purusha Tattva

The notion of person is equated with *purusha,*[39] as the twelfth principle *(tattva)*[40] of the thirty-six principles *(tattvas)* of manifestation *(âbhâsas),* consequently, it is important to examine this term in relation to the *tattvas.* The *purusha tattva* becomes important not when considering a notion of person in *Pratyabhijñâ,* but also in terms of revelation, of how the divine reveals Himself to the world. This process of revelation through the *tattvas* also related to the movement from the divine 'I-consciousness' to that-

---

[39] Even though in the term *purusha* can be correlated to a notion of person and expressed as such in the *tattvic* categories, the preferred term to indicate individual is not *purusha* which is only mentioned once directly in the text of the *IPK* (*see IPK,* 2.19, p.44). Neither is it *jîva* which is mentioned once in *IPK* (*Ibid.,* 1.4., p.2); or *pashu,* which I could only find mentioned four times (*Ibid.,* 3.7, p.61; 3.14, p.64; 4.4, p.71; 4.6, p.71); or *anu,* of which I found six references (*Ibid.,* 1.3, p.2; 1.8, p.4; 1.9, p.4; 1.39, p.17; 2.24, p.46; 2.47, p.55) not including the references to the *ânava-mala* or coverings of finitude (*Ibid.,* 3.15, p.64); but *pramatr* (experient) which is mentioned at eighteen times (*IPK,* 1.57, p.24; 1.65, p.27; 1.67, p.27; 1.69, p.28; 1.70, p.29; 1.76, p.31; 1.83, p.34; 1.85, p.35; 1.88, p.36; 2.12, p.41; 2.31, p.49; 2.38, p.52; 2.44-45, p.54; 2.48, p.55; 3.9, p.62; 3.13, p.63; 3.14, p.64). Also Abhinavagupta in *PSA* seemed to prefer the term *pashu* (*PSA,* 5-6, p.16) to indicate individual, though he does utilise *purusha* at least once in the same text (*Ibid.,* p.36)

[40] From *tat* or that, hence the *tattvas* describes that-ness. The *PBH* stated that, "Tat (that) means the universe" (translation by Singh, *PBHs,* p.52), or the exterior aspect of divine action in relation to personal consciousness. See also, *A Descriptive Analysis of the Kashmir Series of Texts and Studies,* p.4; Chatterji, *Kashmir Shaivism,* p.89; Swami Lakshmanjoo, *Kashmir Shaivism,* (USA: 2003), pp.1-10; Tagare, *The Pratyabhijñâ Philosophy,* pp.24-31.

ness, or manifestation (*âbhâsas*). This relationship of the divine to the world comes to indicate on the human level types or modes of existence and consciousness by which the divine is expressed. As such the *tattvas* were related to the divine act (*kriyâ*), or revelation, as principles of manifestation (*âbhâsas*) in the *Âgamâdhikâra* of Utpala's *Ishvarapratyabhijñâkârikâ,* which included the *purusha-tattva*.[41] However, the term *purusha-tattva* is not expressly stated but inferred through the word *pramatr* which indicated finite subject. Utpala stated:

> That subjective condition, void, having entities other than itself as its objects, and being wrapped by five limiting elements known as time and so on, is itself an objective element, appearing as a subjective one.[42]

This part of the work examines the relationship of how the experient (*pramatr*) relates to the *tattvas*, especially the *purusha-tattva,* to understand how concrete existence is to be understood in the light of *Pratyabhijñâ* seeming negation of individuality.

The Tattvas of Manifestation

The *tattvas* of manifestation or cosmological categories of Utpala in the *Ishvarapratyabhijñâkârikâ* were not given as a straight forward list, but were expressed through a philosophical-cum-theological context.[43] Within this context, the notion of person related not only to principles of manifested existence, but how individual consciousness is raised to a level where divine participation changes the mode of the *purusha* from impurity to purity.[44] The definition of a notion of person also has to be considered within this context, where any term does not rest at a certain level but evolves until

---

[41] *IPK,* 3.9, p.62.

[42] *yash ca pramâtâ shûnyâdih vyatirekini/ mâtâ sa meyah kâlâdika-pañcaka-vestitah, IPK,* 3.9, p.62; translation by Pandit, *IPKp,* 3.1.9, p.167. See also Chatterji, *Kashmir Shaivism* p.54; and *MT,* p.xix.

[43] *IPK,* 3.1-3.31, pp.59-69; *IPKp,* pp.155-188.

[44] *Ibid.,* pp.159-163.

placed within a context of pure existing within the category of *tattvas*.[45]

The first *tattva* was *Shiva,* who as the highest deity (*Anuttara*) was ontologically and existentially undifferentiated with the highest *Âtman* or *Paramâtman*.[46] This divine state was not to be considered an unconscious substance but was "the very essence of Consciousness",[47] having the highest 'I Am' awareness. This conscious awareness allows for the second *tattva*, which was the dynamic aspect of the first *tattva*. The second *tattva, Shakti,* was also ontologically undifferentiated to the "divine essence"[48] but becomes existentially differentiated in that it indicated how the activity (act or *kriyâ*) of the *Self*-contained Absolute reality comes to express itself in an outward movement, creating the world and then revealing itself to the world.[49] Here, the notion of person

---

[45] The *tattvic* categories related to the first five "pure", the first being *Shiva*. The second *tattva* was the divine *Shakti*which expresses the desire and power to create which is dynamic, having movement, where there is both 'I am' (*ahanta*) and this-ness (*idanta*), but where divine activity is still intrusive. Through God's infinite consciousness and *kriyâ-Shakti, tattvic* manifestation occurs. The first two *tattvas* are expressed in the first stanza of the *Âgamadhikara* of *IPK* where *Shiva* is inferred by *evam* (thus or alone), see *IPK* 3.1, p.59; see also S. Vasudeva working on the seven perceivers' in *The Yoga of Mâlinîvijayottaratantra*, p.152.

[46] Which states that consciousness indicates "Self-sufficiency of God as well as His extraordinary divine essence (*paramâtmanah*), *IPK,* 1.44, p.18; translation by Pandit, *IPKp,* 1.5.13, p.62.

[47] *IPK,* 1.44, p.18; translation by Pandit, *IPKp,* 1.5.13, p.62.

[48] *IPK,* 1.44, p.18; translation by Pandit, *IPKp,* 1.5.13, p.62.

[49] Utpala states: "Thus the divine action, vibrating inwardly as well as outwardly in accordance with time sequence, belongs to none other than the infinite Subject of knowing. Therefore infinite knowledge and action are mutually inseparable", *IPK,* 3.1, p.59; *IPKp,* 3.1.1, p.155; see also *MT,* p.xxiii. *IPK,* 3.1, p.59; *IPKp,* 3.1.1, p.155, There has to be made a distinction between *eva* and *evam,* the first emphasises really, actually, just, alone, entirely, while *evam* means like this, thus, in this way. The text actually states *evam* to mean thus, as to support what went before, which is the conclusion of Raffaele Torella, see *IPKt,* p.189, and then *eva* to indicate "knowing subject alone" (*Ibid.*)

comes to be better understood in this dynamic of non-difference and difference, and in the observed downward movement or unfoldment (*unmesha*) of the divine activities by which person (*purusha*) attains *being*.

In the third *tattva* (relating existentially to *SadâShiva* or *Sâdâkhya*),[50] interior divine movement increases, where the interior aspect of the divine knowledge and action are further revealed, and where the revelation, *aham asmi idam* ('I am this') is born.[51] This movement allows expansion to the fourth *tattva, Ishvara,*[52] where the extroversive aspect of divine unfoldment (*unmesha*) is reflected in the understanding "this is I (*idam asmi aham*)".[53] The *Ishvara tattva* had also been correlated to *tatpurusha* by Abhinavagupta[54] to underline this extrusive activity of divine consciousness which comes to indicate, in the notion of divine person (*purusha*), a concrete sense of movement to the objectified universe, but which manifests a consequent *gulf* between the divine and the world.[55] The subject of how this *gulf* was resolved in *Pratyabhijñâ* will be examined in the following parts of this work.

In relation to the *tattvas* this *gulf* begins to allow the notion of individual to become more concrete, but at the expense of participation with the divine. In the fourth *tattva* or the *Ishvara tattva* the notion of divine person becomes specifically related to how the divine comes to communicate with the world and hence there is a context of relationality, which paradoxically resolves the

---

[50] *IPK*, 3.2, p.59.

[51] It is, as Tagare states, "the first creative aspect or vibration of *Parama Shiva* (*Anuttara*, the highest deity)", see Tagare, *The Pratyabhijñâ Philosophy*, p.26.

[52] *IPK*, 3.3, p.60.

[53] See Tagare, *The Pratyabhijñâ Philosophy*, p.27.

[54] Abhinavagupta, *Mâlinîslokavârtika* (200-212); translated by Hanneder, *Abhinavagupta's Philosophy of Revelation*, pp.93, 205.

[55] *Ibid.*, (207-209); p.205.

dilemma of an uncommunicative unmoving essence in relation to the world, through the revelations of personal divine principles. This relationality is expressed in the further outward movement from the divine centre, and expressed in the fifth *tattva, shuddha-vidya* (correct knowledge or *sad-vidyâ*),[56] which allows knowledge of the divine to be grasped. At this point Utpala refers to individual entities experiencing these types of consciousness, yet retaining some form of individuality, where partial unity is experienced in a state of diversity.

> (This viewpoint is pure and correct knowledge) because one may see even entities that are well known through an idea of 'this-ness', through the correct perspective; that is, Consciousness is seen as their essence.[57]

In the *shuddha-vidya tattva* there is a distinction between 'I-ness' and 'this-ness'. This tattva is the last pure *tattva,* which represents a dual consciousness of both unity, of pure 'I' and this-ness, where there is purity and impurity. The *sad-vidyâ tattva* indicates a state of qualified unity or *parâpara* (highest-non-highest-knowledge).[58] It is in *sad-vidyâ* that a model of unity-in-diversity comes to be apparent (*bhedâbheda*), which allows individual personhood to be expressed in terms of concrete existence in relation to unity. This points to the qualifying of subjective awareness, the pure 'I am', with some impurity, which allows the *pashu* (bound creature) to discover his real nature in the connection between the pure knowledge and impure consciousness. Although these five principles are often taken to indicate the first aspects of revelation, actually only the last three represent true *tattvas* as the first two, *Shiva* and *Shakti* do not represent a *dualism*, but aspects of Absolute *being*. But this too is incorrect for from an absolute point of view in *Pratyabhijñâ,* all manifestation is nothing but the light of divine

---

[56] *IPK,* 3.3-6, p.60-61.

[57] *idâm-bhâvopapapannânâm vedya-bhûmim upeyushâm/ bhâvânâm bodha-sâratvâd yathâ-vastv avalokanât, IPK,* 3.4, p.60; translation by Pandit, *IPKp,* 3.1.4, p.160-161.

[58] *IPK,* 3.5, p.60.

consciousness. Hence in *Pratyabhijñâ*, as Pandit poetically remarks, there is "a beautiful and satisfying unity between theism and absolutism of a monistic character".[59]

While the first two *tattvas* indicated purity, the next three indicated purity-impurity, all the rest related to impurity. As the divine unfoldment becomes greater so the principles (the sixth to the eleventh *tattvas*) become equated with the metaphysical coverings of ignorance (*kañcukas*)[60] that have wrapped self-awareness in finitude and limitations as Utpala stated:

> All bound beings, including the gods in heaven, are undergoing rebirth and are defiled by the three impurities; but among these, the defilement caused by past deeds is the most important cause of their transmigratory existence. Subjective consciousness, being wrapped in finite creative power (*kalâ*, counted among the *kañcukas*), and appearing finite in character, stands here as a quality of unconscious elements like the void (*úûnya*).[61]

It is due to these coverings that the deluded souls come to experience reincarnation.[62]

---

[59] *IPKp*, p.151.

[60] *IPK*, 3.21, p.66; also *IPKp*, pp.165-168. The five *kañcukas* are: *kalâ* (brings limitation in respect of doer-ship); *vidyâ* (brings limited knowledge); *raga* (brings worldly desire); and *kâla* (brings idea of limited time); also see Chatterji, *Kashmir Shaivism*, p.81; and Rudrappa, *Kashmir Shaivism*, p.78. In the thirteenth *tattva* relates to the notion of matter, *prakrti* (*IPK*, 3.10, p.62) which is "the diverse manifestation of the objective world, when it appears under the effect of that very impurity is called mâyâ" (*IPK*, 3.16, p.65; translation by Pandit, *IPKp*, 3.2.5, p.175).

[61] *IPK*, 3.21-22, pp.66-67; translation by Pandit, *IPKp*, 3.2.10-11, pp.179-180.

[62] Because the above passage refers to reincarnation it is appropriate here to state that the Byzantine tradition rejected reincarnation in the Second Council of Constantinople, see 'The Anathemas Against Origen' in *The Seven Ecumenical Councils* (NPNF 14), pp.318-319. Reincarnation seemed to deny the freedom of grace and salvation, and God's creation of each new individual soul at the human birth. However, from a philosophical point of view, the individual consciousness reincarnates or changes many times even in one life

From a position of consciousness, reincarnation only points to the path of bound-ness, to limited consciousness, and does not relate to fulfilment and thus is irrelevant from the position of completed consciousness. Nevertheless, in relation to the concrete identity of a single and unique individual, reincarnation seems to denude such a concept, especially the relationship of that identity to the physical body. But this should not be considered as an unmoveable obstacle, for what is argued in this work is a qualified sense of individual through the term person, where the emphasis is first on unity which negates the stress on reincarnation. As the focus in work is upon the relationship between a notion of person to consciousness and essential being, reincarnation points to an incomplete notion of person, a deluded individual, and as such only indicates the natural *physis*. The natural condition has to be overcome through a union with the highest nature which can be experienced within a "flash of true knowledge"[63] through the activity of the "brilliance of the real subject pure Consciousness (*samâvesha*)".[64]

In the light of consciousness, reincarnation is dissolved, as within a notion of *deification*. In the experience of *samâvesha* while in the body, the *yogî* lives in what is called the *turyâ* state (or *tutyâtîta*),[65] which can be called a *Cid-âtmanic* mode of existence, and because it is in the body it can also be affirmed as *hypostatic,* and relating to a concrete existence. The relationship of the transformation of consciousness and thus the overcoming of the bound state, or reincarnation is confirmed in *Pratyabhijñâ's* focus on the release from bondage. This release is also expressed through the four states of consciousness, waking, dream, deep sleep and the

---

Maximus referred to many types of births of a single person, of the physical birth, baptism and new birth in the resurrection, see Maximus, *Ambig. 42* (PG 91) 1316A-1349A.

[63] *IPK,* 3.23, p.76; translation by Pandit, *IPKp,* 3.2.12, p.181.

[64] *Ibid.*

[65] *Ibid.*

turyâ state.[66] In the bound condition, relating to the coverings of *mâyâ*, the individual experiences the first three states of consciousness, where there is an erratic and unequal rhythm of *being* in the forces of existence, to the energies of the body, mind and breathing.[67] This is rectified in the upward energetic movement (of *udâna* force) which was "fiery in character and functions"[68] and refers to the *kundalinî* energy,[69] which rises up in the central spiritual channel to the *sahasrâra-cakra* and *brahma-randhra* giving enlightenment. This points to the secret experiences of the *Siddha Yogis* and *yogic* texts dealing with such ideas.[70] The upward movement of this energy and union with *Shiva* establishes the *yogi* within the *turyâ* state.

These practices relate to the process by which enlightenment is experienced and had within a concrete individual or *purusha*. The term *purusha* was equated with the twelfth category of the *tattvas* and also related to types of sentient creatures. Hence the generic term *purusha* indicated a category of life, not particular human life.

The thirteenth *tattva* was *prakrti* or nature, which allowed a generic category for the lower or impure nature of objects and finite beings. The impure *tattvas* represented levels of *mâyâ* descending from the finer aspects to the subtle and the gross aspects of existence.[71] Also the impure *tattvas* were not systematically explained in the *Ishvarapratyabhijñâkârikâ*, but were considered in the text in verses 10-11 of Chapter 1 of the *Âgamadhikara*.

---

[66] *IPK*, 3.23-31, pp.67-69.

[67] *IPK*, 3.29-30, p.68, which also relates to inhalation and exhalation.

[68] IPK, 3.31, p.69; translation by Pandit, *IPKp*, 3.2.20, p.187.

[69] As it states in the *Hatha-yoga-Pradeepika*, 1.27, that "with daily practice it arouse the *kundalinî*"; translation by *Brahmânanda, Hatha-yoga-Pradeepika of Svâtmârâma* (Madras: 1972).

[70] As highlighted in the *Shiva Sûtras*; the *Hatha-yoga-Pradeepika*, and the *Kulârvana Tantra*.

[71] *IPKp*, p.209.

The fourteenth to the sixteenth *tattvas* related to mental operations, *buddhî* (intellect), *ahamkara* (ego) and *manas* (imaginations, concepts of mind); the seventeenth to twenty-sixth *tattvas* were related to the senses and activities of living and deal with the five senses, objects of action and perception; the twenty-seventh to the thirty-first to the qualities of the elements; and the rest of the *tattvas* dealt with principles of materiality, the earth, or the five *bhûtas*.

The Tattvas and the Seven Pramatrs

The levels of *tattvas* also correlated to levels of consciousness within seven classifications of experients (*pramatrs*) or types of souls, which experienced specific cognitions on specific *tattvic* levels. When correlating these classifications to person, the focus is to be placed on many types of awareness possible in categories of person. The first type of experients in the *Ishvarapratya bhijñâkârikâ* related to purity[72] and those souls who experienced unity with the *Shiva pramatr.* On this level, everything is *Shiva* and there is no differentiation. This level also corresponded to the *Shaktitattvas* and *Œakta pramatrs,* where beings experienced *Shivahood* or *aham-vimarsha.* The *Shaktipramatrs* were

---

[72] According to the *PBH* (*PBHs,* p.30) the pure *pramâtâs* are: (1) *Shiva (Shakti),* (2) *SadâShiva,* (3) *Ishvara,* (4) *Úuddha vidyâ* and (5) *Mahâmâyâ,* correspond to the first five pure *tattvas* and divine operations. After this come the remaining *pramâtâs* within *mâyâ.* These 5 levels relate also to differing levels of pure souls: (1) *Shiva Pramâtâ;* (2) *Mantra-Maheshvara;* (3) *Mantreshvara;* (4) *Mantra;* and (5) *Vijñânakala-pasu* covered with slight individuality (*pralayakala-pashu* covered with individuality and *kârma, sakala-pashu* covered with individuality, *kârma* and slight delusion). The impure *prâmâtas* have total individuality, *kârma,* delusion and total difference. The first five *pramâtâs* also relates to conscious awareness of: (1) pure 'I-ness', *Aham vimarsha,* 'I Am' *Shiva*; (2)'I-ness' with faint this-ness (*idam*); (3) 'I-ness' with more this-ness and notion of that-ness; (4) balance of 'I-ness' and this-ness with that-ness; (5) this-ness and that-ness; and then in the impure universe only that-ness and deluded or impure 'I-ness'. For a full list and chart of categorisation see Tagare, *The Pratyabhijñâ Philosophy,* p.80.

incorporated into this first experiential mode of existence as non-different to *Shiva* These levels correspond to non-difference within a concept of person.

The second level of experients correspond to the *tattva* (*SadâShiva*) and to purity-impurity. These were the *mantra-Maheshvara* experients (*pramatrs*) who had a dim consciousness of the world. The next level (third) of experients were the *mantreshvara pramatrs* who correspond to the *Ishvara-tattva* having *self*-perception (*aham*), and consciousness of the world (this-ness/ *idam*). Both the *mantra-Maheshvara* and the *mantreshvara pramatrs* related to pure knowledge or *Vidyâ*. The last, or fourth level of pure *pramatrs,* were called the *vidyeœvaras* who experienced partial impurity, having pure-impure knowledge. They were called *Mantra* beings, having both 'I-ness' and this-ness, and were related to the *Œuddha* or *Sad-vidyâ-tattva* and represents a focus on relationality in person, which is exemplified in Utpala's arguing that *Œuddha* or *Sad-vidyâ* pointed to pure knowledge qualified through impurity and represented purity-impurity qualifying the unity of these subjects as unity-in-diversity.

The fifth level of souls related to impurity, to souls who begin to experience a mode of existence under the power of *Mahâmâyâ* and thus difference in manifestation. Although these souls are under the control of *mâyâ*, they too have to be considered in relation to divine unity as Abhinavagupta highlights that this level has to be considered in *non-dual* terms through the highest experience of consciousness. At this level, the experients are also ultimately non-different to the divine and identical to *Cit,* which is the reality of "both perceiver and doer".[73] The souls under *Mahâmâyâ* are able to experience the lower states in relation to considering the higher. At the *mâyâ pramatr* level the experients can be correlated to a sense of individual and were divided into four levels. The first had

---

[73] *IPV*, 3.1.6 translation by Pandey, *IPVp*, p.195.

a "finer aspect"[74] of consciousness and were called *Vijñânakalas* or *Vijñâ-kevalins* (*kevalin* indicating alone-ness) who were bound only by coverings of ignorance or *ânava-mala*. This also represented a *dualistic* category. The next category related to impure beings, who were called *pralayâkalas,* which represented a type of existence of bound (*pashus*) with *ânava-mala* and *kârma-malas*. The third category of impure *pramatrs* were called *Sakala* beings having a gross aspect and related to bound *pashus* having *ânava-mala*, *kârma* and *mâyîya-malas,* and the last level indicated those beings having gross bodies.

The sixth level of *pramatrs* are under the *mâyâ tattva* and related to *úûnya* (void) *pramatrs* experiencing lower states, to void. The last experients in the seventh category experienced the remaining *tattvas* and see complete difference, having a beast like consciousness.

Philosophical Implications of the Purusha Tattva

The notion of person or *purusha*[75] cannot be reduced to an object,

---

[74] See *IPKp*, p.208.

[75] The term *purusha* was understood as indicating the individual person; mentioned in the *Rig Veda* 10.90.1-2, stating "a thousand heads hath purusha, a thousand eyes a thousand feet...this purusha is all that yet hath been and all that is to be", translated by Griffith (Pelikan). This refers to the embodied spirit of "Man" as a collective term, a principle of the personal in all animated humans, hence referring to "a thousand", see footnote. The term *purusha* is also mentioned in the Upanishads, exemplified in the *Katha Upanishad,* 1.iii.11, in a theistic context stating "the Purusha is higher than the unmanifested. There is nothing higher than the Purusha. He is the culmination, He is the highest goal", (Swâmi Gambhîrananda). This model was also taken up by the Bhagavad Gîtâ (8.8, 10) which refers to the Supreme Person (*Paramam purusham*) and stating, "This is the Supreme person, O Son of Pritha! In whom abide all existence and by whom all this is pervaded, who is attainable by answerving single minded devotion", *sarvam tatam* Bhagavad Gîtâ, 8.22 (Vaidik). This notion of Supreme Person or *Parama Purusha* will be correlated to the Supreme or *Parama Shiva* in *Pratyabhijñâ*, see *PBHs*, p.54.

or mere principle of manifestation (*âbhâsa*),[76] hence further explanation is needed to describe how the *tattvic* categories[77] related to a real and concrete concept of person. This approach was affirmed by Utpala who argued that conscious awareness (of the *pramatr* or *purusha*) and existential life is intrinsically related to the "Subject of knowing",[78] which provides meaning to a concept of person. This meaning allows person to be considered as something more than an isolated, material and "self dependent entity"[79] as argued by the *Vijñânavâdins*. The individual or person is dependent on the divine, is relational and also is real. This does not detract from what is spiritually real or negate person as existentially real, for without the divine, person could not attain its sense of real existence. There is a relationship quality of *pramatr,* as a created being, to the divine *being* (*Paramâtman*), power (*Shakti*), will (*icchâ-Shakti*) and activity (*kriyâ-Shakti*) of divine consciousness (*Citi*), which informs the experient of the true nature of itself. Also *Citi* is not a material cause for that would bind God and individuals to that nature and deny divine freedom, consequently Kshemaraja stated, "Cit and free will are inseparable".[80] This freedom is not bound by the natural *physis* or created principles, but allows the conscious subject to rise above that nature to attain an awareness that moves from that-ness (*tat*), to 'I am this' (this-ness or *idantâ*), or a bound mode of existence to a mode of existence that expresses the true 'I am' state. This represents not only a reciprocal movement of human persons to experience the divine, but indicates in the divine (*Siva*) the desire and freedom to create.

---

[76] For the philosophy of *Âbhâsavada* see Rudrappa, *Kashmir Shaivism,* p.44; Tagare, *Philosophy of Pratyabhijñâ,* p.37.

[77] *IPK,* 3.2, p.59.

[78] *IPK,* 3.1, p.59; translation by *Pandit, IPKp,* 3.1.1, p.155.

[79] See *IPK,* 1.12, p.5.

[80] *PBH, Sûtra* 2 (commentary); translation by Singh, *PBHs,* p.51.

The desire to create allows a higher mode of existence to be attained, which is intimately related to the divine *being* in that it is God Himself who desires to manifest Himself as creation:

> SadâShiva and other appropriate forms flashes forth (*prakashamânatayaâ sphurati*) at first as non-different from the light (of consciousness) (*prakashâbhedena*) but not experiencing the unity of consciousness...He unfolds Himself in the totality of manifestation (*tattvas*), worlds (*bhuvanas*), entities (*bhâvas*) and their respective experients (*pramâtâras*) that are only a solidified form of (*âshyânatârûpa*) of Cit-essence.[81]

The mode of the higher existence then becomes the divine mode of existence intended for the lower modes and *tattvas*. When relating the movement of one mode to another consciousness, the movement from *tat* to pure I-consciousness indicates a disturbance in which pure consciousness (vimarsha) itself becomes pure-impure consciousness (*parâpara*).[82] This *vimarsha* then reveals itself to itself. The pure consciousness experiences a throb or movement (*Shakti*) which *re-cognises* this-ness (*idantâ*) and then the pure 'I am' state. The levels of a descending movement of consciousness, from non-difference to levels of difference (pure 'I-am' to that-ness), corresponds to descending levels of *tattvic* manifestations and created phenomena. As the process of divine unfoldment (*unmesha*) continues, the descending movement within the divine, or outward movement from God *ad-intra* (*nimesha*) to God *ad-extra,* manifests a greater space and distinction between the divine subject and the objectified world and a difference between modes of existence.

There is also in the beginnings of *tattvic* manifestations within the divine, a corresponding distinction between 'I-ness' (*ahanta*)

---

[81] *PBH, Sûtra* 4 (commentary); translation by Singh, *PBHs*, p.55

[82] Utpala stated that "such a state (of vidyâ) is thus superior (to phenomena) and perfect, one hand, and inferior and imperfect, on the other hand since it is the state of unity in diversity, indicating both purity and impurity, *paratâhantayâcchâdât parâpara-daûâ hi sâ//, IPK*, 3.5, p.60.

and this-ness (*idantâ*) so as to fulfil the free will to create. The movement outwards from the divine *being* allows the *vidyâ-Shakti*(revelatory operations) to manifest, which are then juxtaposed to manifested phenomena. This also corresponds to the differentiation of awareness in the movement from 'I Am' to 'I am this' or an awareness of otherness, in which unity-in-diversity is expressed. In this awareness the notion of person comes to be related to an inner reality through the outward expression of concrete existence. In the awareness of otherness, there is purity and impurity in the middle level of manifested diversity[83] in which this-ness indicates a move from pure consciousness to an outward awareness. The outward expression of consciousness, or an outward looking individual, represents a movement in which total difference (indicating also impurity) is experienced. Difference indicates that individual conscious awareness of manifested phenomena is experienced, or that-ness. That-ness (the *tattvas*) or a complete identification with the objectified universe results in a continued identification with impurity and levels of concrete identity with the lower *physis* (*tat*). The movement from pure 'I-consciousness' to this-ness and that-ness is attributed to differing operations of *vidyâ-Shakti* and *mâyâ-Shakti*[84] which are equated to differing levels of experients (*pramatrs*). Through these descending levels of consciousness, consciousness itself moves from pure divine awareness to a limited condition. It is this true knowledge or *vidyâ-Shakti* that allows an ascent to the divine where the aspirant begins to understand his or her divine nature while living as a bound being. While it is the divine activity of knowledge that allows a movement to the divine, it is another divine activity, the *mâyâ-Shakti* that "conceals the truth under ignorance".[85]

---

[83] *IPK,* 3.5, p.60.

[84] *IPK,* 3.5-6, pp.60-61.

[85] *IPK,* 3.7, p.61; translation by Pandit, *IPKp,* 3.1.7, p.164.

It is in a concept of person that both knowledge of the divine or ignorance is experienced and thus becomes a vehicle of the divine to express the divine in both conditions.

As a consequence, the individual soul (*jîva*), or *purusha,* comes to represent a principle of being and consciousness by which the divine is understood within a concrete individual, and by which an existence is had. This existence can be called personal,[86] and also reflects the possibilities of many types of consciousness, culminating within a full sense of unity while existing as a person. However, even in ignorance, at the core of *tattvic* diversity is unity. Unity is vouchsafed even in *tattvic* distinctiveness through the activity of *Citi-Shakti,* which is the light of consciousness (*prakasha*). The *prakasha* allows a sense of freedom (*svâtantrya*)[87] within the individual to be experienced as it mirrors the freedom of the divine,

---

[86] Mishra believes that in *Pratyabhijñâ* the term *purusha* has a central *role* in the understanding of *being,* in relation to divine revelation, and the nature and activity of God and states: "it would not be far from the truth to say that the whole *Pratyabhijñâ* system centres around the concept of person. It seeks to know the real nature of the person and his relationship with the rest of the World. The Divine or the Absolute is in reality the divine one; reality is absolutely personality", Kamalakar Mishra, 'Person in the light of Pratyabhijñâ Philosophy', *Indian Philosophical Annual* (1972), pp. 206-214. Also unlike the pure absolutism of Shankara's monism, *Pratyabhijñâ* does not view manifestation in a negative context as illusion, *mâyâ,* but views manifestation as non-different to the Absolute. For this reason, Aleaz argues that in Shankara's philosophy, there is no real anthropology (see K. P. Aleaz, *A Convergence of Advaita and Eastern Christian Thought*, p.177) as individual persons do not have any real existence, which is not the case in *Pratyabhijñâ.* While the absolutism of *Advaita* presented a seemingly unbridgeable gulf between transcendent and immanent, in *Dvaita,* an ontological *gulf* is developed between *Ishvara* and *jîva* making true participation difficult to argue. For this reason Panikkar stated: "in fact neither dualism, nor pure monism can solve this problem. Dualism digs a gap that it cannot afterwards overcome. Monism over simplifies the issue, and does not so much explain the problem as it explains it away", see Panikkar, 'Ishvara and Christ as a Philosophical Problem', p.10.

[87] *PBH, Sûtra* 1 (commentary).

which is the very nature of the divine existence. This freedom is expressed in the active *Citi,* will and luminosity of the *Âtman,* which is continually active, unfolding itself as the *tattvas*, including the *purusha tattva.*

Within these complex models of principles, experients and types of consciousness, the model of pure and impure manifestation (*âbhâsa*) in *Pratyabhijñâ* allowed the term *purusha* to take on a dual role, indicating bound-ness and also limitless in *re-cognition*, within a dual cognition. To underline this point Kshemarâja gave a long list of philosophical traditions[88] to argue that *Pratyabhijñâ* accepts a paradoxical position, of the one and the many, accepting both the immanent and transcendent (*Âtman*), where unity is simultaneously expressed as multiplicity.

> He is a single centre in universal consciousness but he becomes twofold form, threefold, fourfold (*âtma*) as a subjective reality, and appears as seven pentads (*tattvic pramâtâs*) in the expression of his inherent nature in manifestation.[89]

In the state of unity amid *tattvic* diversity, the empirical self (individual *purusha*) is to be understood as the Absolute *Self,* where "mundane manifestation"[90] relates to the unfolding of His nature (*Paramâtman*). This unfoldment is also continuous through divine maintenance (*sthâpakatâ*)[91] where the act of grace[92] allows a continuous relationship between the manifested world and the "unfoldment of the essential nature (of consciousness)"[93]

---

[88] From the *Cârvâkas* (who believe that the self same as body), to the *Nyâya* (materialists who consider *self* as the intellect), the *Vedântins* (who view *prâna* as *Self*), and the *Sânkhya s* (who see duality), see *PBH, Sûtra* 8 (commentary), *PBHs*, pp.65-68.

[89] *sa caiko dvirûpas trimayapas trimayaú caturâtmâ sapta-panÞcakasvabhâvah, PBH, Sûtra* 7; translation by Taimini, *The Secret of Self Realization* (Adyar: 1997).

[90] *PBH, Sûtra* 10 (commentary); translation by Singh, *PBHs*, p.74.

[91] *Ibid.,* p.75.

[92] *Ibid.*

[93] *Ibid.*

This continuous relationship or communion of the essential nature of the divine in relation to phenomena, followed on from the teachings of *Mâlinîvijayottaratantra* where the manifested world becomes intimately related to non-difference. As Kaul shows, the *jîvas* were included in the list of ontological "acceptables" (pure universe) for the *jîvas* or *purusha* and participate in the pure universe and in an undifferentiated experience.[94] The notion of *purusha* indicates a subjective and concrete existence, in an immaterial-material sense, and thus juxtaposing the individual existence to the divine reality. Hence the human level becomes informed by the divine, which changes the way in which the type of existence of the *purusha* is understood. Even the term *purusha* indicated a certain type of limited existence as the twelfth *tattva* in the relational capabilities of that existence to experience the higher. However, the lower nature cannot by itself understand the divine without the grace of the divine. It is *Shiva* who, as the supreme *Purusha,* gives this grace, and it is grace which allows the observation that it is God who enters into a state of becoming so that individual *purushas*[95] can attain a pure consciousness. The bound soul realises his *Shivahood,* which at the same time does not detract from the concrete human experient. In this context the concept of person can be equated with the term *purusha,* where the nature of the divine person or *purusha* informs the human person or *purusha* of his or her true nature, so that the human experient rises above the natural *physis* in the experience of divine consciousness.

There is consequently a relationship of the personal God to the human person (*purusha*) where the *purusha* becomes more that an empty principle, evident in the free divine power (*Shakti*) and

---

[94] *MT*, p.xvii. Tagare argues though that *purusha*: "means not merely human being but includes all sentients, *Purusha* is *Shiva* who has subjected himself to the *Kañcukas* of Mâyâ like *Kalâ, Vidyâ* etc. and due to the absence of his original omniscience, omnipotence etc., got himself reduced to an atom (*anu*)", see Tagare, *The Pratyabhijñâ Philosophy*, p.29.

[95] See Hanneder, *Abhinavagupta's Philosophy of Revelation*, pp.63, 93.

love of the divine *Purusha,* through the extrusive *Citi*[96] to commune with the created world through the creation of individuals. Also the light of consciousness (*prakasha*),[97] becomes intimately related to the subject awareness of the *purusha* (person). This relational and thus outward motion of God was expressed by Abhinavagupta, who referred to the "face of God which is consciousness",[98] recognising the relationship of objects to the divine, but which remains "unstained" by them. Abhinavagupta stated:

> When therefore God through the power of his will truly wishes the objects, they become grounded in his will, yet the will remains unstained by them, for they are in contact (*sprshanti*) with the unity of consciousness, by being identical with it. The objects, however, are then hidden by the will that is affected by limitation as a cover. But God remains in his own will. This face of God, which is consciousness, is turned away from the light is not occupying the highest, replete state and therefore appears to be in deep sleep.[99]

The term 'face' as an *âbhâsa* (manifestation) qualifies the single *Self* of *Maheshvara,*[100] as the 'face' in manifestation, which becomes the 'face' of the individual (*purusha*). The term *purusha* in this context, as the 'face' of the *Self,* becomes the outward 'face' and indicates the possibilities of the concrete person and also unity. This is affirmed by Abhinavagupta who argued that the "highest face",[101] is of *Shiva.*

Pratyabhijñâ's categorization of the individual reflects this sense of difference and unity, through the term *pramatr*

---

[96] Or "the power of *unmesha* (*cid*)", Abhinavagupta, *Mâlinîslokavârtika* (206-207); translation by Hanneder, *Abhinavagupta's Philosophy of Revelation,* p.93.

[97] *Ibid,* p.63.

[98] *Ibid.* (216), p.95.

[99] *Ibid.,* (213-216), pp.94-95.

[100] *Ibid.*

[101] *Ibid.,* (20); commentary, p.143.

(experient),[102] for "every *pramatr* is *Shiva* in a contracted form",[103] the "Highest Lord".[104] God consistently experiences His own *aham* or 'I-ness', as an "unbroken consciousness, 'I am this universe'",[105] and manifests existence (*âbhâsas*)[106] as *idam* or this-ness, which is the object of the "Lord's consciousness".[107] Through *Shiva* entering into a becoming as the world, in a simultaneity of *common* and *uncommonness*, experients come to understand their bound-ness and also their true identity.[108] This indicates simultaneity of modes of existence which does not point to confusion, but a layering of existence on multi-experiential platforms united through the *Âtman*. While the bound individuals see difference,[109] the liberated, the *Siddha* experiences *Shivahood* and experiences non-difference[110] This *Shivahood* also has a revelatory context for *Shiva's being* (*Satta*)[111] and is also non-different from the "mass of endless Tattvas".[112]

---

[102] See *IPKp*, 3.1.9, p.167; and *PBH*, 4. For a good analysis of *pramatr* and the seven experients or perceivers, see Vasudeva, *The Mâlinîvijayottaratantra*, pp.151-178.

[103] *PBH*, 4.

[104] *IPV*, 4.1; translation by Pandey, *IPVp*, p.219.

[105] *Ibid.*

[106] *Ibid.*, 4.7, p.225.

[107] *Ibid.*

[108] *Ibid.*, 4.7-4.12; pp.224-228.

[109] *Ibid.*, 4.13; p.227.

[110] *Ibid.*, 4.16; p.229.

[111] *Ibid.*, p.75.

[112] *Ibid.*, 4.14; p.228. While the first *tattva* can be said to represent philosophically that which is *non-dualistic*, the rest of the categories evidence *dualism* in varying degrees (see *MT*, p.xvii; see also Vasudeva, *The Yoga of Mâlinîvijayottaratantra*). The first five classes of beings in the *Mâlinîvijayottaratantra* were the list of acceptables, as *Shiva, Shakti, Vidyesa, Mantra, Mantreœvara*; and the *Jîvas*, which were added to the list. The last two, the avoidables, were the impure experients and actions, who experienced

modes relating to *Mâyâ* and the world. Within the seven levels of experients of the *Ishvarapratyabhijñâkârikâ* and *Pratyabhijñâhrdayam* the souls corresponded to the *pramatr* levels in the *Mâlinîvijayottaratantra*, see *MT*, pp.xxi-xxii; *IPKp*, pp.157-163; *PBH*, Kshemarâja's commentary of *sûtra* 3; and Tagare, *The Pratyabhijñâ Philosophy,* p.80; see also Vasudeva, *The Yoga of Mâlinîvijayottaratantra,* pp.151-167.

CHAPTER 8

Personhood and Unity of Being

Introduction

In the remaining parts of this work a notion of person will be centered in *Pratyabhijñâ*: around the application of unity of *being* (*Âtman*); the inclusion of conscious awareness (*Cit*) within divine activity (*Citi-Shakti*), which discloses levels of consciousness; and juxtaposed to revelation in manifested phenomena (*âbhâsa*) through a model of unity-in-diversity. Each part will correlate to the theological discussion of *Shiva, Cit* (*Shakti*), and manifestation (*âbhâsa*) respectively in relation to person. These divisions also correlate to modes of personal existence within the *purusha* and which have, on each level, a basis in unity. The three parts constitute an apparent downward or outward flow of consciousness. The emphasis is firstly, upon the condition of *being* (or *Âtman*) and then secondly, on how this level of *being* reflects unity within manifestation. The focus will be upon revealed levels of consciousness within person, from *Cit* to *citta* and then back to *Cit*, and how separation is overcome or at least accepted in a qualified model.

Person through Âtman

Although the *Âtman* can be viewed as a monist static reality, it is also, in *Pratyabhijñâ*, connected to everything as the substratum of all personal *being* that is in relation to personal existing and thus also has this quality of reflecting activity. Abhinavagupta describes the *Âtman* in relation to the world in the following way:

> Just as the disk of the moon appears to be moving when reflected in flowing waters and just as it looks to be static in still waters, so does this great *Âtman* appear in multifarious variety in the different categories of bodies, senses, organs and worlds. Just as *Râhu* (shadow of the earth) shine and appear in the disk of the moon, though otherwise invisible, so does this *Âtman* shine only in the mirror of psychic apparatus while witnessing objective reflection, though it is present everywhere.[1]

The essential condition of *Âtman* when viewed from *below*, or in relation to existing as a concrete unique but separated person, is to be considered in three ways: firstly, as a generic term that can be applied as the metaphysical centre of all persons (as a principle of *being*); secondly, in relation to the world, where the *Âtman* is to be considered as a revelatory principle of the Divine and thus having a relational value; and lastly, the concept of *Âtman* is to be considered in relation to the personal experience, which informs the person who she or he is and thus allows a change in the way in which that individual perceives the concept of person itself.

The *Âtman* in *Pratyabhijñâ* while ontologically appearing beyond material being having a non-dual centre, has from a position of individual "an appearance of duality"[2] in that it is viewed as distinct from the individual. This vision of the individual allows *Âtman* to be considered not only as the form of absolute *being,* or *being* beyond *being,* but allows a sense of divine relatedness to the world. Relatedness is not constricted within a static substance, but has the quality of freedom, the freedom to *act,* and in relation to the bound individual. Abhinavagupta stated that:

---

[1] *PSA*, 7-8 (Pandit), p.24.

[2] *SS*, 'First Section'; translation by Singh, *SSs*, p.1.

> He (the Lord) is free…and that His freedom is manifold and consists
> in bringing about diversity in unity and unity in diversity by internal
> unification.[3]

This passage includes the three aspects of the *Âtmanic* reality in relation to person or diversity: the value of diversity through unity; how unity expresses itself within itself as an expression of freedom; and the character of that freedom (in unity) from an ontological perspective, which implicitly relates to the existential characteristics of person. The nature of this freedom can initially be said to expresses a dynamic of unity in relation to an internal movement within the divine person allowing person in the human context to express individual characteristics. These characteristics, even when considered through an experience of unity with the divine, are indicative of the general ontological disposition of person that are expressions of the divine being. While this appears to be tautological it shows how *Âtman* leads to person which leads back to *Âtman.* The movement within the divine manifests a *stir*, pushing outwards from the divine reality and manifesting the world, which cannot be viewed as separate or self-created but is created by divine will and power.

The movement of the divine as an expression of free will (*svâtantrya*) to create and to reveal itself is initially expressed through a divine pulse (*spanda*).[4] This pulse or throb of the divine is not due to an indirect impersonal force but a free act of the divine *being.* This implies that the *Âtman* is not to be considered as an impersonal nature, only capable of expressing itself to itself, but related to a movement of itself outwards through its consciousness (*Cit*).[5] Within this understanding, a notion of person

---

[3] *IPV*, 1.1, p.11; translation by Pandey.

[4] Spanda is the *Shakti* or power of God to create the world. It is the essential nature of the divine and the creative pulse, *svarûpaspanda* (*Spanda Kârikâ*, ed. J. Singh, Delhi: 1980, p.3).

[5] See the 'Commentary' of the text of *Sûtra* 1 of *SS*; SSs, p.7.

is conditional to the *Âtmanic* condition as a reality and thus consciousness.

The conscious awareness of the *Âtman,* as the *Shiva Sûtras* state, is the very characteristic of *Âtman,*[6] and expresses the Absolute 'I Am' in an outward flow in the desire to create within a personal Self-aware existence and when establishing a form of personhood in *Pratyabhijñâ* this context has to be included. Thus implicit to a model of person, developed through *Pratyabhijñâ philosophy,* is the qualifying of the *Âtmanic* ontological condition through consciousness. But because *Pratyabhijñâ* is addressed to the world, to an audience of deluded others as persons we can say that *Pratyabhijñâ* is dedicated to resolving human personhood in relation to Divine existing. Thus *Âtman* is static for it has extrusive activity and consequently has a relational dynamic. This relationality expresses the dependence of creation upon the Lord's will and grace. Consequently, there is always this relational dynamic between the extrusive activity of God and the world, of subjects and objects in relation to the true subject,[7] through the admittance of the real-ness of creation. By considering the divine freedom, will and activity of the divine to create, and the "One develops multiplicity"[8] through the *Âtmanic* nature, a sense of person is developed in the admittance of multiplicity, where person also reflects those same qualities due to the inherent nature of person. This affirms the importance of person to express concrete existence as an act of unity in multiplicity, while also indicating the inherent nature *Âtman.* This nature allows person to be considered as not superficial or outward looking but as having ontological depth. The *Âtman* allows the nature of person to be revealed which in turn points to the truth of *Âtman,* it provides a point by which person informed of itself in the field of personal

---

[6] *Caitanyamâtmâ, SS.*1; translation by Singh, SSs, p.6.

[7] This argument is developed in the first chapter of the *IPK* from verses 12-30, pp.5-13, through its epistemology which rests on the premise of the unity of phenomena through a single entity, the Absolute God.

[8] *IPK,* 2.10, p.40; translation by Pandit, *IPKp,* 2.2.2, p.116.

concrete existence by which *Âtman* comes to be revealed as the underlying reality of existence. This is possible due to person being an expression of the *Âtmanic* effulgence or the "light of consciousness" or *prakasha*.[9]

Person as an Expression of Prakasha

The constructing of a model of person through *Pratyabhijñâ*, as a concrete entity, is also supported when considered through the 'light of consciousness' (*prakasha*).[10] It is the theological use of *prakasha* which upholds a relational condition of the divine activities to the world, while affirming the validity and concrete identity of both. The *prakasha* is the support of creation, which is the pure 'Self-awareness' of the divine and:

> described as a (shining) pulsation, as supreme existence not conditioned
> by time and space, and as the very heart of the Supreme, because it
> is the real essence (of all existence).[11]

The "Lord manifests His own Self...the objective world is not a thing existing separately from Him".[12] Here the objective world is affirmed and so too a sense of person must also be admitted, while confirming person through *prakasha* as intimately related to the divine. Through *prakasha,* the activity of the highest reality expresses itself as the aspect of divine consciousness, or *vimarsha,* by which "phenomenon becomes evident".[13] This illuminates the manner by which ordinary knowledge (*vidyâ*) gives way to *jñâna* in an inward informing of the nature of *being*, where the discovery of *Self* leads to a *re-cognition* of the true nature of *being* in an

---

[9] *IPV,* p.187.

[10] *IPK,* 1.42, p.18.

[11] "*sa sphuratta mahasatta desha kalavisesini/saisha saratya prokta hrdayam paramesthinah//*" *IPK,* 1.45, p.19; translation by Pandit, *IKPp,* 1.5.14, p.63. The very nature of the *prakasha* is the divine essence, which is the underlying reality of existence.

[12] *IPK,* 1.46, p.19; translation by Pandit, *IKPp,* 1.5.15, p.64.

[13] *IPKp,* pp.156, 176, 233.

event of *Âtman* within the *purusha*. It is within the experience of
re-cognition that the value of person, of *moi*, is comprehended as
an expression of *prakasha,* which allows the other, that is other
persons, to be comprehended through *prakasha,* which does not
negate concrete person but places person within a context of a true
value and qualifying person in the same way as *hypostasis* qualifies
individual. This value underlines that, within an ontological context,
person indicates the possibilities of *being* through the condition of
having not only a mundane nature, but a higher nature. This higher
nature is not an unconscious lump within the person, but the
substance of eternal conscious *being.* The higher nature allows
person to *be* what it should be, for it has at its very core, *Self-*
awareness which is reflected within each person and allows the
notion of finite *self.* As Kshemarâja stated:

> "Therefore this (i.e., Caitanya or consciousness which is Absolute
> Freedom) is Âtmâ or Self, not anything else of varied nature as assumed
> by pluralists (those who propound the doctrine of bheda or difference
> among selves) (Are these different selves conscious beings or non-
> conscious beings?) If Âtmâ or varied nature is assumed to be non-
> conscious, then it would be inconscient matter and thus not Self. If
> it be considered to be of the very essence of consciousness, then there
> can be no valid reason for considered to be of the very essence of
> consciousness, then there can be no valid reason for considering on
> *âtmâ* or self as different from another self. Difference in the case of
> *cit* or consciousness cannot be established either by means of space
> or time or form, for if these are different from *cit* or consciousness
> then being deprived of the light of consciousness, they cannot appear
> at all and are thus unreal; if they appear, then they are consciousness
> itself (for it is only consciousness that can appear.[14]

For this reason the *Shiva Sûtras* state that the very nature of the
Âtman is consciousness (*caitanyamâtmâ*),[15] and thus at the very
core of selves is the activity of divine consciousness. This definition
of the *Self* is at the heart of *Pratyabhijñâ* and thus at the heart of
a theology of person. Utpala himself cites the *Shiva Sûtras,* stating

---

[14] 'Commentary' of the text of *Sûtra* 1 of *SS.*

[15] As already stated above; *SS, Sûtra* 1.

that the "Self has been defined as Consciousness as the activity of awareness"[16] and due to the reality of Absolute *being*, the *Âtman*.

In each conscious *being*, this essential reality and awareness manifests the unique consciousness specific to that experient (*pramatr*), which in turn is a reflection of the highest awareness and reality, even in mundane consciousness. This is because the mundane consciousness shines as the light of consciousness (*prakasha*). But what is *prakasha*? Firstly, Utpala approaches this question by affirming that matter has no independence, stating that "independent existence cannot be proved even through inference",[17] and argued that matter is due to *prakasha,* where the "entire phenomenal existence (is) contained within Himself (His divine potency); otherwise the throb of His will (*icchâ*) to manifest it outwardly could not proceed".[18] If this were not the case then *prakasha* "even though bearing the appearance of an object, could at most be compared to some insentient elements like crystal".[19] Divine awareness is the "essential character of consciousness",[20] which itself has the character of divine luminosity expressing itself as each person, for every conscious being, or person, is aware of himself/herself. This consciousness then is a reflection of the divine consciousness or *vimarsha.*

Hence, this double dynamic is expressed in relation to person, firstly, in the condition of a specific consciousness in each person, and secondly, where this consciousness reflects the power and capabilities of the divine consciousness. If *prakasha* implied a mundane consciousness and an ordinary luminosity "devoid of *vimarsha*"[21] then it could be likened to a reflective light or an

---

[16] *IPK,* 1.43, p.18; translation by Pandit *IPKp,* 1.5.12, p.61.

[17] *IPK,* 1.40, p.17; translation by Pandit, *IPKp,* 1.5.9, p.58.

[18] *IPK,* 1.401 p.17; translation by Pandit, *IPKp,* 1.5.10, p.59

[19] *IPK,* 1.42, p.18; translation by Pandit, *IPKp,* 1.5.11, p.60.

[20] *Ibid.*

[21] *IPKp,* p.60.

insentient nature. Consequently, *prakasha* itself highlights the condition of the divine essential reality contained within the *Self* and the divine awareness contained within that nature. This also indicates the capabilities of person and the ultimate resting place of consciousness within person. As a result Utpala stated:

> To be Self-aware is the very essence of Consciousness. It is the supreme speech, rising out of its own ecstasy, and is itself the special Self-sufficiency God as well as His extraordinary divine essence.[22]

When correlating this notion of person to the divine Person and to the awareness of Supreme Consciousness, there is evident within the divine essence the awareness and freedom to act in relation to objects or the world. Utpala declares that this apparent movement is due to the Lord Himself objectifying Himself where "objective existence is not a thing existing separately from Him".[23] Through the capabilities of free will, the Absolute essence (*Maheshvara, ParamaShiva*)[24] creates all things, manifesting all phenomena. However, the *Âtman* entering into the process of creation does not get "enmeshed in any sort of diversity".[25]

Here, Utpala expressly indicates that the *Âtman* is not a static reality and is perceived through movements, where the *Âtman* enters into manifestation but does not experience change within the many activities such as individual consciousness (*buddhi* or intellect) within a person. Thus there is a succession of perceived movements within a process and single intention. This makes apparent, in the many movements or series of movements, a dual cognition, will and activity within a united cognition, will and activity of the divine. There is one relating to ordinary or mundane existence and that

---

[22] *citih pratyanamar satma paravak sva rasodita/svatantrya etan mukhyam tad aishvaryam paramatmanah//*, *IPK*, 1.44, p.18; translation by Pandit, *IPKp*, 1.5.13, p.62.

[23] *IPK*, 1.46, p.19; translation by Pandit, *IPKp*, 1.5.15, p.64.

[24] IPK, 1.1; 1.2; 1.7; 1.64; 4.1.

[25] *IPK*, 1.48, p.20; translation by Pandit, *IPKp*, 1.5.17, p.65.

relating to the divine, but where both are intimately related to *Âtman.* In these movements an indissoluble link, or relationship, is established between *being (Âtman),* act *(kriyâ),* and will *(icchâ).*

While Pandit argues that "at the level of the limited self *(purusha),* the sense of non-duality is totally lost",[26] this is not the case in *Pratyabhijñâ* as it accepts that mundane existence is intimately related to the non-dual state, whether it is *re-cognised* as such within the *dualistic* condition. A sense of person does not negate the highest reality but is confirmed through that reality, for *Pratyabhijñâ* accepts many types of existences. Abhinavagupta's *Vimarúinî* endeavors to explain this antinomic model through a balance between *being,* awareness, and act, stating:

> The Lord is naturally self-luminous and preserves the world by bringing about its existence...His being freedom...That is transcendental motion – characterized by a slight flutter, quiver or motion.[27]

This motion is to be correlated to the light of consciousness *(prakasha),* which is inseparable from *Self*-consciousness *(vimarsha)* as the power of action.[28]

Due to the dual aspect of *being,* awareness and activity, the bound individual experiences both aspects, though they are unaware of the higher. Thus Abhinavagupta argued that "the limited subject has both being and its negation, bliss and its negation"[29] because of the apparent power of limitation or obscuration, emanating from the lower nature. It is only the revelatory activity of the *Âtman,* through *Cit-Shakti*that allows both a sense of individual and whole or *deified* person, of a limiting condition and an unlimited awareness, where all conditions are accepted as the *prakasha.*

---

[26] Pandit, *The Trika Shaivism of Kashmir,* p.215

[27] *IPV,* 4.6 (commentary); translation by Pandey, *IPVp,* p.222.

[28] *Ibid.*

[29] *Ibid.,* p.223.

Allowing for Modes of Person

Thus through *Pratyabhijñâ* the notion of person has to be accepted as an activity of *prakasha* and that person also indicates concrete existence, otherwise a negation of either statement negates the purpose, will and activity of the Lord who manifests the conditions for both. This provides a way to view person in real (concrete) and existential terms and yet providing for an essential condition underpinning its existentiality. Hence, a person has the freedom to exist and to *be* in truth, reflecting the freedom and *being* of the divine, which through the *prakasha*, reveals the true nature of *being* to the person (*purusha*), and a *way* in which persons should exist.

The *prakasha,* while conferring a sense of personhood, allows a person not to be dominated by the lower nature, but encourages ascents to the higher. This freedom is constitutive of the nature of *Âtman,* and allows the person to live within a consciousness and type of existence in the world that is relative and also *Âtmanic.* In the highest condition the person can be said to exist within an *Âtmanic* consciousness that is reflected within a *Cid-âtmanic* mode of (*hypostatic*) existence through the experience of *re-cognition.* The prefix *Cid* implies that the *Âtmanic* nature exists within an awareness of its own reality having awareness of the world. This implies, within the human condition, there exists within each person a dual consciousness, one pertaining to the limited awareness and the other pertaining to the divine state. The experience of *re-cognition,* of the divine condition (of *being*) as the true reality of existence, does not preclude cognition of the ordinary life but allows mundane existence to be considered in a true way as a play of the light of consciousness. In this sense the human person living in the *Cid-âtmanic* mode of *hypostatic* or personal existence, as an *Âtman-hypostasis,* attains an awareness in *re-cognition* of the divine reality that can also be expressed in terms of a communion of substance, through this *Âtmanic* nature. This experience indicates a sense of unity within the individual experience of the *Âtman* through the communion with the essential reality of *being.* In *Pratyabhijñâ* the ontological reality of the *Âtman* allows God to force Himself into the world through the divine consciousness, piercing the levels and coverings of ignorance through the active awareness of God's *Self,* allowing a communion or relationship with the world.

The very fact of *being* pushes the notion of the world into a sense of objectification in relation to the subject (*Âtman*), but in *Pratyabhijñâ* the world is not to be considered in terms of separation as an outer object, or something different to the *Âtman*, but intrinsically related to divine *being*. The objectification of phenomena from a view-point of the divine reality does not hinder a sense of real existing, or a type of existing, from the perspective of the object but affirms two things. Firstly, the object is real having a real existence apart from the divine condition and secondly, that the true sense of reality of that object relates to its interior nature, the *Âtman*. The conscious awareness, of the subject, objectifies the world as that-ness (*idantâ*), which has as its backdrop the *Âtman*, or the *what* of *being,* but which is not divided or separated from "that" or objectified phenomena. Thus the way in which persons come to understand themselves relates as much to their own existence as a material type or mode of existence, which comes to be understood in relation to the light of *being*, and to the underlying reality or the *what* of *being*. Through the experience of the higher consciousness, a person comes to live in a higher type or mode of existence. Thus there are not different types of *being* but types of existing, where all modes of existence reflect a particular existence within a specific nature, but which exist through the essential reality of *being*. The type of existence a person experiences reflects the level of consciousness of a particular subject (person/*purusha*), where consciousness allows an awareness within the existential condition or type of existence a person is experiencing, and then the evaluation of the nature of that existence.

The conscious awareness of an individual can experience a movement towards accepting a notion of unity, but this initially does not disclose a higher level of or a change in the type of existence. Through the limited cognition in the individual, true cognition underpinning that existence comes into the field of the person's consciousness. It is important here to underline again that consciousness is informed by *Âtman* and not itself, for if that were the case, unity would be based on a consciousness associated with the natural or biological *physis*. In this condition consciousness would not be able to disclose truth to existence, and unity would stand distinct and separate from multiplicity. The lower nature would also not be able to create itself for this would make unity impossible to attain within an inescapable prison. The natural *physis* can neither reveal the truth to itself or manifest itself to itself without the activity of the divine *being*. Consequently, in the natural model individuals could not attain knowledge or awareness of themselves but exist within a mode of existence that would be incapable of experiencing another. Hence it is the divine consciousness, whose nature is self-awareness and has the characteristic of consciousness (*Cit*) that allows not only for awareness of individual persons, but of the highest *being*. It is the luminosity and activity of *Cit* in manifestation which overcomes the *gulf* between the divine and creation, where the natural *physis* becomes a "reflection" (*pratibimba*)[30] of the divine.

Existence and Non-existence

The correlating of creation to *prakasha* does not indicate the non-existence of objects or person, or non-being, but rather it reflects the fullness of objects and persons. *Pratyabhijñâ* does not imply a non-existence of manifestation or person as with a reflection of the moon in a mirror, it affirms that objects have a dependency. This does not denude a sense of *being* or existence but rather confirms that the ontological existence of a thing or person is affirmed in its difference, through the will and power of the Lord to create. The Lord (*Parameœvara*) is the 'cause'[31] of substances and objects, which do not have themselves as cause. Utpala stated:

---

[30] Abhinavagupta, *Tantrâloka*, III.11, (Walli).

[31] *IPK*, 2.40, p.52; translation by Pandit, *IPKp*, 2.4.8, p.140.

> It cannot be within the power of any inanimate object to bring into existence anything that is non-existent. Therefore the essence of the relation between cause and effect is in fact, the relation between a manifesting subject and a manifestable object. A non existent entity is always non-existent; the existence of a non-existent entity is not possible...even when the cause-and-effect relation is talked about in the world, (the effect) can (at the most) be just an exterior manifestation of some internally existent entity (the cause, which assumes) the position of an object of knowing through (a persons) interior and exterior senses. Such a thing can happen only through the divine power of that unknowable Authority (God).[32]

In other words persons do not manifest God, but God manifests persons and through this relational position a sense of person acquires meaning. It is because all substances and objects have as their cause the divine substance and radiance, which reflects through those substances and objects, that the solidity of material form is accepted. The world has to be thus considered real and existent due to the cause and is reflected through the activity of *prakasha*.[33] This reflection is not the type perceived within a mirror, where in that reflection forms are confused and have no true reality. But as Abhinavagupta shows, through *Cit*,[34] hollow objects gain significance where just as in a mirror, the mirror acts as a medium by which the exterior object is perceived. So too it is through *Cit* that reflected objects attain significance. But the notion of reflection may cause some problems due to an inherent lack of concrete existence of the reflection. Conversely, the clarity of the image of the reflection in the mirror may indicate that an object has a real or self-caused nature. Another dynamic relates to the perception of objects by the senses of the human person, which allows individuals to gain a concrete sense of themselves and through false identification with the objects, a sense of separation and ignorance.

---

[32] *IPK,* 2.34-36, pp.50-51; translation by Pandit, *IPKp,* 2.4.2-4, p.136-137.

[33] *IPV,* 3.4.19 (commentary); translation by Pandey, *IPVp,* p.185.

[34] *Ibid.*

However, objects and the subject perceiver, all shine with the light of consciousness and are consequently able to be perceived and perceive through divine consciousness. In this sense person, while in one condition can be viewed as a reflected object, becomes related to the source of reflection and attains a sense of true *being* through that context. It is the nature of perception itself which allows objects, and thus persons, to reflect the nature of the true *Self.* They may appear to be false from a position of truth, but are themselves true having concrete existentiality due to the activity of *Cit. Cit* manifests as such objects and due to the nature of *Âtman,* allows objects to be considered real. Consequently, the reality of objects is not conditioned through their own existence for otherwise how could objects be perceived outside of a *self*-awareness if not reflected through the divine awareness? Objects do not attain a sense of reality through sense perception, but because of the created nature by God and His will to allow self-perception and in the perception of objects.

It is because unity shines through the objects, due to the radiance of the divine *being* and the activity of the light of consciousness radiating from the *Âtman* that objects attain a sense of real-ness and this is not due to self-causation or material causation. Due to the true cause of objects, God, perceived as non-existence, becomes real because of the real-ness of that causation. If objects were unreal then the source of that unreality would also be unreal. As a consequence objects are to be considered real, as is the perception of them and of the perceiver. However, if any sense of falseness arises, this is also due to 'the *Âtman*', for nothing arises or exists without the *Âtman* whether good or bad, pure or impure, for without this luminosity no objectification would be perceived at all. But when the mind shines as the light of consciousness all objectified manifestation is viewed as related to the Lord. In this sense the objectified world and concrete persons can appear to be real but at the same time unreal, and attain a true sense of reality through the light of consciousness. As Utpala stated, the world's activities whether pure or impure are experienced "within the Lord decorated by the (reflective) manifestations of various different phenomena".[35]

Conversely, if oneness and unity of the *Self* were to be argued without affirming the reality of manifestation, then the world would have to be admitted as unreal or *mâyâ* or *avidyâ*. But it has to be asked, to whom does this non-knowledge belong? Not to *Brahman* which is pure *being*, or to itself, for an unreality cannot be real to itself. There cannot be *non-duality* in itself for there is plainly *duality*, or *duality* in itself for *duality* cannot support itself. Even the admittance of *non-duality* implies an exterior element in the affirming of the non-ness of *duality* in the first place. In other words it would seem *duality* is prior to *non-duality* for *non-duality* would not manifest *avidyâ* on account of its own perfect *being* and knowledge. But even this would be true if it were not the activity of *Citi-Shakti*creating *duality*. Consequently it is the Supreme personal Lord, *Maheshvara*, desires to manifest and does so out of His will and capacity to do so.

As such, the human experient, person, cannot be called a product of *mâyâ* or *avidyâ* as his or her *being* (*Âtman*), is connected to the Divine will to create a real person with a spiritual dynamic and thus the human personal existence is intimately related to the divine *Citi-Shakti.* However, the individual consciousness may be covered with a lack of awareness of this truth (*kañcukas*), living certain types of modes of existence (*gunas*) that support a limited view, and thus is unaware of the true nature of a personal existence. Indeed any awareness that supports finitude (*ânava-mala*) is only due to an apparent "*ânava*-impurity".[36] It also seems that separateness and bound-ness or individuality has come to be considered as a proper definition for a human person, when

---

³⁵ *ittham aty-artha-bhinnârthâvabhâsa-khacite vibhau/ samalo vimalo vâpi vyavahâro 'nubhûyate//* , *IPK*, 1.77, p.32; translation by Pandit, *IPKp*, 1.7.14, p.92.

³⁶ *IPK*, 3.16, p.65; translation by Pandit, *IPKp*, 3.2.5, p.175.

according to Utpala the opposite is true. The human person is not truly a whole person in the natural condition, where an entity experiences a loss of an "independent active power and active identity".[37] In the deluded and separated condition the individual cannot understand its true condition due to the "loss of the awareness of one's real nature".[38]

This loss of ones real nature, due to perceived coverings (relating to *kañcukas*) of ignorance, can be correlated, in the Byzantine tradition, to the coverings of Adam and Eve with "garments of skins" (Gen 3:21). This, Maximus the Confessor argued, could be correlated to the covering of the true nature of human persons in the blending of the soul and body together.[39] This blending of the immaterial and the material natures, due to transgression, paradoxically allows for a capacity for change, and it is this capacity for change that allows an existential movement from individual to person. Within the notion of change, a change of awareness and existential conditions in both traditions, were at the root of an incorrect mode of existence, which is full of irrational love (eros),[40] and opposed that mode of life which leads to truth and fulfillment.

The fulfillment of the human person, that is the moving out of a natural condition in *Pratyabhijñâ* terms, was equated to an experience of *re-cognition* of one's true condition, as being non-different to the luminous shinning *Self* of the Lord. But if one's *being* is divine, then is one's ego, *Shiva's* ego? This is the crux of the ontological dilemma in the qualifying of the *non-dual* condition in concrete existence and the need not to completely nullify *dualistic* existence in *non-dualism*. In complete *non-dualism* a kind of gnostic dualism becomes evident in the separation of the divine from the

---

[37] *IPK*, 3.15, p.64; translation by Pandit, *IPKp*, 3.2.4, p.174.

[38] *Ibid.*

[39] Maximus, *Ambig. 8* (PG 91), 1104B-C (Blowers).

[40] *Ibid.*

world, or the development of a complete monist unity, which dissolves individuality. In a qualified *dualistic* model however, as in *Pratyabhijñâ, duality* is affirmed but then contextualized through the light of consciousness (*prakasha*). Utpala argued that *prakasha* is the "essence of an object",[41] otherwise, objects would remain unmanifest, thus they have "consciousness as its very soul".[42] Indeed, all existence would be non-existence if it were not for the light of consciousness, or the activity of *Âtman* which remains the basis for all "mundane activities".[43]

It could be argued that the *Pratyabhijñâ* model, which views everything through the light of consciousness, may denude a notion of concrete person in reducing a person to a divine manifestation, but as already shown, a notion of concrete person is only understood as such when the person experiences the freedom of true *being* rather than being conditioned through *ânava-mala.* Hence, personal egoity attains a sense of true *being* and freedom only when related to divine "Egoity".[44] But *ânava-mala* and egoity do not imply a kind of non-being even though the teaching of non-being (*abhâvavâda),* in *Trika* has been applied to the divine.[45] Dyczkowsky argues that the philosophy of *abhâvavâda* in the *Shaivism* of Kashmir is more common than previously thought.[46] He demonstrates that in *Pratyabhijñâ* the concept of "absolute ego"[47] reflects a positive ontological context, 'I am' *being* (*ahambhâva*) rather than 'I am' not *being.* This sense of *being,* allows for a full sense of *being* where the ego experiences its selfhood, and yet unity when related to divine 'Egoity' through the light of consciousness. This type of

---

[41] *IPK,* 1.33, p.14; translation by Pandit, *IPKp,* 1.5.2, p.50.

[42] *Ibid.*

[43] *IPK,* 1.37, p.16; translation by Pandit, *IPKp,* 1.5.6, p.55.

[44] Mark S. G. Dyczkowski, 'Self-Awareness, Own Being and Egoity', in *A Journey in the World of the Tantras* (New Delhi: 2004), p.29.

[45] Dyczkowski, *A Journey in the World of the Tantras,* p.13.

[46] *Ibid.*

[47] Dyczkowski, 'Self-Awareness, Own Being and Egoity', p.29.

existence (*Cid-âtmanic*), which is had in a "flash of true knowledge",[48] gives rise to pure Consciousness of the "real Subject",[49] or the true knowing person.

Knowing Person

The question is asked, who is the knowing person or "knowing subject"[50] and what are the implications to person? These are difficult questions for while *Pratyabhijñâ* affirmed that subjects and objects are dependent on the divine cause and this dependency infers that perceptions, non-perceptions, reasoning, faculties of existing, all emerge "fundamentally out of one common knowing subject".[51] As Pandit stated that according to *Pratyabhijñâ*:

> all knowing is thus in fact, an inseparable quality of the inner divine knower who alone shines as Himself in the form of such activities as perception, conception, recollection, imagination, contemplation, recognition, realisation and so on.[52]

The question of how knowing relates to person and a single *Self* becomes not an ontological question in the sense of awareness, but dependent on how one perceives consciousness within a concept of person. The consciousness of person when directed to false perceptions becomes incomplete in those false perceptions, but when directed to the divine consciousness, to a relationship with divine consciousness (*Cit*),[53] the individual consciousness becomes transformed through a union with the true knowing subject. The question of a knowing subject, as person, does not become

---

[48] *IPK*, 3.23, p.67; translation by Pandit *IPKp*, 3.2.12, p.181.

[49] *Ibid.*

[50] *IPK*, 1.67, p.27; translation by Pandit, *IPKp*, 1.7.4, p.84.

[51] *Ibid.*

[52] *IPKp*, p.46.

[53] Or Supreme Consciousness, see *PBHs*.1, pp.46-51. But *Cit* can also be understood as *Citi* (singular), as the *Shakti* of the divine within a sense of conscious aware energy (*Ibid.*). *Citi* is viewed as the cause of the universe as the Lord's power (*Ibid.*).

constrained within mundane consciousness (*citta*), but is related to the real subject or person. This model considers a notion of concrete person[54] in relation to a unifying field of consciousness or unity within an *Âtmanic* experience and how this experience is not in conflict with, or invalidated by, a simultaneous condition of divine consciousness and mundane consciousness. The knowing person at once indicates the vehicle by which mundane awareness and a true cognition takes place, the material condition, and the nature of true knowing, where the person is transformed, within an experience of unity with the divine and attains an awareness or consciousness of the "knowing Subject".[55]

Difference and Subjectivity

In *Pratyabhijñâ*, the stress on difference and subjectivity was to affirm the nature of dependency in those conditions, and to highlight where doer-ship belongs. The notion of concrete person, while partly relating to a concrete material existence also includes an aspect of awareness, or the identification of doer-ship. In this identification, objective phenomena can be considered as isolated and disconnected but are truly established through and in relation to a unity of being. Without this unity, materiality and the body becomes a fleshy lump of useless substances. It is the unity of awareness that establishes a link between material substances and cognition, even that of finitude, which is established through the unity of *Self*. Hence there has to be a focus on how particular subjectivity relates to awareness in relation to doer-ship. Who is the real doer? Of course most persons would affirm that they are the doer, but the task of *Pratyabhijñâ* was to question this assumption. If finite beings were the real doers they would become

---

[54] B. Pandit never explains how *purusha* indicates person. In one instance he tends to see the terms indicating "finite persons" (*IPKp*, p.193) and in another in absolute terms without satisfactorily bringing the two models together where a notion of person can mean different things in *Pratyabhijñâ* depending on whether a pure or impure *pramatr* is being discussed.

[55] IPK, 1.83, p.34; translation by Pandit, *IPKp*, 1.8.6, p.96.

independent beings, which would have two effects. Firstly, they would be self-caused, and secondly, they would not be able to communicate or even be aware of other self-caused entities, for what would be the unifying relational constituent by which relationality could be affected. Hence, *Pratyabhijñâ* asserted that worldly activities are conditional to unity, which is provided by the "unity of *prakasha*: *Prakasha* is the common Subject",[56] whereby subjectivity and objectivity are existent and conditional to a single 'I-consciousness' or "knowing Subject"[57] established through an inherent unity. All observable phenomena attain subject-to-object relationality or "mutual unity"[58] due to the dependency on divine unity and divine doer-ship. Consequently, when relating doer-ship to a "single cognisor: the Self"[59] individual doer-ship is negated, which may seem to negate the place for concrete individual and consciousness, but this is only from a position of ignorance.

In *Pratyabhijñâ,* cognition thus was intimately related, not only to ordinary knowledge,[60] but to divine cognition, where the

---

[56] *IPK*, 1.87, p.36; translation by Pandit, *IPK*, 1.8.10, p.100.

[57] *IPK*, 1.83, p.34; translation by Pandit, *IPKp*, 1.8.6, p.96

[58] *IPK*, 1.26, p.11; translation by Pandit, *IPKp*, 1.4.3, p.40.

[59] *Ibid.*

[60] As highlighted by Peter David Lawrence, see D. P. Lawrence, 'Aspects of Abhinavagupta's Theory of Scripture', *Satya Nilayam; Chennai Journal of Intercultural Philosophy* 5 (2004), pp.5-26; and D. P. Lawrence, *Rediscovering God with Transcendental Argument* (Delhi: 1999). Lawrence focuses on the role of word (*Vâc*), speech and syntax (Lawrence, *Rediscovering God with Transcendental Argument,* p.24) mantra, ritual and gnoseology (Lawrence, 'Aspects of Abhinavagupta's Theory of Scripture', p.5) in the role of 'self-recognition', and in relation to the 'transcendental argument' as a "contemporary interpretation of monist *Kashmiri Œiva* Philosophy"(*Ibid.*). He highlights that any new interpretation has to be placed within the prevailing theological discourse and philosophical narratives such as postmodernism, relativism and "non-epistemic factors" (*Ibid.* pp.2-33) of Jean-Francois Lyotard, Thomas Kuhn, and Michael Foucault. Lawrence offers an adapted form of epistemological relativism to understand *Pratyabhijñâ* through "cross cultural dialogue" (Lawrence, 'Aspects of Abhinavagupta's Theory of Scripture', p.24) in which

divine power of differentiation (*apohana-Shakti*)[61] manifests in knowing subjects (*pramatrs*) the notion of difference (*bheda*). But even within a concept of difference there are acceptable levels of difference and unacceptable levels of difference. This is highlighted by Utpala, who develops a complex cosmological system, based on already accepted constructs as exemplified in the *Mâlinîvija yottaratantra,*[62] where *Shiva* and *Shakti*form part of the "pure" planes of existence[63] and the pure-impure universe correlated to

---

he highlights the deconstructive role of *Pratyabhijñâ,* which undermines previous discourses of other traditions without denuding the truths of those traditions. He places his approach to *Pratyabhijñâ* within a model (Lawrence, *Rediscovering God with Transcendental Argument,* pp.14-16) where epistemological categories (*pramânas* or 'means of knowledge'; see Lawrence, 'Aspects of Abhinavagupta's Theory of Scripture', p.7) are self-informing principles, and this becomes the foundation of his methodological approach. Lawrence seeks an interpretation which relies on the external, the phenomenological, where transcendence is disclosed in "philosophical rationalisation" (Lawrence, *Rediscovering God with Transcendental Argument,* p.23) and identifies relation and action as constantly the manner in which *Pratyabhijñâ* is understood in a "narrative or mythico-ritual narrative ontology" (*Ibid.*). But in using Western philosophical models to contextualise *Pratyabhijñâ,* does he miss the ontological implications of *Pratyabhijñâ?* It can also be asked whether he reduces *Pratyabhijñâ* to a narrative of syntax of the metaphysical and transcendent, capable of being accessed merely epistemologically, viewing *Pratyabhijñâ* as "an exercise in 'pure reasoning'" (Lawrence, 'Aspects of Abhinavagupta's Theory of Scripture', p.17) where the *Âgamic* epistemological categories inform the experient of *re-cognition.* While Lawrence understands ontology in Abhinavagupta in a Heideggerian type model where a relationality becomes the focus in understanding *being,* where form, action and relation are coalesced through scripture and syntax, I relate person in *Pratyabhijñâ* to true *being,* to a re-discovery of *being* and consciousness. Lawrence in his over-stating of the epistemological argument, develops his interpretation of *Pratyabhijñâ* to accomplish an over-nuanced narrative as a polemic for a postmodern deconstruction of the *metanarrative,* but does not inform us how to approach a whole model of *being* and existence.

[61] *IPK,* 1.22-23, p.10.

[62] See *Mâlinivijayottaratantram* (KSTS, 37), ed. P. M. K, Shastri.

[63] *IPK,* 3.1, p.59; and also Pandit's 'Cosmology of Kashmir Shaivism', *IPKp,* ('Appendix'), p.209.

SadâShiva, Ishvara and *Sadvidyâ.*[64] The impure universe was related to the rest of the *tattvas* including *purusha.*[65] The important point here is that a dual aspect of purity-impurity (or non-difference-difference) is incorporated within a single model, enabling me to argue for a simultaneous acceptance of multiple cognitions. Even though the notion of individual (*anu*) initially indicates finitude and separation, it also indicates the possibilities of a higher consciousness through a process of purification and prayer (mantra repetition). Through this process the *anu* begins to change its perception and thus the relationship of individual to the divine changes, as does the perception in relation to the world and God. This intimate relationship between cognition and *âbhâsas* reveals the philosophical depth of *Pratyabhijñâ* to overcome the dilemma of the divine reality and revelation in relation to apparent diversity.

There is, in this revelation a perceived movement from the divine to the world where the divine consciousness (*Cit*) comes to participate on an intimate level of activity (*kriyâ*) with individuals and thus raises the level of individual awareness (*citta*) to the divine awareness (*vimarsha*). This divine activity is exemplified in the force of mantras or *matrika-Shakti* which "brings about knowledge in a limited form such as 'I am imperfect' (*ânavamala*)"[66] in the covering of finitude. This is highlighted in the *Shiva Sûtras* which stated that the "subtle basis of mundane knowledge lie in the properties of sound".[67] Consequently, it is the Lord's power or covering (*ânava mala*) that makes an individual believe himself or herself to be incomplete and have a sense of mundane difference as compared to other objects of manifestation. In this context of *Shakti,* which is the power of the mantra, ordinary awareness (*citta*)[68]

---

[64] *IPK,* 3.2-6, pp.59-61.

[65] *IPK,* 3.7-29, pp.61-69.

[66] *SS.*1.4 (commentary); translation by Singh, *SSs,* p.26.

[67] *Jñânâdhisthânam mâtrikâ, SS.*4; translation by Singh, *SSs,* p.25.

[68] As it states in *SS* that the mind-consciousness is the nature of mantra, *cittam mantrah, SS,* 2.1; translation by Singh, *SSs,* p.82.

through the repetition of the mantra allows a person to attain an identity in the highest reality (*Annutara*),[69] whose power is contained in the mantra and thus "becomes identical with that Reality".[70] Cognition then becomes related to the perceived movement from *Para* (Supreme) to *aparâ* (non-supreme) which come together in a model of *parâpara* (supreme-cum-non-supreme).[71] This allows, in the experience of the Supreme, a unity of consciousness and change in cognition. In the *parâpara* cognition there is both the experience of the concrete personal existence and the cognition relating to difference, which allows for the possibilities of Absolute consciousness (indicating non-difference) and difference. Both levels of consciousness are possible through *parâpara* for they simultaneously exist within a person.[72] It is within the higher consciousness, relating to *Para,* that there is both the experience of concrete identity and *re-cognition* or divine consciousness.

In the *aparâ* state the cognition of a particular experient (*pramatr*) is bound within an "impure" state and to a perception which views objects and God as completely distinct from itself. This does not indicate that there are different types of persons but

---

[69] Abhinavagupta stated, that "'the anuttara or the unsurpassable one is the unsurpassable even to the proximate one' or 'anuttara means even the answer amounts to no answer'. The plan of creation in accordance with kula abides in the ether of my heart", *Parâ-Trîshikâ-Vivarana* (Singh), p.65.

[70] Singh, *SSs*, p.82

[71] *Parâ-Trîshkâ-Vivarana* (Singh), p.209.

[72] K. Mishra sees equates personhood only with cognition and personality, confusing a notion of person with aspects of personhood such as personality, or abnegation of the concrete person in divine union. He states that, "*Pratyabhijñâ* is the total spiritual transformation of the person...a transformation of the personality" (Mishra, *Kashmir Shaivism*, p.259). But he does develop a complex epistemology, identifying two types of ignorance and two types of knowledge or illumination to explain types of knowing in human personhood (*Ibid.*).

that there are different levels of consciousness within the human condition. But as Abhinavagupta argues, that if such a limited cognition rests not on pure 'I-consciousness', then that *pramatr* would not be able to experience a cognition outside of its own subjectivity or would only be able to assert "I am this" or "I am that".[73] Cognition is always expressed through the words 'I-am', which reflects the self-luminous expression of the 'I' (*Aham*) of the divine and through the determinative knowledge which follows. In determinate knowledge there is an awareness of the specific reality of an individual and the objects of perception, which come to be expressed through and eventually as the cognition of the divine as luminous expressions of the true subject. Utpala stated:

> Whether the form of determinate knowledge be 'I see this' or 'this is jar', it implies that the indeterminate cognition rests on the subject as one with it. Because the experience or perceiver has various cognitions: 'I see', 'I saw', 'this', 'that', therefore, it is clear that both the knower and the known in their distinctive nature, shine in the subject.[74]

Non-Difference and Subjectivity

Utpala continued to argue that if the objects are not one with the light of consciousness (*prakasha*) then objects would remain unmanifest. Consequently, the "subjective light is not essentially different from the objective"[75] and this light is the essence of objects. Knowing cannot be divorced from the subject of knowing otherwise knowing would only be related to a limited knowledge of the object. If an object were only able to know itself, then it would be constrained to the limits of that knowledge. Hence, that knowledge arising from the light of consciousness is the basis of all cognitions as Utpala stated:

> If the light of consciousness (*prakasha*) be different from the object and homogenous in itself, then confusion of one object with another

---

[73] *IPV*, 1.4.1 (commentary); translation by Pandey, *IPVp*, p.41.

[74] *IPK*, 1.30-31, p.13; translation by Pandey *IPVp*, pp.50-51.

[75] *IPK*, 1.33, p.15; translation by Pandey, *IPVp*, p.55.

would follow. Therefore, the object, that is made manifest, is not different from light. For, what is not light cannot said to exist.[76]

If the subject perceives objects as "the other (*bimba*)"[77] and as other than itself and unrelated to itself, then the subject becomes isolated within a self-conditioned reality and not able to observe anything outside of the subjective experience. Another result would be that the subject would become dependent upon other objects for its own identity and knowledge. However, the objectified or determinate knowledge is not known or experienced in isolation but related to the universal 'I-consciousness', being the divine conscious light (*prakasha*). This universal consciousness, which has the freedom (*svâtantrya*)[78] to act, allows the objects to *be,* as the object and the objects are not divorced from this activity. As Utpala argued, there is the possibility of "both the jar and not-jar, which are essentially different from each other"[79] and although these objects seem different from *prakasha*, the *prakasha* shines in these objects and the objects exist in the light of consciousness. Therefore differentiation (*apohana*) is due to both objectified difference and yet indicates the reality behind this differentiation. Utpala stated:

> Thus there is no doubt about it that the objects shine within the universal subject in remembrance, determinate knowledge, which depends upon the differentiation, and in indeterminate cognition.[80]

Thus individual *pramatrs* and objects are "one with the knowing Subject"[81] for they are one with "pure Consciousness"[82] and it is

---

[76] *IPK,* 1.34, p.15; translation by Pandey, *IPVp,* p.57.

[77] *Ibid.*

[78] *IPV,* 1.6.8; *IPVp,* p.95.

[79] *IPK,* 1.54, p.23; translation by Pandey, *IPVp,* p.87.

[80] *evam smrtau vikalpe vâpy apohana-parâyane/ jñâne vâpy antar-âbhâsah sthita eveti nishcitam//; IPK,* 1.60, p.25; translation by Pandey, *IPVp,* p.94.

[81] *IPK,* 1.83, p.34; translation by Pandit, *IPKp,* 1.8.6, p.96.

[82] *Ibid.,* 1.84, p.34; 1.8.7, p.97.

due to this consciousness, by virtue of His "Self-awareness...pure knowledge...pure action,"[83] that the *pramatrs* not only attain cognition but attain a higher cognition through the absolute subject (*Pramatr*).

But in relating the concept of person to knowledge and to cognition, which is actually God's cognition, the question has to be asked as to whether those *purushas,* who have not attained true knowledge, are to be considered as non-persons? *Pratyabhijñā* does not have a concept of non-*purushas,* or non-persons, it is just that different experiences of knowing indicate different levels of awareness or consciousness. This view is supported in Abhinavagupta who affirmed that, regardless of the levels of experience, we are all "'persons'"[84] for persons are from the Lord and do not exist in isolation.

Abhinavagupta argues this from the point of "Universal Consciousness",[85] which is responsible not only for fulfilment but also obscuration or relative cognition, due to the divine freedom of the Lord to create. In manifestation relative cognition reflects this freedom within the concrete person. However true freedom is reflected in a way of existing where union with the divine reflects in a particular cognition, the 'I-consciousness' of the divine.

It is freedom that allows the *act* of *re-cognition,* where the *Self* or *Âtman* brings into existence of the one who has had the experience of *re-cognition* the freedom to *be,* for the individual by himself or herself cannot alone achieve true *Self-hood* or even perfect knowledge of the relative *self.* It is not any ordinary act that brings *re-cognition,* but only the grace or *Shakti* (power) of God for the Lord is both the subject and the object of grace, or individual *pramatrs.* The light of knowledge is imparted through the activity

---

[83] *Ibid.,* 1.88, p.36; 1.8.11, p.101.

[84] Pandey, *IPVp,* p.9.

[85] *IPV,* p.2.

of *Citi-Shakti*as the light of consciousness (*prakasha*), by which knowledge informs the nature of *being* through the *Self*-luminosity of *Cit*, for without this, all manifestation would be in darkness and no cognition could occur. The awareness of 'I' reflects this activity and of *Citi,* which also has the quality of a divine throb (*spanda*). This allows a movement from the divine to the limited 'I' (*citta*) and then to a true 'I-consciousness'. In this activity, of *Citi,* the individual person is able to experience his/her own sense of individuality and at the same time experience true personhood in a unified experience with the divine *pramatr* (*Shiva*).

The notion of person is therefore to be conceived on many levels and is intimately related to the divine functions, which manifests a sense of person in the first place within the individual in a *self*-cognition, or knowing person. The ability of the person to recognise his or her true personhood, as the "knowing subject"[86] is due to the relationship of an individual with the divine. It is the divine person who reveals His a true sense of knowing within the knowing human person. Through this relationship an individual experiences relational *self*-awareness, which become expanded to include *re-cognition,* or an awareness of one's true condition. This again is due to the activity of divine *Self*-awareness (*vimarsha*), which pushes outwards from its own condition to reveal *jñâna* and *kriyâ* to limited knowing, to the limited knowing person. The Divine activity reforms limited knowing through the experience of *re-cognition* within a *non-dual* cognition, even though experiencing degrees of difference. Consequently, within a concept of person, this acceptance of difference through non-difference indicates the place for multi-cognitions to be accepted. But the experience and awareness of the divine becomes the true experience meant for human persons, whose very nature and existence reflects the divine nature and existence.

---

86 *IPK*, 2.11, p.41; translation by Pandit, *IPKp*. 2.2.3, p.117.

Unity-in-Difference: Revelatory Context

Here I will examine a notion of person in relation to difference (diversity/ *bheda*) or created manifestation (*âbhâsa*). This highlights that *Pratyabhijñâ* allowed for a sense of what is concrete through the admittance of 'this-ness'[87] and 'that-ness', where "the relative and finite subject and the object appear (manifestation) within one basic subject"[88] (the *Âtman*). The metaphysical focus in *Pratyabhijñâ* is not disconnected from the concrete but becomes the concrete essential nature and the principle of existence, allows for a real revelatory principle and context. Utpala stated that: "it is because of this that the Lord manifests His own Self objectively. Objective existence is not a thing existing separately from Him".[89]

Hence dependency not only becomes a feature of difference, and thus of person, which is to be viewed from a context of finitude as conditional to the divine, and also relational. This allows revelation to become fruitful in that phenomena attain fullness through that dependency.

In the context of relationality, between 'mundane objects', objects become 'justified' only through relations with the divine, "established in one and the same knowing subject".[90] From the perspective, of being justified through a single 'knowing subject', person becomes directly related to a single reality and pure 'I-consciousness'. This may seem to denude the notion of person, and indeed in the *Ishvarapratyabhijñâkârikâ* the tone in the latter part of Chapter 1 (*Jñânâdhikâra*) shifts, stressing more dynamically a non-dual stance where "exteriority is just an outward attribute".[91]

---

[87] 'This-ness', or 'idantyâ' (IPK, 1.51, p.21) is an important issue in *Pratyabhijñâ* in relation to awareness, which shows how individual consciousness of otherness (objectified universe, *âbhâsas*) reflects the divine movement from pure 'I am' to 'this is' and thus accepts the universe as real as 'that' (*tat*). 'This-ness' reveals the true nature of *Self* behind 'this'.

[88] *IPK*, 1.31, p.13; translation by Pandit, *IPKp*, 1.4.8, p.46.

[89] *IPK*, 1.46, p.19; translation by Pandit, *IPKp*, 1.5.15, p.64.

[90] *IPK*, 1.65, p.27; translation by Pandit, *IPKp*, 1.7.2, p.83.

[91] *IPK*, 1.82, p.34; translation by Pandit, *IPKp*, 1.8.5, p.95.

Here *Pratyabhijñâ* philosophy seems to become Platonic in the stress on interiority as a focus for "eternal existence" and the negation of exteriority, where objects "are brought into outward manifestation by *mâyâ*".[92] This seems to negate a previous stress on the divine will creating the universe, not as a predicated principle. It certainly has repercussions for a notion of whole person. This view is later qualified by Utpala in a unity-in-diversity model where a relationship between 'self limited' objects and *Self* is established because of the single reality and not through a limiting condition, where Utpala's monism or "absolute realism"[93]is clarified. This clarification is based upon dividing existential reality into three categories: 'absolute realism'; conditional realism and that which is non-real.[94] The first category conditions manifested phenomena through the Absolute reality.

> The Lord, being all powerful, manifests spatial sequence by creating
> wonderful variety in the forms of creation, and also brings about time
> sequence by manifesting variations in actions.[95]

The second category admits that subjects, objects, actions, substances time, and the like, are real, and emphasizes the real-ness of entities, while the third category considers thoughts such as imaginations to be unreal because they have no substantial reality. As a consequence, the whole tone of *Pratyabhijñâ* is qualified to allow for difference, while contextualizing difference through non-difference or the "one knowing subject",[96] through a model of unity-in-diversity (*bhedâbheda*).[97] *Pratyabhijñâ* argues that the "objectives of a person

---

[92] *IPK*, 1.84, p.34; translation by Pandit, *IPKp*, 1.8.7, p.97.

[93] *IPKp*, p.115.

[94] *Ibid.*

[95] *mûrti-vaicitry ato desha-kramam âbhâsayaty asau/ kriyâ-vaicitrya-nirbhâsât kâla-kramam apIshvarah//*, *IPK*, 2.5, p.38; translation by Pandit, *IPKp*, 2.1.5, p.110.

[96] *IPK*, 2.12, p.41; translation by Pandit, *IPKp*, 2.2.4, p.118.

[97] See *IPK*, 2.15, p.42; 2.51, p.57. *Bhedâbheda* is central, for it allows an acceptance of all relational activities and mundane activities in relation to the Absolute *being* and activities. For a full understanding of the philosophy of

desirous of mundane attainments are fulfilled"[98] having both "unity and diversity as their character. Such a thing is not illusion".[99] The model of *bhedâbheda* allows a sense of concrete person to be argued while at the same time qualifying existential person (*purusha*) through the completed state of *re-cognition*. Through this model, difference, or *bheda,* is qualified through non-difference within a simultaneous acceptance of both conditions. It is the admittance of the divine activities in the world and the intention behind those activities that allows person to especially gain significance through the relational context implied in those activities.

Revelatory Activities

Through the divine activities or revelatory activity (*kriyâ-Shakti*)[100] of the divine the world comes to be accepted in *Pratyabhijñâ* as real. This real-ness allows person to be accepted as a real ontological condition, without denuding that condition by relegating person to a mere principle of manifestation. Although the concept of person can sit within such a category, the reality of *being* a person must have existential and ontological significance. This significance is vouchsafed through the free will (*Svâtantrya-Shakti*)[101] and activity of the Lord, divine consciousness (*cid-âtmani*)[102] to create each unique person. But person cannot be left in this isolated condition as a separate individual within a material nature, which is taken in *Sânkhya* to be the cause and effect,[103] but attains true significance

---

bhedâbheda see, P. N. Srinivasachari, *The Philosophy of Bhedâbheda* (Madras; 1934, 1996); see also Mishra, *Kashmir Shaivism*, p.166; and Sanderson 'The Doctrine of the Mâlinîvijayottaratantra', p.295, who shows that this development comes from the *MT*.

[98] *IPK,* 2.15, p.42; translation by Pandit, *IPKp,* 2.2.7, p.120.

[99] *Ibid.*

[100] *IPKp,* p.105, which establishes the divine active power of the Lord to negate atheistic or Buddhist arguments of non-being or creation by some natural condition (*Ibid.*).

[101] *SS,* III.43; translation by Singh, *SSs,* p.225.

[102] *IPK,* 2.51, p.57.

[103] *IPK,* 2.49, p.56.

through a relationship with the divine. This relationship is established through the divine will and activity, as are the relations between persons, due to "their dependence on the knowing subject",[104] for the Absolute Consciousness is the basic cause and source of all phenomena".[105] This activity is not 'justifiable' in the case of the nature (*prakrti*),[106] because it could not allow both unity and diversity, only diversity, and is justifiable through *Âtman*, which "consists of pure consciousness (*cid-âtmani*) *cid-âtmani* with the capacity of appearing diversely".[107] Through the experiencing of the divine state, the truth of this position is *re-cognised* by the person who "becomes a citpramâtâ"[108] and attains full personhood. This becomes possible through the movement of the divine to and in the world through the *kriyâ-Shakti*. The *Shiva Sûtras* stated:

> The divine consciousness with a desire to display the variegated panorama of the universe, at first adopts the principle of contraction, assumes the state of limited experients (*jîvas*) who are a form of *prakasha* – the universal life force which brings about the manifestation of the entire universe in a limited form and also appears in the form of the world as *grâhya* or object.[109]

It is the Lord who becomes so related to the world so as to allow the world to be expressed in a real way and in turn provides meaning to person for the world is not negated as in a *Advaitic* model but is viewed as real. Hence a dual approach was evidenced, which allowed for both unity stressed in the *Âtmanic* experience and difference through the levels of *âbhâsas*. However, this view was also qualified for the world cannot reveal truth to itself, as Utpala stated, "the activity of creation is not possible at all on the basis of the two apparently different realities (*Âtman* and world)".[110] Utpala

---

[104] *IPK*, 2.48, p.55; translation by Pandit, *IPK*, 2.4.16, pp.146-147.

[105] *IPKp*, p.147.

[106] *IPK*, 2.51, p.57; translation by Pandit, *IPKp*, 2.4.19, p.149.

[107] *Ibid.*

[108] *SSs*, p.lxv.

[109] *SS*, III.43; translation by Singh, *SSs*, p.225.

[110] *IPK*, 2.52, p.57; translation by Pandit, *IPKp*, 2.4.20, p.150.

also argued that "such a thing is not justifiable in the case of an insentient entity (matter), on account of contradiction between unity and diversity",[111] but this dilemma is overcome in that the *Âtman*, which is pure consciousness and has the capacity to 'appear diversely'. Utpala stated that:

> The Lord, by virtue of His divine power, manifests these apparent phenomena simply through the power of His divine will (without resorting to the use of any other cause or means). That is what is known as His active nature and His creative aspect.[112]

It is because the manifested world is due to divine activity, and is not separated from God, that the mundane activities are fulfilled by the divine, where entities have both "unity and diversity (*bhedâbheda*) as their character",[113] which are not illusions.

However, such a viewpoint is only from *below* for in the highest awareness, all manifestations (*âbhâsas*) are viewed as intimately related to the divine, as Utpala stated: "God is taken to be numerous types of finite persons".[114] The sense of finitude infers that a dual consciousness and will is apparent, that of relating to the divine experience and that of the entity experiencing his or her existence as the object of existence or the egoistic 'I'. This sense of finitude or *anavamala* indicates that ordinary or mundane thoughts and life are not rejected but ultimately are also considered as the divine. There is an implicit relationship of the divine consciousness to the world and so the *Ânâvopâya* of *Shiva Sûtras* develops a process by which the individual comes to know his or her true state.

---

[111] *na ca yuktam jadasyaivam bhedâbheda-virodhatah/ âbhâsa-bhedâd ekatra cid-âtmani tuyujyate//*, IPK, 2.51, p.57; translation by Pandit, *IPKp*, 2.4.19, p.149.

[112] *esha cânanta-Shaktitvâd evam âbhâsayaty amûn/ bhâvân icchâ vashâd eshâ kriyâ nirmâtrtâsya sâ//33//IPK*, 2.33, p.50; translation by Pandit, *IPKp*, 2.4.1, p.135.

[113] *IPK*, 2.15, p.42; translation by Pandit, *IPKp*, 2.2.7, p.120.

[114] *IPK,* 4.3, p.70; translation by Pandit, *IPKp*, p.193.

While *Pratyabhijñâ* developed a more sophisticated philosophical explanation of the divine activities in relation to the world than the *Shiva Sûtras,* the *Shiva Sûtras* did begin to express how the divine comes to be related to the mundane condition through the aphorism, "*Atmâ* is Citta".[115] This statement allows the divine nature to be directly correlated to the lower condition without confusing either. In the individual consciousness (*citta*), the *Self* becomes *self,* where knowledge in that condition becomes bondage (*jñânam bandhah*).[116] The *Ânâvopâya* thus concerns itself with the *yoga* of the individual, so that the individual can attain the consciousness (*Cit*), which is its true reality. *Cit* becomes "reduced to citta"[117] in the apparent movement to the world from the divine, and then there is an apparent reciprocal movement from the world or individuals to the divine in which the *yogî* experiences "over and over again the awareness of the divine both inwardly and outwardly".[118] This view is confirmed again in the *Pratyabhijñâhrdayam,* which affirms that the individual experients (*pramatrs*) are "Citi in a contracted form"[119] or a "solidified form (*âshyânatârûpa*) of Cit-essence".[120]

From Individual to Person

The movement of the divine to the world is reciprocated in an upward movement. These movements can be viewed as continuous expressions of the divine activity and at a certain point seem to attain a sort of *stasis* in which a pause is evident. There is a simultaneous affirmation of all conditions. At this point there is evident, difference and non-difference, absolute *being* and individual human existing. This allows individuals, as *âbhâsas*, to be considered

---

[115] *Âtma Cittam, SS,* 3.1; translation by Singh, *SSs,* p.126.

[116] *SS.* 3.2.

[117] *Ibid.,* 'Exposition', *SSs,* p.128.

[118] *bhûyah syât pratimîlanam, SS,* 3.45; translation by Singh, *SSs,* p.230.

[119] *PBH,* 4; translation by Singh *PBHs,* p.55.

[120] *Ibid.,* (commentary).

as real, having as their cause the divine Cause. The real-ness of individual in *Pratyabhijñâ* is not denied but confirmed in the context of *âbhâsas,* as Abhinavagupta argued, because of the knowledge of differentiation or determinate knowledge,[121] difference is expressed. However, due to the continuous activity of the divine, individuality does not rest but changes within a continuous movement, and can be viewed as evolving a sense of person, where a divine mode of existence becomes the goal. Individual (*anu*) becomes person/ *purusha* (*hypostasis*), which allows a sense of true *being* (*Âtman*) to be experienced.

In differentiation, *âbhâsas* do not to appear to have any relational context to the divine in themselves, which is true of human individuals who exist according to the nature of each specific individual. It is because human individuals experience themselves in difference that the quality of difference continually changes due to the force acted upon it by the divine activities. If this were not the case the material nature of individuals would not allow a fluctuation or change of consciousness. Nevertheless, initially individuals only exist as a form of manifestation as does the knowledge relating to difference. Abhinavagupta stated:

> The *âbhâsas* of time and space impart particularity and exercise the function of as it were destroying eternality and omnipresence...among the best known *âbhâsas* mentioned above, the *âbhâsa* 'man' is the best known, because in 'man' are found many *âbhâsas.*[122]

Consequently, there are *âbhâsas* relating to love, desires, greed, and the intellect, in short, relating to all things that indicate differentiation. Even the power of differentiation or *apohana-Shakti*[123] is an *âbhâsa* of the Lord. But it is because all *âbhâsas* are a consequence of the true 'I-consciousness', becoming objectified manifestation, fluctuations, changes and movement occur in individuals, even when considered as *âbhâsas,* which in turn allow

---

[121] *IPV*, 2.3.4-5 (commentary); translation from Pandey, *IPVp*, pp.148-149.

[122] *Ibid.*

[123] *IPVp*, p.40.

for changes in awareness. These changes allow an individual to be considered as relational to the divine as a person and then as a *deified* person.

As the perception of manifested phenomena comes to be recognized as "that" and different to the cognition of 'I Am', a space is created between objectified phenomena and individual consciousness. This initially is observed as such affirmations such as *cogito ergo sum*,[124] which relies on a sense of separation and observance of objects (*âbhâsas*) outside of one's own existence. These observations provide conclusions with regard to the nature of objects and individual subjects in relation to existence. In addition, the power of differentiation allows the beginnings of an exterior perception and awareness of the divine reality. Through this differentiation the individual comes to perceive an awareness of 'I am' in relation to 'Thou Art', and so the 'I-Thou' relational model begins to develop in which a sense of relational person allows the individual to develop a relationship with the divine. In addition, Utpala relates the notion of individual to a context of *prakrti*[125] and shows how individuals enter into a process of becoming for the *Ishvarapratyabhijñâkârikâ* elucidates how to understand this process. The aim is to "initiate a concern with God"[126] so that, through the revelatory divine power (*Shakti*), the world can be overcome and the delusion of false perceptions, fall away. Utpala explains that it is the Lord Himself through His infinite power (*Shakti*) and will (*icchâ*) who creates the world, and it is His power and will that allows a human reciprocity.[127] Even though there is the affirmation of the individual consciousness and a distinction between the states of consciousness, such as the *pashu* (bound), there is also a recognised movement from this state to that of the *pati,* or realised[128]

---

[124] Descartes, Key Philosophical Writings, (UK: 1997), p.198.

[125] See *IPKp*, p.149.

[126] *IPK*, 2.32, p.50; translation by Pandit, *IPKp*, 2.3.17, p.133.

[127] *IPK*, 2.33, p.50; translation by Pandit, *IPKp*, 2.4.1, p.135.

[128] *IPK*, 4.6.

condition of super-conscious, the *turyâ* or fourth state.[129] In this state of awareness mundane knowledge and experience comes to be fulfilled in divine Self-awareness, which permeates all realities.

The outward flow of the divine *kriyâ* or activity manifests a link between the internal divine state and the outer world, or *âbhâsas*. Within a sense of difference, non-difference allows the individual to attain the highest consciousness. This is because within the depth of a person/*purusha*,[130] there is an ontological relatedness to the divine, who as the Cause allows difference as a reflection of divine freedom. Mundane or individual consciousness is not denied, but as an *âbhâsa,* is related to the divine act. Utpala stated:

> His individual creation, not being common to all beings, remains dependent on God's creation. But even such a phenomenon, though appearing erroneously, is 'true' because of its being created by God appearing in the form of this individual being.[131]

---

[129] *IPK,* 3.31, p.69.

[130] The difficulties of interpreting how person relates to *purusha,* is exemplified by Bede Griffiths who determined that *purusha* in the *Brahman* and *Âtman non-dual* model points to an impersonal underlying *Reality,* Bede Griffiths ('The Adwaitic Experience and the Personal God in the Upanishads and the Bhagavad Gita', *Indian Theological Studies* 15/1; 1978, pp.71-86), where personhood is correlated through an impersonal experience of *Âtman.* Even though Bede Griffiths presented an *Advaitic* Christian perspective, he highlighted the problem of the antinomy generally present in *Advaita,* that of the personal in relation to the impersonal.

[131] See *Chandogya Upanisad,* 6.2.1. It could be interesting also to correlate ideas relating to personhood in *Pratyabhijñâ* to *Vedânta* in the context of *Neo-Vedântic* understanding of the concept of person where the *Atmopanishad*'s, notion of *purusha* could be utilised, see Swami Madhavananda, 'Atmopanishad', in *Minor Upanishads* (Calcutta: 1988). In this model, *purusha* has three *Âtmanic* components, the "Outer-Âtman, the Inner-Âtman and the ParamÂtman", Swami Madhavananda, *Minor Upanishads,* verse 2, p.12.The *Outer-Âtman* refers to the body, the *Inner-Âtman* to the individual perceiver or the one who experiences, and the *Paramâtman* to the Supreme Lord who dwells within. The Supreme in the *Atmopanishad* is non-dual, non-being, but also has a personal quality in Subjective awareness, and thus it is stated: "He is the Purusha who is called the *Paramâtman*" (*Ibid.*). He is the awareness of *being Paramâtman.* Thus the *Âtman* indicates what a

Thus *Pratyabhijñâ,* in its accepting of the world as an *âbhâsa* of the Lord and thus real, had to incorporate notions of revelation, within a theocentric model, to allow reciprocation, otherwise the *âbhâsas* would only be relational to themselves. To accomplish this revelatory activity, *Pratyabhijñâ* utilised the notion of *Cit.*[132] The *âbhâsas,* as the contracted form of *Citi,* come to reflect the divine reality because of the awareness of *Cit* in *âbhâsas,* which can be said to leak out and it is this leaking or outward flowing of the divine consciousness in *âbhâsas* that starts to reveal how *âbhâsas* are related to the divine consciousness (*Cit*). In this respect the individual starts to attain an existential condition more related to relational person. It was not sufficient to express *Cit* purely within a *non-dual* doctrine, but God and the world were to be brought together through the outward flowing activity of *Citi-Shakti,* which ultimately reveals the true nature of the *âbhâsas.* This relationship between *âbhâsas* and *Cit* was underlined through the philosophical usage of *bhedâbheda,*[133] which allows difference within the non-different state. It must be stressed here that *bhedâbheda* does not impinge on the *non-dual* outcome of *Pratyabhijñâ,* but rather complements it by incorporating it in a sense of the *dualistic* and the accepting of *âbhâsas* as an aspect of divine condescension, where the presence of the Lord exists in those *âbhâsas.* This exemplifies an acceptance of both unity and diversity,[134] and the

---

person truly is and how the person in truth reflects an essential reality of *being.* What distinguishes this model from that of *Pratyabhijñâ* is that in *Pratyabhijñâ* the all-pervading *Cit* of *Self* distinguishes *being* from act, though at the same time upholding unity, and that it is this Supreme 'I-Consciousness' that informs the person of his or her true identity. Thus the Lord enters into participation with the individual through the activity of *Cit,* although the individual or *purusha* may not understanding in what way, but ultimately participating as *Cit.*

[132] *IPK,* 4.9, p.71; translation by Pandit, *IPKp,* pp.198-199.

[133] *PBH,* 1-20.

[134] K. Mishra does not accept that the Absolutism of *Kashmir Shaivism* (new Trika), can be considered in a qualified manner. He also seems to centre his criticism of qualified models through Hegelian and *Visisht-advaitic* notions

admittance of the real-ness of the world. Manifestation (as *âbhâsas*) in the context of revelation and immanency (*vishvamaya*)[135] is not unreal or dreams of the impersonal, but rather it is a tangible and luminous manifestation of the divine *Cit-Shakti,* and due to this luminosity is ultimately non-different to the transcendent (*vishvottîrna*) personal Absolute. Abhinavagupta states that "Paramasiva, the Absolute God, thus plays His wonderful game of

---

(Mishra, *Kashmir Shaivism*, p.101). In the former model the notion of free act is negated through evolution of matter, and the latter distances the Divine from creation. While I accept this, I would state that the *bhedâbheda* of *Pratyabhijñâ* is not of the type considered by Mishra, in that, it views the world as a luminous expression of Supreme consciousness. While Mishra negates a model that would affirm a qualified position and a Hegelian type interpretation, Manoranjan Basu embraces a comparison of Hegelian doctrine with *Pratyabhijñâ* (Manoranjan Basu, *Fundamentals of the Philosophy of Tantras,* Varanasi: 1986, p.141). I believe that such a comparison only reflects Basu's interest in Hegel and Kant and is not viable, for *Pratyabhijñâ* does not purport an impersonal moral imperative or a phenomenological cosmogony (as in *Sânkhya*), but allows the place for divine will and freedom, which is not evidenced in a law of "logical necessity" (Mishra, *Kashmir Shaivism,* p.101). Nor does the qualified nature of *Pratyabhijñâ* imply a *dualistic* role in its concept of the divine act (*Shakti*). As Sudhendu Kumar Das shows, *Shakti* is a "sort of reflex relation of self-Identity" (Sudhendu Kumar Das, *Shakti of Divine Power* (Calcutta: 1934), p.600. *Shakti* is an appellation of the divine power, but it also came to take on its own existential character, representing a dualistic consort to *Shiva,* but as Kumar Das argues in *MT, Shakti*"belongs to the one unified Self of *Shiva,* and is not really a distinct principle at all" (*Ibid.*, p.72). In *Pratyabhijñâ, Shakti* is the 'vimarsharûpâ' or "the vibration of Consciousness of real Egoity" (*Ibid.*, p.60). For Mishra the notion of *kriyâ-Shakti* does not necessarily indicate *dualism* as in the case of the qualified *non-dualism* in the *Vira Shaivism* of Southern India which gives a *dualistic* character to revelation. This is not what is being developed in *non-dual Kashmir Shaivism.* Mishra states that "Shaktiis not an attribute, or quality, of Shiva, but the very nature of Shiva" (Mishra, *Kashmir Shaivism*, pp.101, 102). But the very affirmation of *kriyâ-Shakti* in itself seems to qualify in some way Mishra's absolutist view of *non-dual Kashmir Shaivism* (new *Trika*) and so in *Pratyabhijñâ* we too have to conclude that divine act and the world are not at odds, and while there is non-differentiation, there is at the same time some kind of differentiation at play.

[135] *IPK,* 2.14, p.42.

bondage and liberation".[136] All *âbhâsas* are not independent but are dependent upon the divine luminosity which reflects within the *âbhâsas* not only the objectification of manifestations but within each subject, individual cognition and the possibilities to experience true 'I-consciousness'. It is this experience of true 'I-consciousness', reflected through mundane cognition, that allows the ability to observe objects as different, but ultimately allows a *re-cognition* of *Self.* The sense of difference that a subject experiences, paradoxically becomes the medium by which manifested phenomena and finite subjectivity are qualified through non-difference in the highest experience through the nature of *Citi,* which establishes the bridge between *âbhâsas* and the world.[137] But there has to be a vehicle of correspondence by which a condition is mediated to another state.

Hence, Kshemarâja concludes that what is important is the focus on the perception or awareness of a subject, that "when the bliss of *Cit* is attained, there is stability of the consciousness of the identity with *Cit* even while in the body".[138] The consciousness attained in *Cit,* in the attainment of *samâveœa* or the experience of unity of consciousness with the divine *Self* (*Âtman*) within the body, paradoxically allows the observance of manifested diversity and limited consciousness. In the experience of the mundane consciousness of the individual, the force of impressions, due to an association with manifested phenomena, prohibit the consciousness of *Cit* to be experienced. But in the experience of unity with *Cit,*

---

[136] David Peter Lawrence argues that the dichotomy of immanence and transcendence is overcome through a model of "unity to unity-in-multiplicity" (David Peter Lawrence, *Rediscovering God Within the Transcendental Argument* (Delhi: 1999) pp.136-137). Lawrence interprets appearance through *emanation* and addresses the issue of manifestation and *being* in a relational context through "soteriological return"

[137] trough the unity-in-multiplicity paradigm. The Supreme engages in a descent through principles in unity-in-manifestation, which firstly involves *being,* it is the Lord who descends and is conscious in that descent, and secondly through act, through the will (*icchâ*) of the Lord to descend.

[138] *PSA,* 33 (Pandit), p.40.

these impressions are "left behind in the unity-consciousness"[139] by the *jîvanmukti* or the one who is liberated (saved) while alive. In this consciousness, *Samvit* or universal consciousness is experienced in which the manifested world *âbhâsas* are experienced. Also in this condition, the role of *mâyâ-Shakti*is dissolved and the various types of *âbhâsa* mechanisms, which Kshemarâja considered as having a "descending" movement, from Brahman to the "rib of a palâúa leaf",[140] and are cognized, not through the lens of differentiation, but through universal consciousness. *Being* is therefore, not a question of considering ontological difference, but of how types of consciousness are expressed, and how individuation relates to becoming as person. One type recognizes (individual) material manifestation as different to the divine, and another (person) perceives the possibilities of participation with the divine.

Relational Person and Re-cognition

The hermeneutical approach to person has been constructed by qualifying a notion of outward looking person, or what has come to be known as concrete person in contemporary personhood studies, so as to consider person as related to both difference and non-difference. The notion of whole person should be considered within a relational context through an experience of unity through the notion of *re-cognition*.

In *Pratyabhijñâ* the world has to be as considered as intimately related to the divine activity and presence, and equated with "manifestations of a single, changeless entity".[141] As such, when placing person in a relational context to the divine, the notion of relationality has to be re-considered. A *Pratyabhijñâ* type of relationality based on unity does not indicate a person-to-person

---

[139] See *IPK*, 2.18-20, pp.56-57.

[140] *cidânandadalâbhe dehâdishu cetyyamâneshvapi cidaikâtmaya-pratipatti-dârdhyam jivanmuktih/*, *PBH*.16; translation by Singh, *PBHs*, p.91.

[141] *Ibid.*, (commentary), p.92.

type of relation but of person as *Âtman*. *Pratyabhijñâ* does not consider this as a contradiction, for while a person-to-person model is usually constructed to place person in relation to others, or as an objectified manifestation, *Pratyabhijñâ* structures its relationality through unity. It questions the validity of seeking a relational construct, of objectifying others, when considering the lack of inherent unity between objects. It argued that unity and thus relationality can only be developed through an existential realism[142] of the true subject, through dependence, where the notion of concrete person becomes, not isolated or *self*-reflective, but unified through a "unitary awareness"[143] within an essential nature.

Personhood reflects the divine condition through the *Âtmanic* reality and the will of the divine to bring individuals out of their state of isolation otherwise there could be no *self*-cognition and no perception of the divine state. *Self*-cognition cannot therefore be only related to an inward condition of divine consciousness but also to observable manifestations. An awareness of manifestations also reflects a relational context to person, for the ability to be aware of these objects within a sense of *self*, in *Pratyabhijñâ*, is due to the nature of *self*-awareness reflecting the capabilities of divine awareness. In a purer or higher form of awareness the natural individual condition can be said to be raised to another, which can be correlated to a notion of relational person. This does not mark the end of awareness of person but the beginnings and culminates in an experience of *re-cognition*.

In the pure state of consciousness the world and oneself is *re-cognised* as existing as the light of consciousness, while still admitting the reality of those cognitions that seem to be outside of this *re-cognition*. Without limited perception there could not be a cognition of the *Âtman*, which would be self-reflective, having an inward perception and not able to consider the world. Hence, there

---

[142] *PBH*.17 (commentary); translation by Singh, *PBHs*, p.93.

[143] *IPK*, 2.18, p.56; translation by Pandit, *IPKp*, 2.4.18, p.148.

is a need to affirm the place for the outer perception in the individual as well as the inner in the highest cognition (of *Âtman*) by which the *hypostatic* existence comes to experience its sense of worth. There comes to be evident existence (diversity or difference) and also unity through the *Âtmanic* experience within a model of person which can be called an *Âtman-hypostasis*.

Through differentiated cognition, there is the admittance of the differing states of experience because of the nature of the revelatory activity (*kriyâ-Shakti*)[144] of the divine. This activity manifests the world and then interacts with the world in the most meaningful way where there is also the acceptance of difference and objectified phenomena. The human person comes to be correlated to a form of manifestation, yet the human person having *self*-cognition is able to understand its true sense of person and allows the notion of person to change and be restored, thus changing the way manifested phenomena are viewed. The model in this work allows the cognition of *Âtman*, within a *Cid-âtmanic* mode of existence, to affirm that the personal consciousness of individual soul *deified* does not detract from both the specific concrete existence and also unity. The notion of unity within manifested diversity can be argued through the words "while in the body",[145] so as to make clear that the divine state is not divorced from the somatic existence. The bodily existence reaches its pinnacle in true 'I-consciousness', which affirms the true reality of the human person, as Kshemarâja stated:

> Then is attained the awareness of the ultimate reality as a result of entering the perfect I-consciousness or Self which is in essence Cit and ânanda (bliss) and of the nature of the power of the great mantra. There is the attainment of the lordship over the one's group of deities of consciousness that brings about emanation and re-absorption of the universe. All this is the ultimate reality or the nature of Shiva.[146]

---

144 *IPKp*, p.115.
145 *IPK*, 2.52, p.57; translation by Pandit, *IPKp*, 2.4.20, p.150.
146 *IPK*, 3.53, p.58.

Consequently, mundane existence is ultimately due to the divine Cause (*Shiva*), who accepts that such manifestations are due to Himself as a perfect expression of "His own Self",[147] where the spatial sequence (objects), pertaining to finite subjects, appear to be "the infinite Subject, His Self...and filled with His own existence".[148] In this condition the (interior) reality is one, and that "One alone develops multiplicity".[149] Objectification does not infer a disparity between mundane consciousness, or objects and the divine, for such objectification is the external unfolding of the divine,[150] and thus the universe and persons are in essence the nature of *Shiva*.[151]

Conclusion

At the start of this part of the part of the work it was asked whether *Pratyabhijñâ* had a concept of person and how can such a concept be understood within *Pratyabhijñâ* philosophy? This part of the work represents a general examination of person, where this examination was understood from a perspective of *Pratyabhijñâ*. There was a focus on the term *purusha* to correlate ideas of concrete personhood to that term, whilst recognising that this notion of personal concrete existence (*hypostasis*) was qualified through an experience of the essential reality of *being* (or *Âtman*). It is in this experience of the *Âtman* that a full mystical sense of person was developed and correlated to a spiritual mode of existing, which allowed for both individual existence and unity in the divine experience. This manifested a model which qualifies *non-dualistic* aspects of *Pratyabhijñâ* and the *dualistic* within the model of unity-in-diversity. In this model the world is viewed as the light of

---

[147] *PBH*.16.

[148] *PBH*, 20; translation by Singh, *SSs*, p.106.

[149] *IPK*, 2.7, p.39; translation by Pandit, *IPKp*, 2.1.7, p.112.

[150] *Ibid.*

[151] *IPK*, 2.10, p.40; translation by Pandit, *IPKp*, 2.2.2, p.116.

consciousness (*prakasha*) and as such the human person gains significance to freely be a person in the highest condition and not be restrained by what John Zizioulas called "ontological necessity",[152] where the human person is dominated by instincts and lower impulses.

However, while the Byzantine theology of John Zizioulas was dependent on an existential model to overcome the lower nature of human personhood, or the biological *hypostasis,* it was argued that this type of existential model should be qualified through an experience of the essential reality of *being,* or *Âtman.* In this experience the lower natural *physis* of the human person is overcome through grace to attain a mode of life in the experience of *Âtman,* having conscious awareness of this state in the material life within a spiritual mode of existence. This approach allowed me to present a model which accepts the place for individual concrete existence as a mode or type of human existing and the overcoming of the natural *physis* in another type of existence or conscious awareness, an *Âtmanic* existence and awareness.

The notion of person is not dissolved in that experience, but on the contrary it allowed a sense of freedom where a human person attains a true sense of personhood in that state as an *Âtman-hypostasis.* If a person were not able to have this experience he or she would be bound to the biological condition and have no freedom to escape the prison of the natural existence. It was argued, in relation to the *Âtman-hypostasis* model of person that this model allows for a real sense of being as a human person without displacing the important stress on *essential* being. It was also argued that *Pratyabhijñâ* does have a sense of the personal in the stress on divine awareness of the true subject (*Shiva-pramatr*), which when translated into the human level allows for a sense of true personal

---

[152] Utpala stated: "*Ishvara* is the extroversive aspect of the Absolute and *SadâShiva* is the introversive one, the former being known (in the Âgamas) as *unmesha* and the later as nimesha...", *Îshvaro bahir unmesho nimesho 'ntah sadâ-Shivah,* IPK, 3.3, p.60; translation by Pandit, *IPKp,* 3.1.3, p.159.

cognition, made possible through the *Âtmanic* reality. The *Âtman* reality has at its core both pure *being* and pure awareness or *Cit,* which implies that on the divine and human levels, personhood includes notions of existence within an essential condition of (restored) *being.*

The *Âtmanic* model when correlated to human personhood affirms the place for personal consciousness on both a limited and a *deified* or *re-cognised* level, which is made possible through the divine unity and the divine expansion of the Supreme *Purusha* (*Shiva*). The many levels of human consciousness considered in *Pratyabhijñâ* did not divide personhood but allowed for a harmonisation of many types of consciousness through the Absolute Consciousness. Despite the admittance of both *citta* and *Cit* in human personhood, concrete existence was not denied but affirmed. In this sense *Pratyabhijñâ* can be said to have an understanding of person/*purusha,* harmonising the sense of ordinary existence and the possibilities of what can *be* in human personhood through the experience of *re-cognition.*